Praise for *Usurping Suicide*

'Sometimes the depth of an economic crisis can only be fathomed when suicide, that most personal of acts, accrues political meaning and consequence. The authors bring committed insight to political suicides in our time, from Tunisia to Syntagma Square.'

Terrence McDonough, co-author of *Contemporary Capitalism and its Crises*

'An original study of those moments when the act of ending one's own life can acquire public and political significance. The authors bring a fresh approach to an old problem: why individuals choose to end their lives and what meaning the act can have for those left behind.'

Aamir R. Mufti, author of *Forget English! Orientalisms and World Literatures*

ABOUT THE AUTHORS

SUMAN GUPTA is a professor of literature and cultural history at the Open University, UK, and honorary senior fellow at Roehampton University, UK.

MILENA KATSARSKA lectures in American studies at the Paisii Hilendarski University of Plovdiv, Bulgaria.

THEODOROS A. SPYROS is a post-doctoral fellow of historical sociology at the University of Crete, and adjunct academic staff in the sociology and anthropology of sports at the Hellenic Open University.

MIKE HAJIMICHAEL is an associate professor at the University of Nicosia, Cyprus, in the Department of Communications.

USURPING SUICIDE

The Political Resonances of Individual Deaths

SUMAN GUPTA, MILENA KATSARSKA,
THEODOROS A. SPYROS AND
MIKE HAJIMICHAEL

Zed Books
London

Usurping Suicide: The Political Resonances of Individual Deaths was first published in 2017 by Zed Books Ltd, The Foundry, 17 Oval Way, London SE11 5RR, UK.

www.zedbooks.net

Typeset in Bulmer by Swales and Willis Ltd, Exeter, Devon
Cover design by Andrew Brash

ISBN 978-1-78699-099-0 hb
ISBN 978-1-78699-098-3 pb
ISBN 978-1-78699-100-3 pdf
ISBN 978-1-78699-101-0 epub
ISBN 978-1-78699-102-7 mobi

Contents

Acknowledgements

This book arises from the collaborative project *Framing Financial Crisis and Protest: North-West and South-East Europe* (2014–16). The authors are very grateful to the Leverhulme Trust for funding the project.

The research and analysis which inform this book were discussed in some detail during a project workshop in London, 15–16 July 2016. Comments by participants there have helped shape the final draft.

Thanks are due to John Seed, P. K. Vijayan and Fabio Akcelrud Durão for reading early drafts of some of the chapters and making perceptive comments.

The authors alone are responsible for shortcomings in the following pages.

Introduction

One of the conundrums of liberal democratic politics is that individuals are constantly courted but cannot be seen or heard. The individual does not have a material presence. This is a pervasive conundrum, not confined to specific constitutional and institutional arrangements. Some degree of adherence to liberal democratic principles are claimed in an overwhelming majority of political states at present, and those principles provide an ostensible operating system for global economic, governmental and media operations. So, political discourses are constantly and ubiquitously centred on concepts of individual freedom, individual choice, individual rights, in-principle equality of individuals (e.g. in the eyes of the law), dignity of the individual, and so on. However, the individual can only be politically apprehended in the abstract. This could be as a statistical aggregate in relation to certain indicators (usually as components in majorities, minorities and proportions), or by way of a sampling of some collective attitude or experience. More often, the individual can be seen or heard as extraordinary in some way and therefore in the public eye and commanding the public ear, such as political representatives or celebrities. But the constantly highlighted extraordinary individual is not really the individual of liberal democratic discourse. Simply by being seen and heard this person becomes more than an individual, collectively significant in a way that the individual cannot be. The individual in liberal democratic discourse is relevant to *all* individuals, both ordinary and extraordinary. To distinguish those who are not seen and heard from those who are, and who are therefore more akin to the individual in general, we may designate them *ordinary individuals*.

The obvious fallout of this conundrum is that, while the individual (which means *all* individuals) seems to confer democratic legitimacy on the state, and the state claims to have responsibilities towards and courts the individual constantly, the individual cannot be meaningfully thought of as being politically determinative. The individual can only be *acted upon* collectively (for instance, by legislation and persuasion); the individual cannot be a political *actor* or exert political *agency* unless she surfaces as extraordinary and thereby surrenders her individuality.

The tensions that arise from this are most keenly felt when the politics of death-dealing is contemplated. Death, in an immediate sense, is the great equaliser of all individuals – each will die. In various ways, the management of unnatural death seems like an ultimate test of liberal democratic principles. The liberal democratic claim of being confirmed by individuals and protecting individual interests seems to have a particular bearing on securing the lives of individuals – every individual. Thus, when the state considers the acceptance and formal processing of some kind of unnatural death of individuals (usually through legal provision following the principle of the "rule of law"), the most passionate and inconclusive debates arise. Few political debates have been as heated as those concerning the legal status of euthanasia (assisted suicide), recourse to capital punishment, the legitimacy of killings by state agents (by soldiers of civilians in conflict situations, by police of suspects in custody or in encounters, etc.). Innumerable advocatory and analytical treatises of philosophy, jurisprudence, sociology, ethnography, politics and history seek to clarify the liberal position with regard to dealing with unnatural death.

Similarly discomfiting from the liberal democratic perspective is the contemplation of an ordinary individual's suicide. In an immediate manner this might be regarded as an instance of irreversible failure on the part of the state or as an irrevocable rejection of the state's ability to offer security to an individual. However ordinarily unseen and unheard an individual might be, an individual act of suicide could become a most damaging gesture for the liberal democratic order, undermining some of its fundamental principles and claims, *if it were to assume political dimensions and instantiate a political debate.* Consequently, discussion of individual acts of suicide as being political is largely discouraged or tends to be muted – not only in formal discourses (in legal processing or media reportage) but often also by a kind of self-censorship or moral anxiety within society. Thus, discussions of individual suicides by, for example, interested specialists and academics tend to prefer analytical framings that discount political implications or consider them only after carefully de-individuating such acts. An individual suicide that appears to have a political dimension, perhaps because the act was explicitly performed as a political gesture, is generally regarded by authorities as nevertheless resulting from narrow individual concerns – a mental health issue or stressed personal circumstances (e.g. domestic discord). Considered thus, the act of suicide assumes a contained significance and is removed from political reckonings. Analyses of suicides with clearly articulated political interests usually focus on trends from a large number of suicide acts rather than on an individual act (de-individuation). Thus, a rise or fall in suicide rates could be variously analysed as reflecting political and social realities.

Such circumspection is typically abandoned when an individual suicide is performed ostensibly on behalf of a collective or organisation that refuses liberal democratic subscriptions (such as religious cult suicides or extremist suicide bombers). These acts are by definition de-individuated in their performance, and the individual simply disappears in the collective statement made through the performance of suicide. They are analysed without restraint as confirming liberal democratic principles by evidencing the abnormality or depravity of undemocratic and illiberal formations.

However, despite – and perhaps deliberately against – the more usual circumspection, acts of suicide by ordinary individuals do at times acquire powerful political resonances within, and have repercussions for, liberal democratic societies and establishments. In doing so, the ordinary individual's suicide seems to confer an extraordinary status to that individual posthumously. But this is inevitably a contradiction in terms: the ordinary individual committed suicide as ordinary, but their individuality was wiped out in the act, and no posthumous reconstruction can really change that. The challenge to liberal democratic orders that such cases present then seems beyond resolution: they are a fissure in the liberal democratic fabric that can only be managed into gradual forgetfulness rather than explained away into quick oblivion. At any rate, over the preceding decade, in contexts of severe economic stresses and political disaffection and under crisis conditions, such cases have caused widespread consternation. Some acts of suicide by ordinary individuals have made them household names in their countries and beyond, through local or global media discussion, for shorter or longer periods of time. These include Mohamed Bouazizi's suicide in Tunisia on 17 December 2010, Dimitris Christoulas's in Greece on 4 April 2012, and Plamen Goranov's in Bulgaria on 20 February 2013. Numerous other acts of individual suicide have been similarly registered with individual markers, though fleetingly, as bearing immediate political resonance. The attribution of political resonance in such cases appears to have a consistent bottom-up thrust, working against the establishment order. Such cases are now familiar enough to constitute a distinctive political phenomenon that calls for reflection, and they cannot be blithely dismissed as anomalous or freakish occurrences.

This study is devoted to analysing the phenomenon of suicides by ordinary individuals with anti-establishment political resonance. The focus here is on this phenomenon amidst recent crises, those which surround the so-called "Arab Spring" and the crash of 2007–08 in Europe and the resulting austerity measures. This focus delimits the phenomenon to specific geopolitical contexts. The phenomenon itself is of considerably wider and longer-standing import across various contexts, taking in farmer suicides and numerous self-immolation protests in India, starvation suicides by political prisoners in Turkey, Northern Ireland and elsewhere, and so on. Elements of such cases in other contexts have been variously analysed, but not from the perspective assumed here. The purpose of this study is to understand how such cases came to be regarded as politically significant, what sort of resistances they fed into, how they were managed in the short and long term, and, ultimately, what they indicate about the prevailing national and global political order – especially among institutions claiming adherence to liberal democratic principles, and particularly with their current neoliberal functioning.

Such a project naturally goes against the grain of the dominant and familiar approaches to the politics of suicide outlined above. Before exploring specific cases and contexts, therefore, it is necessary to articulate a consistent rationale and methodology. Received convictions and widely disseminated analytical frames for this area do not necessarily serve this project well; when writing this, the authors found that strongly held preconceptions about how suicides should be viewed are common amongst our everyday interlocutors – and, indeed, that the authors themselves were far from being critically aware of their own preconceptions. Chapter 1 therefore provides an account of broad disciplinary approaches to the politics of suicide and current debates about political suicide. Through this account, a methodology for this study is clarified. Briefly, this consists in not trying to gauge whether specific cases of suicide were *intended* to be political statements or had political *causes*. Instead, one could say that the emphasis here is on the receptive field: how political resonances were perceived or activated *after* the act, through what means, by whom, and to what effect.

The four chapters that follow are the substance of this book, dealing with specific cases of suicides by ordinary individuals with anti-establishment political resonances. Chapters 2 and 3 focus respectively on two of the cases mentioned already, grounded in their socio-political contexts and the relevant mediascape: Mohamed Bouazizi and Dimitris Christoulas. Chapter 4 takes a wider view of such suicides amidst prolonged protests in Bulgaria, particularly in 2013. It covers the third case mentioned above – that of Plamen Goranov – alongside a number of other cases that were received as acts of protest, irrespective of whether they were intended as such or not. Chapter 5, finally, broadens the picture further by considering individual acts of suicide that were fleetingly registered as symptomatising the effects of austerity – acts that were not regarded or received as protest gestures but seemed to encourage protest. In particular, the so-called "economic suicides" in Italy and "eviction suicides" in Spain are considered before drawing this study to a close.

Suman Gupta, Milena Katsarska,
Theodoros A. Spyros and Mike Hajimichael
1 January 2017

ONE | On suicide archives and political resonances

Suman Gupta

Approach of this study

This study examines a distinctive situation, the general contours of which may be outlined as follows.

A person commits suicide in a public space, in a manner which ensures that only this individual's life is extinguished. This person has not been in the public eye; on the contrary, the person has been veiled from public attention by ordinary circumstances and unexceptional conduct. More importantly, this person has made no explicit claim on behalf of any particular political alignment in committing suicide, and no such alignment has discernibly driven this person towards suicide. The suicide cannot be understood as enacted for or on behalf of a political party or organisation; it is recognised as an individual act. Nevertheless, political resonances accrue around this individual act after its occurrence, and specifically anti-establishment resonances. It is received in some tractable way as if the suicide were a protest against, or has subversive implications for, the prevailing political establishment. The political resonances may be of two sorts: *active*, in feeding an exacerbation of anti-establishment action, being recruited to oppositional political (including party political) advocacy or into the mobilisation of collective protests; or *tacit*, in calling upon establishment agents (such as government spokespersons, experts, investigators or publicists) to diffuse anti-establishment resonances (by censorship, propaganda, selective interpretation, etc.).

The anti-establishment political resonances of such an individual suicide have to do with the manner in which this act is articulated so as to generate a response, whether active or tacit. For this study, the articulation of the act is not a straightforward matter of recognising what the individual intended or what their motives were. In fact, this study does not investigate motives and intentions, and it does not speculate on their veracity or establish their probity. The articulation of the act, in this instance, is not to do with how the act was produced but with how it was received and acted upon. It is understood, then, not as an expression of the individual's intent but as embedded in what we dub the *suicide texts* that appear with the act. How the political reverberations of such an individual suicide appear in any given period after the act depends upon the aggregate of suicide texts that are available: we think of this aggregate of suicide texts as the *suicide archive* that pertains to the case of suicide in question.

The suicide archive for such an act is a complex formation which is available to interpretative and affective response, and which consists of everything that renders a response possible and allows for the tracing of such a response in suicide texts. Suicide texts that form the suicide archive may include explicit statements by the person committing suicide (such as a suicide note), the manner and setting of its performance (in public or private, as spectacle or ritual, etc.), the testimonials of witnesses, and so on, so that intent, motive and significance can be *attributed* by those contemplating the act. The archive also includes suicide texts in the form of records for public purposes, such as reports and media accounts, and findings and assessments by various investigators (for the legal record, for news reportage, etc.). The suicide archive further incorporates possible linkages and framings that may already be publicly anticipated: for example, in relation to other such acts and their suicide texts, in terms of pressing social concerns, everyday associations and common-sense speculations. The suicide archive is thus a fluid formation: it is constantly updated and modified initially and remains open to change even after it becomes relatively stable. The relationship between a suicide archive and its (activated or diffused) political resonance is not a linear one. Every new turn in political responses generates further suicide texts which in turn modify the suicide archive, and each updated version of the suicide archive has a bearing upon further political responses. How the suicide archive is shaped and received depends on the contexts and concerns of those contributing to it.

This study focuses on the relationship of the suicide archives for specific cases to their anti-establishment political resonances, which were either tractably activated or diffused between 2010 and 2015. The four chapters that follow are devoted to analyses of case-specific suicide archives. The cases of suicide in question appeared against the background of the so-called "Arab Spring" and, in a more sustained way, the financial crisis and anti-austerity protests in Europe from 2008 onwards, particularly in Greece, Bulgaria, Italy and Spain. In analysing such cases we engage with important contradictions in the dominant ideological disposition and political practices of the present.

This, then, is not a study *of* suicide but a study of present-day political regimes through an analysis of specific suicide archives and the resistances they instantiate. The cases in question here are of sudden or unanticipated suicides rather than slow suicides that seem purposive (such as starvation protests leading to death). This spare outline of our study's theme is variously sharpened or complicated as we proceed. The remainder of this chapter explores some of the conceptual and methodological predicates that underpin this study.

Conceptual strands of suicide studies

The above outline of our theme is carefully phrased to draw attention away from the impetuses that motivate suicides and to focus attention squarely on their reception and responses. In this instance, motives are matters of attribution based on what the suicide archive offers – so they too are within the field of response and only indicative. This emphasis is worth underlining because it differentiates this study from the great majority of research into suicide. The study of suicide has been largely concerned with establishing the impetuses (motives, intentions, impulses and objectives, whether individual or social) that precede the act or phenomenon of suicide. Further, such research has made dealing with suicide one of its key drivers (usually the prevention, reduction or management of the impetuses behind suicide), sometimes even where this appears not to be an explicit aim. Both establishing the impetuses for and dealing with suicide are irrelevant to this study. Nevertheless, there is much in this field of research, even with those guiding concerns, that is relevant to this study. It is from this field that the theoretical underpinnings of the analyses offered in subsequent chapters are drawn. There is both obvious recourse to the existing research field to take into account (to studies of suicide protest, for instance), and more tangentially relevant concepts to tease out from such research.

It is therefore expedient to clearly place our approach within the larger field of suicide studies at the outset. Doing so is, of course, necessary to hone our approach; it also has the advantage of delimiting references from a superlatively productive scholarly field. Researchers into suicide have long regarded the scale of the relevant literature with trepidation. Writing early in the twentieth century on the subject, Maurice Halbwachs (1978 [1930]: 3) contemplated an incomplete bibliography of 3,771 works; early in the twenty-first century, John C. Weaver (2009: 19) starts by enumerating early bibliographies of suicide studies up to Norman Farberow's (1969), which covers the period from 1897 to 1967 and lists approximately 3,500 works – and simply notes thereafter: "Libraries today hold an astonishing number of recent titles."

The difference between our approach and that of the wider field of suicide studies, along with our dependence on it, calls for some deft negotiations. There are a number of more or less dominant conceptual strands of suicide studies, from the agendas of all of which this study can be differentiated to a greater or lesser degree, and all of which are relevant here to a large or small extent. The distinctive thrust of this study is most cogently expressed in terms of its agenda. Bearing the above-stated objective in mind (a study of current political regimes through the analysis of specific suicide archives and the resistances they instantiate), the salient point to note about each currently dominant strand is as follows: why is this sort of research into suicide undertaken? The definitions and methodologies that characterise each strand are usually conditional to its predetermined agenda. How suicide is defined, in particular, reveals the predetermined character of the agenda and is always worth noting (multiple definitions of suicide are usefully addressed in sociological terms by Douglas

(1970 [1967]: Appendix II) and in philosophical terms by Cholbi (2011: Chapter 1)). Once the predetermination of agenda is taken into account, each strand enables some clarification of the ways in which suicide texts and suicide archives, and related political repercussions, are generated and the conceptual nuances at work within them – which are useful to this study. Some of these conceptual nuances are relevant here in ways that go against the grain of the strand of suicide studies in which they appear; some are straightforwardly adopted here in the spirit of the strand where they are found.

With a view to clarifying the thrust of this study in relation to four of the currently dominant strands of suicide studies – suicidology and prevention of suicide, sociology and suicide rates, philosophical horizons, and in terms of academic and cultural reflexivity – a strand-by-strand consideration of the field follows.

STRAND 1: SUICIDOLOGY AND SUICIDE PREVENTION
The kind of research that is now called "suicidology", established mainly through the energetic efforts of Norman Farberow and Edwin Shneidman since the 1950s, regards suicide as a pathological issue, a result of psychological dysfunction. It comes with an inbuilt agenda of preventing suicide through the treatment of individuals and via measures of social control of individuals. In a way, this is the current authorised strand, in that such research is powerfully backed by governmental, non-governmental and corporate organisations and policy, especially by the medical and mental health establishment. Much of this prolific and multivalent field of research is devoted to the social, economic and cultural determinants of suicide, insofar as they offer insights

into the psychology of potential suicides with a view to preventing suicide. The definition of suicide that underpins suicidology research – and to which Shneidman devoted a book – provides a useful if hurried purchase on this approach:

> My principal assertion about suicide has two branches. The first is that suicide is a multifaceted event and that biological, cultural, sociological, interpersonal, intrapsychic, logical, conscious and unconscious, and philosophical elements are present, in various degrees, in each suicide event.
>
> The second branch of my assertion is that, in the distillation of each suicide event its essential element is a *psychological* one; that is to say, each suicidal drama occurs in the *mind* of a unique individual. Suicide is purposive. Its purpose is to respond to or redress certain psychological needs. (Shneidman 1985: 202)

Because it is given as an *assertion*, the weight of authority is conferred on this definition – the sort of authority that demands attention. Assertion, as opposed to circumspection, is relatively rare in academic discourse, though commonplace in management and governmental discourses. The two branches of the definition then make two linked moves. First, various disciplinary approaches to suicide are acknowledged, while they are tacitly disinvested of social and political (collective) content; their relevance is confined only to "each suicide event". Second, the definition reiterates that confinement (so that "each suicide event" becomes the province of "a unique individual") by making all the disciplinary approaches secondary to the prerogatives of psychology ("the essential element"). In this definition, a tactical battle against many directions of research is thus won, and the territorial occupation of one area of research is thereby established. In the process, a dictum of authority is also established: the individual is the focus of management and control in suicidology and suicide prevention. Moreover, a particular understanding of the individual is foregrounded – and is taken up via a small detour.

Evidently, suicidology makes the determination of individual intentions and motives its main focus, which immediately places it at some considerable distance from this study. Moreover, our interest in anti-establishment political resonances is diametrically opposed to suicidology's disinvestment from political analysis by focusing on the particular act and the unique individual. But our approach cannot be indifferent to suicidology, the authorised presence of which in academic and establishment – state, medical, corporate – practices means that it is a critical part of the suicide texts we are concerned with. Our interest in suicidology, however, does not address the latter in its own terms but rather argues against those terms. Pursuing this interest involves drawing suicidology as an object within the critical purview extended to suicide texts here. Usefully, such a perspective is far from being unique in contemplating suicidology; strong critiques of suicidology are available, in a polemical vein by Thomas Szasz (1999) and in a measured and convincing analysis by Ian Marsh (2010).

Szasz (1999) turns suicidology's understanding of suicide as a pathological issue that concerns the individual on itself, so to speak, by taking a strong liberal individualist (akin to libertarian) position. He argues that such an approach is a means for the state and the medical establishment to disempower individuals and curtail individual freedom. Marsh (2010) makes a related but broader argument, not by focusing on a loose first principle of freedom and the limits of the state but by drawing on Michel Foucault's methods. Foucault's critical methodology usefully enables habitual social practices and norms to be put into perspective by teasing out the rationales of power – and thereby the exercise of power – that operate through them. In other words, these practices and norms are scrutinised as cohering within a structure of knowledge that embeds control and compliance. At the same time, the methodology also demonstrates the contingent character of the structures of knowledge and rationales of power by historical tracing: that is, by laying out the logic of their development according to historical circumstances and agencies. Importantly, the focus on structures of knowledge allows reflective attention to be paid to knowledge production – specialist pursuits and their complicity with power. Understandably, Foucault's methods have been influential in critical scholarship on suicide and reappear later. Marsh uses all the dimensions of Foucault's method in his analysis of suicidology. This includes, first, a systematic examination of the routinized and normalized practices of suicidology as a "contemporary regime of truth" through which establishment power is exercised. And, second, a historical account is presented of how the discourse of suicide as pathological emerged as the dominant approach from a range of other discourses. This "regime of truth", Marsh argues, is designed to disperse other, more socially and politically disturbing, nuances of suicide, "as [an] act of protest or resistance, of self-determination, choice or will, an event of moral, criminal or political concern, even as a subject of philosophical concern" (ibid.: 4).

The point at which Szasz and Marsh converge is suicidology's construction of the individual who commits or contemplates suicide. Regarded as persons with a psychological dysfunction and subject to pathological disorder, and as objects of mental health concern, suicidal individuals are divested of responsibility for themselves. Thus regarded, their motives and intentions can be disregarded, especially if they are inconvenient to establishment norms. They become involuntary symptoms of a malaise and therefore devoid of rational judgement (which is ceded automatically to the authority of the psychologist), and suicide is thus removed from the possibility of political resonance. Emphasising the *voluntariness* of the act of suicide is therefore essential to understanding the political resonance of that act. In Marsh's words:

> If suicide can be conceived as voluntary, at least to some degree, then the door is also opened to consideration of the act in political terms [...] Such a position then opens up the possibility of interpreting suicide in terms of resistance, refutation or protest. Power relations and questions of social justice and inequalities could come more to the fore in discussions of suicide. (Marsh 2010: 73–4)

Szasz, in a typically defiant tone, extends his critical position by defining suicide as voluntary to begin with: "I use the word 'suicide' to refer to taking one's own life voluntarily and deliberately, either by killing oneself directly or by abstaining from a directly life-saving act" (1999: 2).

Marsh's emphasis on reception – "*consideration* of the act", "*interpreting* suicide" – in ascribing voluntariness and thus releasing political resonance is relevant to this study. In subsequent chapters, our analysis of politically resonant suicide archives reveals that they are a site of struggle for control. On the one hand, those seeking significant political resonance in the suicide archive look for signs of voluntariness, or try to constitute the archive so that a rational (pragmatic) impetus can be ascribed to the suicide. Such ascription potentially releases political resonances that are meaningful in the context. On the other hand, those seeking to diffuse any notable political resonance seek to constitute the suicide archive so that individual psychological dysfunction and mental health concerns are foregrounded. By exerting the authority of suicidological expertise, the potential political resonance of the suicide archive is contained. In fact, suicidological expertise seems to eschew the possibility of "politics" even when engaging with the "social" dimensions of suicide: for instance, an encyclopaedic entry discussing "social approaches" in *The Oxford Handbook of Suicide and Self-Injury* (Heilbron et al. 2014) confines itself to examining the role of "peers, family and neighbourhood" in cases of suicide, without once breathing the word "political". The fluidity of the suicide archive generally presents the trace of this struggle between those who ascribe voluntariness to suicides and those who do not; frequently, the two sides are in opposition, in a mutually confrontational process, producing suicide texts and moulding the suicide archive.

STRAND 2: SUICIDE RATES AND SOCIOLOGY

Emile Durkheim (1952 [1897]) is the continuous point of departure and return for sociological approaches to suicide, and some truisms about his work seem now to be widely accepted. One of them is that Durkheim defined suicide so as to divest it of individual psychological content (motives and intentions) and thereby render his statistical material of pivotal interest. This is too pat, and loses sight of the context of Durkheim's sociological enterprise. His research was undertaken not long after Adolphe Quetelet (1842 [1835]) and August Comte (1896 [1830–41]) had laboriously and formatively teased out a science of studying human collectives ("social physics" or sociology) from the amorphous "study of man", in which individuality and collectivity had slipped haphazardly into each other. Accordingly, Durkheim's study of suicide was, in fact, at pains to account for the individual before focusing on the collective, and, following Quetelet's example, it used statistics as its scientific basis. So, there is a careful disposal – and typological accounting – of relevant psychological states before the sociological exegesis. And Durkheim's (1952 [1897]) definition is not as unambiguously programmatic as is often made out. The definition of suicide that he developed in his introduction has two steps. The first step is perhaps programmatic in the way it is generally understood, and is stated as the "first formula": "the term suicide is applied to any death which is the direct or indirect result of a positive or negative act accomplished by the victim himself" (ibid.: 42). But then there is a second step, driven by the need for greater precision, which consists in adding a clause at the end: "which he knows will produce this result" (ibid.: 44). That opens up a very significant space for considering the individual and for accommodating individual motives and intentions; whether the individual *knew* that death would result is the juncture of individual agency and motivations.

The point, however, is that, although this is a definitive clause, it is also irrelevant to Durkheim's focus on the collective and on his dependence on statistics as indicative of collective features. It is acknowledged, but it does not impinge on Durkheim's study. His dependence on statistical sources rendered it unnecessary for him to delve into the business of determining what the persons committing suicide knew. He could assume that those who collected the statistics, or who provided the base material for statistical collation, had done that already. To be precise, Durkheim took as suicide whatever had been officially recorded as suicide for statistical purposes: in a way, he was constructing a metanarrative on extrapolations from existing suicide texts, which he knew existed but wasn't concerned with. That obviously sharply distinguishes Durkheim's approach – and, indeed, sociological approaches that foreground statistical data generally – from later approaches of suicidology with a view to preventing suicide.

The individuality of the suicides in the suicide archives that interest us seems to offer limited recourse to Durkheim's approach or to statistical data analysis in general. But gauging the relevance of this approach calls for a more precise understanding of how such data, and the sociological project from Durkheim onwards, features in relation to suicide archives – or, to return to that leading question here, with what agenda. Why study suicide in this sociological statistics-based way? At one level, the agenda is academic: a demonstration of the capabilities of sociology's apparatus for scientific practice (those rules of sociological method that Durkheim (1982 [1895]) enumerated a few years earlier), by application to the "social fact" of suicide. The potency of this method was demonstrated precisely in its being applied productively to an area – suicide – which, at the time, seemed *not* to be amenable to such study. At another level, and comparatively tacitly, the agenda seems to be the production of knowledge that could lend itself to social engineering – in this case, the management of suicide, if necessary, through social policy and the manipulation of social structures (institutions, economies, conventions, etc.). In this respect, despite the different definitions and opposing methods, there is a kind of affinity between this sociological approach to suicide and that of suicidology.

The tacit agenda of social engineering becomes clearer if the structural and methodological similarities between Durkheim's study of suicide and Quetelet's earlier (1842 [1835]) study of the "average man" are contemplated. Quetelet's method for studying the "average man" and Durkheim's in studying suicide are analogous in the following respects: the accounting of statistical data according to descriptive categories (gender, race, age, region, religion, etc.) so as to elicit various mean figures, and then their analysis to obtain a description of a collective fact ("man" itself for Quetelet, suicide for Durkheim), and especially the determination of some unbending regularities or norms (i.e. with predictive potential) for that which is described. Durkheim (1952 [1897]) draws attention to these similarities in a substantial discussion of Quetelet's "average man" (ibid.: 300–4) as a kind of model, with reference to which his own method is honed. The difference is principally that suicides are an atypical minority, and statistical reckonings based on this minority have no bearing on the generality represented by Quetelet's "average man". Notably, Durkheim did not fall into the trap of trying to delineate suicide in terms of a "real average" in the way Quetelet did in his later reflections on the "average man" (1849 [1846]). Questions regarding the agenda of this sort of research had already been raised in the mid-nineteenth century with regard to Quetelet's work. Kevin Donnelly (2014) has written illuminatingly on this, quoting the resolution found in an 1848 essay by statesman Pierre de Decker: "Quetelet proclaimed that: *the important role of moral statistics is to show to the legislator the point where he must act to modify the social state!*" (cited in Donnelly 2014: 416, emphasis in the original). This resolution – the production of knowledge for social engineering, where necessary – seems to extend to Durkheim's adoption of Quetelet's statistical methods. Indeed, in many ways, it seems to extend to the subsequent general project of statistics-based sociological investigation of suicide.

The parameters within which social engineering informed by the statistics-based study of suicide could be considered were set between Durkheim's monograph (1952 [1897]) and Maurice Halbwachs' (1978 [1930]) Durkheim-inspired follow-up. Apart from justifying his sociological method, Durkheim followed two steps in studying suicide: first, examining suicide rates to determine what the normal or regular limits of suicide are in society; and second, analysing recent fluctuations (abnormalities), if any, and considering what could be done about them. The second step is evidently where the potential for social engineering is found. Durkheim did find a significant fluctuation in recent suicide rates: a marked increase, well beyond the norm, in the last hundred years. His analysis drew upon the famous and much-referenced typology for suicide he had proposed: altruistic, egotistic and anomic. He suggested that, instead of specific socio-economic factors being the cause of rising suicide rates, the latter are explained by disturbances in the overall social order that arouse anomic tendencies (this argument is elaborated later in this chapter). The final sections of Durkheim's study (especially Book 3, Chapter 3) offer various observations that could have a bearing on social engineering – or on the management of suicide from above for collectives. Halbwachs followed roughly the same steps, but with somewhat different analytical precepts and reaching contrary conclusions insofar as social engineering is concerned. Briefly, the difference in analytical precepts entailed: first, taking account of more advanced statistical methods and updating the data; second, drawing a line of causality so that the place of individual psychology within collective trends is more explicit and graded; and third, consequently offering a more complex account of progressive development and social organisation than Durkheim's typology of suicide allowed. As a result, Halbwachs concludes that the increase in suicide rates that troubled Durkheim was actually normal if adjusted and understood in terms of growing social complexity, and therefore no particular direction of social engineering need be considered.

There are, of course, other directions of sociological research into suicide that depart from Durkheim's formulations – towards theories of social integration, action, ecology, status and so on – and that have various impulses towards social engineering. Insofar as the powerful analysis centred on suicide rate is concerned, the parameters for considering social engineering set by Durkheim and Halbwachs have largely been maintained. Increasingly sophisticated and broad-based statistical analyses of suicide, such as those presented by Christian Baudelet and Roger Establet (2008 [2005], more on this later), confirm this.

As well as focusing on collectivity, the tacit agenda of social engineering seems to distance such research from our interest in the relationship between specific suicide archives and their political resonances. However, as in suicidology, such sociological research provides framing devices within suicide texts, and pushes the textualising process in various directions of advocacy. That is of some importance here. One of the points that emerges from the above summary of Durkheim's and Halbwachs' arguments is that statistics on suicide are a fluid area. While offering apparent scientific precision and objectivity, the statistical method allows for contrary interpretations and advocacy, which are all the more effective because of their scientific appearance. When a suicide text appears to generate political resonance, that resonance may be activated or diffused by advocacy-led framing in terms of suicide rates and their interpretation. Such interpretations may persuasively suggest either that statistical abnormalities (of which an individual case is symptomatic) are indicative of a general political disorder, or that such abnormalities are not really abnormalities at all or are merely temporary blips (so no individual case can be regarded as a symptom).

STRAND 3: PHILOSOPHICAL HORIZON

Suicide has often been a significant consideration in erecting philosophical and theological systems, usually as an anchor for fundamental concepts such as the meaning of life and death, parameters of freedom, limits of subjectivity, and rational and ethical choices. These are concepts that test philosophical first principles and the consistency of systems. This study's focus on contextually grounded suicide archives does not necessarily call for direct reference to such concepts and systems, but the latter constitute a horizon for any contemplation of suicide, and such horizons are not irrelevant here. Even if the subsequent chapters do not refer to fundamental concepts and philosophical systems explicitly, in many respects they underpin the analyses throughout this book as an unspoken but necessary substrate. Anxious engagements with suicide in philosophical or theological terms ripple quietly in the background of any analysis of suicide archives where political resonances are encountered.

If a suicide text allows for the attribution of voluntariness to suicide rather than presuming an individualised pathology, and thereby enables political resonance (as suggested by Szasz and Marsh, cited above), then discernment of a politically meaningful rationale is necessarily admitted. And yet rationalising suicide is troubling – it disturbs the stability of most conceptual systems, of prevailing political and theological orders, and makes the suicide archive a site of impassioned contestations. The discerned rationales are not easily accepted as justifiable – rather, they invite searching scepticism – and responses to those suicide texts that propose such rationales are correspondingly agonised. The contemplation of suicides with political resonances cannot be untroubled. Consequently, analyses of politically resonant suicide archives have a bearing upon – and inevitably lie within – philosophical horizons, even if they do not address them fully.

For the sake of economical exposition, these observations are stated categorically here; a suitably comprehensive demonstration would be a very different undertaking. A brief explanation, however, is possible by noting two of the most familiar – and usefully symmetrically theist and atheist – philosophical (existentialist) contemplations of suicide. The theist line appears in Søren Kierkegaard (1980 [1849]), where he, writing as Anti-Climacus, expands on the unavoidable undercurrent of despair with which living is imbued. Despair rises occasionally or gradually, but more or less inevitably, to awareness – albeit to different degrees in different circumstances. In a way, Kierkegaard constructs the inevitability of despair by systematically reiterating it in the logic of his argument. His concern is with the comprehension of despair as a Christian, and so "before God". As such, surrender to God is a promise of release from despair, but to understand the need for this surrender is also to fully comprehend despair. One alternative to surrender is another sort of escape, the possibility of suicide. Before God, however, Anti-Climacus/Kierkegaard argues, suicide is not a resolution but the ultimate act of despair:

> The person who, with a realization that suicide is despair and
> to that extent with a true conception of the nature of despair,

commits suicide is more intensively in despair than one who commits suicide without a clear idea that suicide is despair; conversely, the less true his conception of despair, the less intensive his despair. On the other hand, a person who with a clearer consciousness of himself (self-consciousness) commits suicide is more intensively in despair than one whose soul, by comparison, is in confusion and darkness. (Kierkegaard 1980 [1849]: 48–9)

So, the fully aware Christian who, before God, commits suicide contradicts that awareness and its concomitant grasp of despair – and thereby contradicts God ("suicide is basically a crime against God" (ibid.: 46)). Contradictory and self-defeating as suicide might be in Anti-Climacus/Kierkegaard's Christian scheme, it is nevertheless rationally understandable. Importantly, the suicidal person's rationale might be misjudged, but it is a rationale nevertheless. And, the philosophical and theological system that Anti-Climacus/Kierkegaard constructs is itself probed uncomfortably by this misjudged rationale. Outside this system (i.e. according to the pagan's world view), this rationale of suicide is meaningless because, of course, for Anti-Climacus/Kierkegaard there is no rationality outside Christian self-consciousness; he feels convinced that pagans therefore take suicide less seriously.

To take the symmetrical atheistic track, in Albert Camus' (1955 [1942]) conceptual system it is precisely the absence of supernal confirmation that is evidenced in an inevitable encounter with something like Kierkegaard's despair. This consists in us encountering a sense of absurdity, whereby all conventions relating to the meaningfulness of life are put into perspective as contingent and non-binding. The resulting freedom of choice to which an individual – any individual – is thereby exposed is the realisation of absurdity, which is akin to despair; it is discomfiting in that it removes reassuring certainties and approved commitments. In Camus' argument, the appropriately uncompromising response is to defiantly embrace this freedom as both inevitable *and* uncomfortable. The other response is to seek to escape it by committing suicide. But suicide, for Camus, presents a compromised contradiction analogous to Kierkegaard's conception, in that it is not an escape but an exacerbated concession to absurdity:

> This is where it is seen to what a degree absurd experience is remote from suicide. It may be thought that suicide follows revolt – but wrongly. For it does not represent the logical outcome of revolt. It is just the contrary by the consent it presupposes. Suicide, like the leap, is acceptance at its extreme. Everything is over and man returns to his essential history. His future, his unique and dreadful future – he sees and rushes towards it. In its way, suicide settles the absurd. It engulfs the absurd in the same death. (Camus 1955 [1942]: 54)

The point is that, in Camus' conceptual system, suicide is also conferred a rationale, but a compromised and contradictory rationale. And arguing against it is a moment of tension in Camus' text that interrogates the constitution of the conceptual system itself, and takes it to the limit of making sense (the quoted passage is very close to being nonsensical).

Such existentialist systems are far from being representative of philosophical systems generally, but they convey something of the character of philosophical and theological engagement with suicide. Relevantly, these show that being placed within a philosophical system confers a rationale on suicide in a general and a universal way – even if that rationale is contradictory or compromised. Moreover, the contemplation of suicide reveals the fundamental concepts (being in the world, being before God, freedom, self-awareness) with a sense of discomfort and foreboding and leaves them open to question. None of this has a particularly direct bearing on this project of analysing specific suicide archives and their political resonances. However, it seems noteworthy that, at some level, political resonances derive from such a substratum of philosophical and theological reckonings. Kierkegaard's conceptual system, for instance, has in view an implicitly political thrust towards the realisation of a Christian polity and Christian citizenship. Similarly, Camus' atheistic philosophical system has in view a political thrust towards anarchist individualism, or perhaps radical liberal individualism. Camus' contemplation of suicide is possibly the most unremittingly individualistic in conception; he allows for contemplation of suicide only as an individual's confrontation with the world, from an individual's perspective of living in the world (it is not surprising that there is no reference to Durkheim's work). But the concept of freedom that is emphasised by this view radiates into a political commitment to freedom and perhaps deliberately collides with liberal, socialist and other conceptions of secular freedom, and does so in a very studied way.

In fact, the contemplation of politically resonant suicide in some recent studies, close to the spirit of this one, makes the substratum of philosophical and theological systems clearly discernible. Concepts of sovereignty and the exercise of power over life, in which subjectivity and bodily presence are implicated, seem to rise from the philosophical depths into the critical nuancing of specific suicide archives. Naturally, such instances are of particular interest to this study, and are considered in brief accounts of aligned projects later in this chapter.

STRAND 4: ACADEMIC AND CULTURAL REFLEXIVITY

Overlapping with all the above, the analysis of suicide texts and suicide archives has often involved putting into perspective methodologies of study – and culturally determined presumptions about objects of study: that is, making visible that which is unquestioningly assumed or silently at work. Thus, histories of particular types of suicide (such as so-called honour suicides, self-sacrifice and martyrdom, heroic suicides and suicide bombings) have often unpacked their own historiographical assumptions by taking diverse or "other" culturally specific discourses into account. The idea is that scholarly methodologies may be based on hidden culturally specific assumptions, which are tacitly taken as natural or normative and which may prejudice or distort analysis. In examining acts of suicide against different historical and cultural contexts, it is necessary to lay bare such hidden assumptions. This naturally also involves rendering the cultural assumptions of the specific context in question explicit. Similarly, literary or artistic representations of suicide often challenge interpretive strategies, philosophical ruminations on suicide frequently test first principles, juridical views of suicide may clarify legal tenets, the sociology of suicide reveals much about methods of social research, and so on. In each such instance, the cultural determinants of how suicides are viewed in particular contexts can be clarified along with the cultures of scholarship and academia themselves.

In the analyses of politically resonant suicide archives in this book, the relevant contextually grounded cultural factors are naturally discussed. The extent to which this calls for reflection on our methods of analysis remains to be seen. By way of anticipation, such analytical self-reflection (in concert with cultural reflexivity) is of particular interest when it seems to run counter to widely held scholarly conventions – and there is some scope for that in this study. An exemplary instance of this is found in the ethnomethodological turn in sociological approaches to suicide of the 1970s. As observed earlier, the focus on suicide rates as the basis for analysis, from Durkheim onwards, worked on the assumption that suicide is verified as being such by those who generate the data (courts, police, publicists, etc.). In conducting a survey of sociological theories of suicide after Durkheim, Jack D. Douglas (1970 [1967]) found himself wondering whether the cases and data on suicide that sociologists have worked with have predisposed their findings. In other words, Douglas suspected that the common-sense notions of suicide that have underpinned such data collection could well lead sociological analysis to simply confirm those notions with the aid of a seemingly rigorous scholarly apparatus. The idea was pursued by J. Maxwell Atkinson (1978: particularly Chapters 7 and 8): after examining the common-sense theories of suicide of coroners and journalists, for instance, in order to provide empirical evidence for sociologists, he found that such theories tend to be confirmed by sociologists. It appeared that common-sense theories of suicide were influencing the research material so that scholars were simply reproducing those theories within academic discourse. This seemed questionable because rigorous scholarship is putatively designed to circumvent common-sense misconceptions and biases, where necessary; at any rate, *unknowingly* reiterating common-sense theories goes against the integrity of sociological scholarship. Interestingly, this argument did not mean that Douglas or Atkinson tried to obtain data from sources other than the customary, or tried to ensure some sort of institutional disavowal of common sense. That would have been an unrealistically complicated, and in some respects self-defeating, project. The approach they preferred instead was to make common-sense theories of suicide, the practice of common-sense understanding itself, an object of sociological investigation. As Douglas put it:

> [Sociologists] have generally used common-sense explanations (and meanings) of suicidal actions as the basis of their explanations, *rather than treating such common-sense explanations as phenomena to be studied by sociologists (or psychiatrists) because such explanations are themselves likely to be part of the suicidal processes.* It is from this latter standpoint that we propose to *make use of*, rather than *take the standpoint of*, common-sense understandings of suicidal phenomena. (Douglas 1970 [1967]: 267, emphasis in the original)

By subjecting the factor of common sense (to a great extent a culturally embedded factor) to sociological research, they could hope to factor it into further analysis of suicide – or render the sociology of suicide *knowing* about the interference of common sense.

In directing this study towards the reception of politically resonant suicide archives, and thereby leaving the determination of motives and intentions outside our remit, a similar sort of academically dubious factor is courted. As noted above, this does not mean that intentions and motives are entirely neglected; it means that they are considered insofar as they can be attributed or interpreted in suicide texts. Within this study, this methodological decision gives a certain salience to *speculation*. The attribution of motives at some juncture within a fluid suicide archive, in various partisan constructions of suicide texts, amidst partial information or misinformation, necessarily gives full play to speculative interpretations. In this study, the traces of such speculations are taken seriously; they are part and parcel of the suicide archives in question and are often crucial in activating political resonances. In academic discourse, speculations tend to be regarded and offered with caution. Evidence and verification processes are arguably of such importance to scholarly work, so much the bedrock of academic rigour, that speculation can be undertaken only circumspectly. In taking speculations seriously here, however, we do not take the standpoint of speculations but rather we foreground their dynamics *as speculations*. Where such speculations are encountered or used in the following chapters, this occurs so that speculation itself – and the culturally specific predicates of speculation – becomes the object of inquiry.

Relevant areas of suicide studies

The four conceptual strands briefly outlined above for the purposes of this study seldom appear in isolation from each other. Most research into suicide focuses on a specific area, described by content. This could include a specific historical or cultural context, particular junctures of socio-political interest, representation in certain media, demographic categories (class, gender, race, etc.), distinctive modes or performances – and, generally, some combination of these. Within such areas, defined by content, conceptual approaches are sometimes adhered to consistently, sometimes called upon opportunistically, and sometimes negotiated to reach methodological syntheses. Arguably, on the one hand, such content-based delimitation enables a reduction of complexity in understanding suicide (i.e. the complexity of *all* that may be regarded or defined as suicide). Equally, on the other hand, such content-defined areas may introduce a different kind of complexity, of the sort that is found in specific suicide archives but may be muted in general formulations.

As observed earlier, our study is also delimited by content: the political resonances we are interested in are anti-establishment ones, and the cases we discuss are associated with political and financial crises, broadly within a demarcated period (2010–15) and framed according to geopolitical territories (Tunisia and Egypt, Greece, Bulgaria, Italy and Spain). Few sustained analyses of these areas are currently available; however, there are studies in other areas that necessarily influence and inform this. It is useful, then, to consider how this book draws upon such studies and the precise respects in which they inform and differ from it. To that end, three such areas of suicide studies are briefly outlined below: suicide bombings (or, more broadly, where killing oneself and others is coeval); suicide rates in relation to the financial crisis of 2008 and beyond; and protest suicides (where killing oneself is not in order to kill others). These areas of study seem aligned to ours because they investigate suicide archives that have had obvious anti-establishment political resonances. In fact, it is likely that such studies would be associated with this one irrespective of direct influence and bearing, and an initial discussion is as much a matter of prudence as scholarly acknowledgement. The current interest in suicide bombings, protest suicides and the financial crisis (in the mass media, in popular political discourses, in every-day reckonings) makes preconceived expectations unavoidable. The following observations on these three areas proceed from the least to the most relevant for this study.

AREA 1: SUICIDE BOMBING

The phrase "suicide bombing" has come to designate – and is taken here to refer to – any act of suicide that is performed to knowingly kill others, where the person committing suicide is using him- or herself as a weapon. This has no relation to the cases with which this study is concerned. It is perhaps necessary to emphasise this obvious point here because such has been the recent public, policy and academic concern with suicide bombings that the contemplation of any politically resonant suicide immediately connects to that concern. In suicide bombing archives, the political resonances are unavoidable, but they are utterly different from the kinds of suicide archives and political resonances in question here.

Nonetheless, some conceptual turns are found within the intensive discussion of suicide bombings that are suggestive for this study. To begin with, the contemplation of suicide bombings challenges the disinvestment of suicide from politics that the dominant discourse of suicidology demands. That means it is difficult to regard such acts as predominantly individual, rooted ultimately in individual psychology, and to overlook the impetus of organisations (which often explicitly claim responsibility as such) behind them. The result is a fault line in establishment reckonings of the phenomenon of suicide bombing, which is less apparent for other suicide phenomena. The fault line is between, on the one hand, those who see a (distorted, extremist or perverse) political or theological rationale in suicide bombing (such as Reuter 2004 [2002]; Khosrokhavar 2005) or a strategic political or military rationale (e.g. Bloom 2005), and, on the other, those who push the suicidological line of psychological dysfunction, grounded in both individual disposition and group dynamics (as in Silke 2003; De Masi 2011). These debates make for fractured suicide bombing archives, open to incommensurable interpretations, within mainstream and popular discourses. The manner in which suicide bombing archives trouble the dominant discourse of suicidology cannot be reiterated for the cases discussed in this book, and yet the latter trouble that discourse too, but in other ways.

More importantly, some sophisticated contemplations of suicide bombing have turned away from a singular focus on motives and intentions (the production of suicide bombing) towards an analysis in terms of reception (how suicide bombing is perceived and understood). That turn is instructive for this study and its focus on reception. Those who examine perceptions of and reactions to suicide bombing suggest that these reveal a dominant political condition, and offer a more tractable grasp of this condition than of the impetuses behind suicide bombing. In this vein, much of Talal Asad's meditation on suicide bombing is a "discussion of some typical explanations of the suicide bomber [which], I suggest [...] tell us more about liberal assumptions of religious subjectivities and political violence than they do about what is ostensibly being explained" (2007: 42). This approach leads him to raise a question that seems too obvious to be asked: "Why do people in the West react to verbal and visual representations of suicide bombing with professions of horror?"; which in turn leads into an argument about the Christian underpinnings of dominant, seemingly secular, liberal attitudes. The latter, Asad argues, are both ethnocentric and imperialist, and enable the perpetration of violence on their behalf under a guise of moral and civilisational superiority. Whether one accepts or rejects Asad's recourse to religious history, the argument is convincing insofar as it presents the receptive field as the space where political resonances are generated. The features of the present-day liberal (neoliberal) socio-political order thus described are also often persuasive. More or less aligned with Asad's approach, but taking a distinctive line, Hamid Dabashi's (2012) focus on the violence of spectacular suicide concretised (almost phenomenologically) in the body – the exploding bodies of suicide bombers – is similarly suggestive here. For Dabashi, "suicidal violence, the self-exploding body, is a [...] *corpus anarchicum* denying the state its sole site of self-legitimising violence" (ibid.: 185). This makes clear a general present-day political condition, summarised as follows:

> My conclusion is that the globalized capital has made the national state apparatus entirely aterritorial and contingent – the equally globalized practice of the political, which no longer corresponds to territorial sovereignty and has had to narrow in on the *human body* as its singular site of self-legitimising violence. Meanwhile, the same amorphous capital has transfigured the Enlightenment integrity of the *human body* and pushed its anarchic defiance of state violence to the formative edges of a *posthuman disposable body*. (Dabashi 2012: 6, emphasis in the original)

Presenting the exploding body of the suicide bomber thus, as a focalized expression of the politics of the present, constitutes a suicide signifier – a synecdoche of what we think of as the suicide text here. That is, Dabashi could be seen as extrapolating one facet (a single resonant signifier) from various suicide bombing texts to convey how those texts in general, as an archive, may actuate multiple political resonances. This project is useful for this study's engagement with suicide archives as a broad formation, composed of various and often contrary signifiers and specific texts. Incidentally, in his conclusion, Dabashi draws a continuous line from the exploding bodies of suicide bombers to the burning body of Mohamed Bouazizi; this argument, while provocative, is in various ways misconceived – as is shown in the next chapter, which is largely devoted to the suicide archive of Bouazizi's self-immolation and the beginnings of the so-called "Arab Spring".

At any rate, studies of suicide bombers have the sort of tangential and limited bearing on this study noted here, and are not otherwise particularly relevant.

Area 2: financial crisis and suicide

The financial crisis from 2008 onwards in Europe provides the context for Chapters 3 and 4. Financial and political crisis has been a notable node in statistics-based sociological studies of suicide from the discipline's foundational stages. Interpretations of suicide rates are pertinent to – indeed part of – the specific suicide archives associated with the crisis of 2008 and beyond taken up later in this study.

Durkheim's (1952 [1897]: Book 2, Chapter 5) account of anomic suicide, which is key to his general concept of social anomie, was given mainly in terms of the effect of financial and political crises on suicide rates. Briefly, his argument went as follows. Given the distribution of suicide rates at his disposal, Durkheim found no straightforward proportional relationship between poverty and suicide: poorer collectives did not show evidence of higher suicide rates than their affluent counterparts – in fact, the contrary was the case – although there was evidence that stressful conditions led to increased suicide rates (especially among the most vulnerable, such as the poverty-stricken or unemployed). It was clear that political (such as civil wars) or financial crises led to significant rises in suicide rates. However, insofar as financial crises were concerned, Durkheim found that sudden impoverishment in the economy caused a rise in suicide rates as well as sudden prosperity in the economy (a sudden boom); Durkheim thought of both sudden impoverishment and sudden prosperity as financial crises. His inference was as follows:

> If therefore industrial or financial crises increase suicides, that is not because they cause poverty, since crises of prosperity have the same result; it is because they are crises, that is, disturbances of the collective order. Every disturbance of equilibrium, even though it achieves greater comfort and a heightening of general vitality, is an impulse to voluntary death. Whenever serious readjustments take place in the social order, whether or not due to sudden growth or to an unexpected catastrophe, men are more inclined to self-destruction. (Durkheim 1952 [1897]: 246)

And the explanation for this inference amounts to the concept of anomie in general:

> Man's characteristic privilege is that the bond he accepts is not physical but moral; that is, social. He is governed not by a material environment brutally imposed on him, but by a conscience superior to his own, the superiority of which he feels. Because, the greater, better part of his existence transcends the body, he escapes the body's yoke, but is subject to that of society.
>
> But when society is disturbed by some painful crisis or by beneficent but abrupt transitions, it is momentarily incapable of exercising this influence; thence come the sudden rises in the curve of suicides which we have pointed out above. (Durkheim 1952 [1897]: 252)

In his follow-up to Durkheim's project, Halbwachs (1978 [1930]: especially Chapters 10 and 11) took into account further statistical data on suicide rates in relation to political and financial crises to undermine some of the neat symmetry of Durkheim's figures (he found that Durkheim had been selective in interpreting his data). He also inserted an analysis of the impact of crises on the psyche instead of going along with Durkheim's abstruse account of anomie, and was more questioning of the "crisis of prosperity". In its fundamentals, though, Halbwachs' inferences and analysis confirmed Durkheim's, concluding with a more emotive account of the anomic condition that financial crises cause, evidenced in rising suicide rates:

> The woes of unemployed workers, the bankruptcies, failures, and downfalls are not the immediate cause of many suicides. Rather, an obscure oppressive sentiment weighs on every soul because there is less general activity, because there is less participation by people in an economic life transcending them, and because their attention is no longer turned towards externals but dwells more, not merely on their distress or on their bare material competency, but on all the individual motives they may have for desiring death. (Halbwachs 1978 [1930]: 244)

This has a clear psychological and individually grounded character, but it is more a fleshing-out of Durkheim's formulation than a departure from it.

Closer to the financial crisis that began in 2008, Baudelet and Establet's (2008 [2005]) analysis of wide-ranging data on suicide rates updates the Durkheim–Halbwachs analysis with various further nuances, but without departing from its spirit. Among other points of interest, this updates the terms of economic measurement. Instead of simply considering gauges of poverty, they look at the relationship of inequality to suicide rates, and find that that in itself (like poverty for Durkheim) does not correspond proportionally to suicide rates. And, instead of merely "financial crisis", they consider slower and longer phases of growth (1900–48, 1949–78, 1979–95) in relation to suicide rates, and find that the relationships are complex: however, in a general trend, strong growth since 1949 has been attended by stable suicide rates and slow growth by rising suicide rates. Data categorised according to geopolitical territories and social strata (India and China in the late twentieth century, the Soviet Union, according to class and gender) suggests that Durkheim and Halbwachs provide appropriate grids and points of departure for inference and analysis. Baudelet and Establet do not extend their observations to an analysis of anomie in the present; that is left to the very general, somewhat oracular, formulations cited above.

Perhaps that is where a space for sociological theorising opens up: suicide rates in relation to aggregate factors (class, country, political system and policy, etc.) are indicative in a symptomatic way, but do not reveal the political dynamics at ground level, at the level of specific environments, work and everyday life. Baudelet and Establet's conclusion says as much. It is unlikely that what Durkheim or Halbwachs understood as an anomic condition in their political periods could be the same as what is regarded as anomic in the present, although the general drift of social anomie and its statistical manifestations are coherent and represent a continuous relation. But the picture is incomplete without a bottom-up perspective from ground level to statistical aggregates – of the sort, for instance, that Franco "Bifo" Berardi (2015: especially Chapter 9) offers. In Berardi's book, we find an account of suicide epidemics experienced in various industrial contexts among workers, which, as Berardi sees it, provide evidence of the deployment of "[h]ierarchy, obedience, submission, humiliation and psychological violence [that] are the weapons employed by Neoliberal philosophy against the political solidarity of the workforce" (ibid.: 109). He points towards an ideological and political structure of the present as producing and reproducing the kind of anomie that politically resonant suicide now symptomatizes. The terms ("What is 'Neoliberal philosophy'?" we may ask) are there to be unpacked and argued with, but Berardi articulates that which, in some measure, is muted in global charts of suicide rates and the generalisation of (ahistorical) anomie.

The macroscopic sociological analysis of suicide rates and crisis contains the ground-level perspective but doesn't quite capture it; this is what the present study addresses. The macroscopic level is implied in all suicide texts, but the individual and specific suicide archives and their political resonances are the focal point of our analysis.

With the financial crisis of 2008 onwards in view, of some interest here are arguments woven around suicide rates in the healthcare sector (which fall within the fold of suicidology studies). To be precise, such arguments are concerned not so much with the crisis itself as with its principal fallout: a widespread convergence on enacting austerity policies among political states, or having such policies thrust upon them by international financial and governmental organisations. Concern about the "neoliberal philosophy" (which Berardi considered) since 2008 has been particularly directed towards austerity policies, although the latter are consistent with policy moves that go back to at least the 1970s. Very briefly, austerity policies consist in states disinvesting from public institutions and services, either to effectively commercialise and privatise them or to leave them to altruistic non-governmental bodies, or simply to gradually redefine them out of existence. Such policies are driven most programmatically – seemingly driven by economic logic – when significant imbalances appear in the account books of a political state's territories (a financial crisis). But such policies may be more determinatively motivated by an ideological and pragmatic convergence (collaboration) between state and corporate interests. Whatever the context, austerity usually results in the cementing of governance practices and of juridical and economic regimes that maximise such a convergence. Under such austerity conditions, parts of the state's establishment – the public sector – may find themselves having to make strenuous arguments for their survival or to push their privileges for increased governmental investment. It appears that, in various European countries after 2008, the healthcare establishment within the state sector has turned to the affective appeal of suicide rates to that end.

There have been numerous calls for a revision of austerity policies and an increase in public health spending that cite suicide rates in relation to austerity. These have appeared principally in medical, psychiatric and public health journals. To confine ourselves to one example, with a well-established academic reputation, the *British Medical Journal* (published by the British Medical Association) has regularly carried research papers on crisis and austerity in relation to suicide rates (Gunnell et al. 2009; Hawton and Haw 2013; Chang et al. 2013; Godlee 2013; Fountoulakis et al. 2013; Michas 2013; Branas et al. 2015). Some of these have aroused significant interest in the news media. In particular, news media noted the evidence cited by Shu-Sen Chang et al. (2013), who presented statistics on the impact of the economic crisis of 2008 on suicides in fifty-four countries, and found "a clear rise in suicide after the 2008 global economic crisis; there were about 4900 excess suicides in the year 2009 alone compared with those expected based on previous trends (2000–07)" (ibid.: 350). The conclusions reached in all the papers cited above are twofold: first, that austerity policies lead to a rise in suicide rates; and second, that suicide needs to be prevented under these circumstances and the medical and healthcare establishment can do that. The second of these conclusions has two elements within it. On the one hand, the medical establishment should inform policy before it is enacted, and has and should be further enabled to gather information and data on public (especially mental) health to that end. On the other, given that austerity policies have been enacted with detrimental effects, the management of such effects depends on further investment in public health and medical services at all levels (from the screening of populations to dealing with disaffected individuals exhibiting suicidal tendencies). The purpose of this use of suicide rate statistics in research is therefore not to analyse the anomic condition and its political dynamics in a general way, but to make a promotional claim on behalf of a particular sector of the establishment, within the establishment, in the public interest. Similar papers have been published in journals such as *The Lancet, Social Science and Medicine, European Journal of Public Health* and *The British Journal of Psychiatry*.

AREA 3: PROTEST SUICIDE

The area of suicide studies with which this book is most closely aligned is a relatively small one: "protest suicide" as distinct from suicide bombing. Works in this area predominantly consider suicides by self-immolation or starvation with political intent or resonance. At this introductory stage, it is useful to clarify some of the differences between this study and those recently published on protest suicides, while acknowledging the conceptual frames that chime with ours.

A sociological approach to protest suicides with a broad (international or global) view, such as that of Michael Biggs (2005; 2011; starvation suicides are not part of his remit), cannot be based on suicide rates. Protest suicides are proportionally so minute in relation to demographic factors (country, age and sex, religion, class, etc.) that suicide rates are of negligible interest. Biggs therefore draws on data relating to the *incidence* of protest suicides rather than *suicide rates*; Hassan (2011) presents similar data for suicide bombings, and for the same reason. Leaving aside any ambivalence of definition and verification in such charting of incidence, this sort of data can only be indicative in limited ways: by foregrounding comparisons across political and cultural domains at specific historical junctures, and by showing patterns of spread and emulation. To make inferences from such quantitative data, it is necessary to call upon qualitative material: Biggs (2005) does so by citing numerous specific and related cases at different historical junctures and in different geopolitical contexts, and taking into account their narrativisations (in news, which is also the source of the data). This qualitative material is given an ethnomethodological slant (this can be traced back to Douglas 1970 [1967]) which in some ways corresponds to this study's method, and which in other ways does not. It is assumed that protest suicide expresses a clear political intent and is thus a way of voicing the protest of the person committing suicide: in Biggs' words, it is "a tactic of persuasion", whereby the suicide addresses "distant audiences, gaining their attention and conveying the gravity of the cause", and "those who already adhere to the collective cause, exhorting them to greater efforts" (2011: 408). The notion that the protest is expressed by the design or intent of the suicide is outside the remit of the present study, since we are not concerned with intentions and motives. From our perspective, in the suicide archive that appears after the suicide, it becomes possible to make an attribution of such intent (and contest or neglect it), as a matter of reception, at the behest of those sensitive to the political resonance of suicide texts. At the same time, Biggs (2011) – and, indeed, others (such as Andriolo 2006; Spehr and Dixon 2013) – usefully suggests that the suicide archive is an expressive if fluid formation, presenting affective and rationalisable signs for interested interpreters.

A preoccupation with conceptualising protest suicide as an explicit and intentional act of protest, by the design of those committing suicide, also structures some of the most sustained recent studies in this area: those by Banu Bargu (2014) and Simanti Lahiri (2014). Both choose case studies to exemplify protest suicides that apparently enable the tracking of an anti-establishment protest ideology *prior to the act or the appearance of the suicide archive* – therefore, an ideology that is clearly owned by those committing suicide. Bargu's cases are drawn from starvation protests, many leading to death, among political prisoners in Turkey between 2000 and 2002. The ideological commitments and political affiliations of the prisoners, and the slow mode of suicidal protest undertaken (starvation), allowed for an explicit protest rationale to emerge prior to the occurrence of death – in a way, the suicide archive was constructed before the suicide. Bargu's ethnological method, drawing on interviews and numerous contemporary documents, allows for this prior construction, of considerable sophistication and complexity, to be carefully traced. That prior authorship of the suicide archive justifies the negligible attention paid to its reception – which, in any case, seems passive. In other words, the extensive authoring of suicide texts by the protesters who undertook suicidal action, and also by the establishment countering the protesters' authoring through its own re-authoring and intervention, puts the fluidity of the suicide archive in the hands of the authors rather than the receivers – the readers and interpreters. Concomitantly, this also gives a particular weight to Bargu's own interpretive voice, as the sole recipient of a suicide archive that, by this time, has a kind of collective authorship concretised by the distance in time. Lahiri's (2014) cases are drawn from South Asia: three connected to issue-specific social movements (protests against particular government policies) in India and one example of suicide bombing in Sri Lanka. Although they have quite different ideological inclinations from Bargu's cases, they are similarly collectively authored and also involve suicides "owned" by movements in advance of the act. Proponents of the movements have a near monopoly on the authorship of the relevant suicide texts, along with familiar government interventions, and the reception of those texts is relatively passive.

However, the ideological differences between Lahiri and Bargu are important for our understanding of politically resonant suicide. Lahiri (ibid.) does not present protest suicide as unambiguously anti-establishment. Protest in general, even suicidal protest, is conceived instead as participating in the establishment order and process. It is understood as a strategy for modifying that order so that establishment and collective interests become aligned, and, interestingly, as a tactic for grounding the establishment solidly in collective social consensus. Lahiri thus announces her project as exploring "the ability of a certain *category* of tactic in favour of movement goals. In other words, this project examines the effectiveness of suicide protests in creating policy shifts in favour of the movement" (ibid.: 2). She seeks to "explain the reasons why suicide protests result in successful contestation against the state for some group, but not for others" (ibid.: 5). Bargu (2014) not only conceptualises suicide protest and the ideology of protest as uncompromisingly anti-establishment, but also generalises them as fissures in the dominant order of the present. In doing so, she calls upon theoretical lines that can be traced to the philosophical horizons which are briefly mentioned in relation to conceptual strand 3 above. This conceptualisation of suicide protest is of particular interest for our study.

In Bargu's work, the philosophical first principles in question refer primarily to Foucault's investigations into discourses of power and governmentality (mainly from Foucault 1977 [1975] and his 1978–79 lectures at the Collège de France on the emergence of neoliberal governmentality (2008 [2004])). Simply put, those investigations traced a historical modification in the primary political concept of sovereignty. The modification involved a shift in the exercise of political power: from the exertion of sovereign will on the bodies of subjects to demand compliance (as citizens in a monarchy, for instance) to a dispersal of sovereign will within institutional practices that effectively enclose subjects and manage their compliance (for example, as citizens in a liberal democracy). The latter mode of governance ultimately ensures compliance through a cost–benefit accounting rationale. The point is that this shift in fact intensifies control from above, taking hold of the very interstices of day-to-day living and interpersonal relations and physical being (Foucault calls this "biopolitics"), while appearing humane and life-affirming and adopting a rhetoric of freedom and individual choices. This intensification of control becomes manifest, despite its ostensible claims, in an exacerbation of social violence and disaffection at various levels. Giorgio Agamben's (1998 [1995]) critique of Foucault's formulation of sovereignty, which involved articulating sovereignty at the more fundamental level of "bare life" than in discourses of power, inspired Bargu to revise Foucault's account of neoliberal governmentality in the present day. She says that the latter entails not so much a shift *away* from sovereignty as a merging of sovereign and biopolitical modes of exercising power: what she calls a "biopoliticization of sovereignty". Attempts at resisting this all-consuming political ordering of the present find few chinks in the armour of neoliberal governmentality to exploit. Meaningful resistance can only meet the dispersed and close hold on life that the biopoliticisation of sovereignty acquires by turning to death-dealing – especially of the self (the subject) – as an equally dispersed mode of anti-establishment politics. The withdrawal of life thereby assumes a general and oppositional significance in the present. Bargu calls this a "necropoliticization of resistance". In her study, suicide protest is therefore conceptualised as a symptom of a pervasive political condition of the present, where the first principles of living (being) and exercising power are in a constant and contradictory tension. This symptom throws forth, as it were, an uncompromising polarity between the exercise of power and resistance to it in the present: "This book casts the death fast struggle as an instance that crystallizes a conjuncture in which the process of the *biopoliticization of sovereignty* meets the *necropoliticization of resistance*" (Bargu 2014: 27, emphasis in the original).

Bargu makes a reasonable case for this argument by focusing on the starvation suicides of political prisoners, where both the "biopoliticization of sovereignty" and "necropoliticization of resistance" are concentrated in the person committing suicide.

It is the political prisoner's body that is imprisoned and it is the imprisoned political prisoner's body that is effaced in protest – and the political prisoners in question are able to voice this relationship and their intent in the process. For the cases we discuss in subsequent chapters, this kind of embodiment of the relationship between biopolitical sovereignty and necropolitical resistance is unavailable. The onus of recognising such a relationship – or of inserting it – in the suicide archives rests with those who respond to the acts of suicide with a politicising or depoliticising effect. In a way, the suicide archives we address are either produced *after* the meeting of biopolitical sovereignty and necropolitical resistance, or *infer* such a meeting in terms of the suicide archives' own posterior dynamics.

The political order of the present

These brief accounts of three areas of suicide studies converge on a single point that is salient for this study: understanding current political regimes via an analysis of specific suicide texts and suicide archives and the resistances they instantiate, and thereby understanding the general and dominant (widely dispersed and extensive) political order of the present. Each of the areas above variously puts the politics of the present into perspective, and opens it up to critique. The distinctiveness of this study lies in its focus on the receptive field, on what happens between the creation of suicide archives and the release or suppression of their political resonances. In that respect, this is less a contribution to suicide studies in the sense of the areas above, and more a series of meditations on the socio-political aftermath of certain suicides, where suicide is rewritten and reconstituted as a political event of anti-establishment import.

The following chapters are each dedicated to specific cases and contexts of individual suicides which were received as politically resonant. Chapter 2 examines the suicide archive that developed after Mohamed Bouazizi set himself on fire in December 2010 in Sidi Bouzid, Tunisia. Chapter 3 then explores a part of the suicide archive – breaking-news texts – which appeared immediately after Dimitris Christoulas shot himself in April 2013 in Athens, Greece. In Chapter 4, a series of self-immolations that were documented amidst widespread public protests in Bulgaria from 2013 onwards are investigated. These three chapters offer case studies of suicide archives where individual suicides were received as acts of political protest. Finally, Chapter 5 takes a distinctive direction by examining suicides that were not regarded as acts of protest, but which nevertheless resonated with ongoing political debates: the so-called "economic suicides" in Italy and "eviction suicides" in Spain, especially from 2012 onwards.

References

Agamben, Giorgio (1998 [1995]) *Homo Sacer: Sovereign Power and Bare Life*. Translated by Daniel Heller-Roazen. Stanford CA: Stanford University Press.

Andriolo, Karin (2006) "The Twice-Killed: Imagining Protest Suicide". *American Anthropologist* 108 (1): 100–13.

Asad, Talal (2007) *On Suicide Bombing*. New York NY: Columbia University Press.

Atkinson, J. Maxwell (1978) *Discovering Suicide: Studies in the Social Organization of Sudden Death*. London: Macmillan.

Bargu, Banu (2014) *Starve and Immolate: The Politics of Human Weapons*. New York NY: Columbia University Press.

Baudelet, Christian and Roger Establet (2008 [2005]) *Suicide: The Hidden Side of Modernity*. Translated by David Macey. Cambridge: Polity.

Berardi, Franco "Bifo" (2015) *Heroes: Mass Murder and Suicide*. London: Verso.

Biggs, Michael (2005) "Dying Without Killing: Self-Immolations, 1963–2002" in Diego Gambetta (ed.) *Making Sense of Suicide Missions.* Oxford: Oxford University Press, pp. 174–208.

Biggs, Michael (2011) "How Repertoires Evolve: The Diffusion of Suicide Protest in the Twentieth Century". *Mobilization* 18 (4): 407–28.

Bloom, Mia (2005) *Dying to Kill: The Allure of Suicide Terror.* New York NY: Columbia University Press.

Branas, Charles C., Anastasia E. Kastanaki, Manolis Michalodimitrakis, John Tzougas, Elena F. Kranioti, Pavlos N. Theodorakis, Brendan G. Carr and Douglas J. Wiebe (2015) "The Impact of Economic Austerity and Prosperity Events on Suicide in Greece: A 30-Year Interrupted Time-Series Analysis". *BMJ Open* 5 (1): e005619. doi: 10.1136/bmjopen-2014-005619.

Camus, Albert (1955 [1942]) *The Myth of Sisyphus.* Translated by Justin O'Brien. Harmondsworth: Penguin.

Chang, Shu-Sen, David Stuckler, Paul Yip and David Gunnell (2013) "Impact of 2008 Global Economic Crisis on Suicide: Time Trend Study in 54 Countries". *BMJ* 347: f5239. doi: 10.1136/bmj.f5239.

Cholbi, Michael (2011) *Suicide: The Philosophical Dimensions.* New York NY: Broadway.

Comte, August (1896 [1830–41]) *The Positive Philosophy of Auguste Comte.* 3 volumes. Translated by Harriet Martineau. London: George Bell.

Dabashi, Hamid (2012) *Corpus Anarchicum: Political Protest, Suicidal Violence, and the Making of the Posthuman Body.* New York NY: Palgrave Macmillan.

De Masi, Franco (2011) *The Enigma of the Suicide Bomber: A Psychoanalytic Essay.* Translated by Philip Slotkin. London: Karnac.

Donnelly, Kevin (2014) "The Other Average Man: Science Workers in Quetelet's Belgium". *History of Science* 52 (4): 401–28.

Douglas, Jack D. (1970 [1967]) *The Social Meanings of Suicide.* Princeton NJ: Princeton University Press.

Durkheim, Emile (1952 [1897]) *Suicide: A Study in Sociology.* Translated by John A. Spalding and George Simpson. London: Routledge and Kegan Paul.

Durkheim, Emile (1982 [1895]) *The Rules of Sociological Method and Selected Texts on Sociology and Method.* Translated by W. D. Halls. Basingstoke: Macmillan.

Farberow, Norman (1969) *Bibliography on Suicide and Suicide Prevention.* Rockville MD: National Institute of Mental Health.

Foucault, Michel (1977 [1975]) *Discipline and Punish: The Birth of the Prison.* Translated by Alan Sheridan. New York NY: Vintage.

Foucault, Michel (2008 [2004]) *The Birth of Biopolitics: Lectures at the Collège de France 1978–1979*. Translated by Graham Burchell. Basingstoke: Palgrave Macmillan.

Fountoulakis, K. N., S. A. Koupidis, I. A. Grammatikopoulos and P. N. Theodorakis (2013) "First Reliable Data Suggest a Possible Increase in Suicides in Greece". *BMJ* 347: f4900. doi: 10.1136/bmj.f4900.

Godlee, Fiona (2013) "Austerity, Suicide and Screening". *BMJ* 347: f5678. doi: 10.1136/bmj.f5678.

Gunnell, David, Stephen Platt and Keith Hawton (2009) "The Economic Crisis and Suicide". *BMJ* 338 (7709): 1456–57.

Halbwachs, Maurice (1978 [1930]) *The Causes of Suicide*. Translated by Harold Goldblatt. London: Routledge and Kegan Paul.

Hassan, Riaz (2011) *Life as a Weapon: The Global Rise of Suicide Bombings*. Abingdon: Routledge.

Hawton, Keith and Camilla Haw (2013) "Economic Recession and Suicide". *BMJ* 347: f5612. doi: 10.1136/bmj.f5612.

Heilbron, Nicole, Joseph C. Franklin, John D. Guerry and Mitchell J. Prinstein (2014) "Social and Ecological Approaches to Understanding Suicidal Behaviors and Nonsuicidal Self-Injury" in Matthew K. Nock (ed.) *The Oxford Handbook of Suicide and Self-Injury*. Oxford: Oxford University Press, pp. 206–34.

Khosrokhavar, Farhad (2005) *Suicide Bombers: Allah's New Martyrs*. Translated by David Macey. London: Pluto.

Kierkegaard, Søren (1980 [1849]) *The Sickness Unto Death: A Christian Psychological Exposition for Upbuilding and Awakening*. Translated by Howard V. Hong and Edna H. Hong. Princeton NJ: Princeton University Press.

Lahiri, Simanti (2014) *Suicide Protest in South Asia: Consumed by Commitment*. Abingdon: Routledge.

Marsh, Ian (2010) *Suicide: Foucault, History and Truth*. Cambridge: Cambridge University Press.

Michas, George (2013) "Suicides in Greece: A Light at the End of the Tunnel". *BMJ* 347: f6249. doi: http://dx.doi.org/10.1136/bmj.f6249.

Quetelet, Adolphe (1842 [1835]) *A Treatise on Man and the Development of his Faculties*. Edinburgh: William and Robert Chambers.

Quetelet, Adolphe (1849 [1846]) *Letters Addressed to HRH The Grand Duke of the Saxe Coburg and Gotha on the Theory of Probabilities as Applied to the Moral and Political Sciences*. Translated by Olinthus Gregory Downes. London: Charles and Edwin Layton.

Reuter, Christopher (2004 [2002]) *My Life Is a Weapon: A Modern History of Suicide Bombing*. Translated by Helena Ragg-Kirkby. Princeton NJ: Princeton University Press.

Shneidman, Edwin (1985) *Definition of Suicide*. Lanham MD: Jason Aronson.

Silke, Andrew (ed.) (2003) *Terrorists, Victims and Society: Psychological Perspectives on Terrorism and Its Consequences*. Chichester: Wiley.

Spehr, Scott and John Dixon (2013) "Protest Suicide: A Systematic Model with Heuristic Archetypes". *Journal for the Theory of Social Behaviour* 44 (3): 368–88.

Szasz, Thomas (1999) *Fatal Freedom: The Ethics and Politics of Suicide*. Westport CT: Praeger.

Weaver, John C. (2009) *A Sadly Troubled History: The Meanings of Suicide in the Modern Age*. Montreal: McGill-Queen's University Press.

TWO | The irresistible rise and fall of posthumous Bouazizi

Suman Gupta

The Bouazizi suicide archive

On 17 December 2010, Mohamed Bouazizi, a twenty-six-year-old street vendor, set himself on fire in front of the Governor's office at Sidi Bouzid, Tunisia. He died of his injuries on 4 January 2011. At the time, this suicide was widely regarded as the spark that set off the uprisings that spread from Tunisia across North Africa and the Middle East, now thought of as the "Arab Spring".

The suicide archive of this most discussed of suicides contains almost every kind of suicide text except the most obvious sort: no judicial ruling, medical report or other official record of Mohamed Bouazizi's self-immolation has featured meaningfully in debates. In their absence, the archive acquires a sort of constitutive malleability. That a specific suicide archive seemingly contains nothing significant bearing the seal of official sanction is an extremely rare circumstance. Here, the power of the establishment over individual life seems suspended; the judiciary, the police, the medical and forensic authorities, insurance companies, and so on, appear to be muted. Circumstances have rendered Bouazizi's suicide archive peculiarly anti-establishment, irrespective of how the act itself is now understood, whether as spurring a revolution or subject to over-zealous propaganda. It always presents a juncture of dramatic instability and regime change, with its effect escalating from Sidi Bouzid to Tunisia as a whole, and then to other populations fed up with oppressive governments – in Egypt, Libya, Syria and elsewhere, the so-called "Arab World" – and thereafter seeping into wider disaffections with austerity policies and neoliberal strangleholds.

Since there is no significant official account to depart from, we need to turn to the speculations found in the initial suicide texts to understand the drift of the later texts. In fact, one preponderant speculation was accepted widely after Bouazizi's self-immolation: that a clear conceptual line had emerged – had been activated – between the ordinary individual and the protesting crowd. The conviction and speed with which this was acted upon was more suggestive of certainty than speculation. And yet, characteristic of speculations, amidst uncertain facts and confident guesses, that conceptual line evinced schisms which would widen in the later suicide texts. This chapter tracks the path from the self-assured speculations of the initial suicide texts to the ambivalences of the later texts in Bouazizi's suicide archive. Seen thus, the suicide archive of Bouazizi traces some general features of current political protest.

Ordinary individual to protesting crowd

Immediately after Mohamed Bouazizi's self-immolation, and particularly after his demise eighteen days later, it seemed self-evident that an ordinary individual can spur a protesting crowd into being, and that the protesting crowd is composed of ordinary individuals. Moreover, the conceptual line from the ordinary individual to the protesting crowd seemed not merely to lead from a spark to a single explosion but to a series of explosions aimed at a number of oppressive regimes.

The line was drawn seemingly without forethought. It appeared as an on-the-ground possibility that soon became a self-fulfilling certainty. However, the conceptual negotiations involved in drawing that line are of considerable interest. Scholarly expositions have constantly denied a coherent relationship between ordinary individuals and protesting crowds. This relationship has repeatedly been conceptualised as discontinuous, in terms of identifiable *individuals* versus faceless *collectives*. Classical and early modern accounts evoked mainly "extraordinary" individuals or demagogues (usually orators) in relation to the crowd. As far as ordinary individuals in modern political upheavals are concerned (especially during the French Revolution and in subsequent periods), they are understood as evincing personal traits that do not cohere with those of the crowds they join. The latter appear as organic entities, subject to an autonomy (of dynamics, of intent and effect) that is not derived from that of an ordinary person. Ideological leanings make little difference to this structuralist approach to crowds and individuals; ideology merely puts different normative constructions on the significance of crowds. The influence of the anti-revolutionary and antidemocratic Gustave Le Bon, who declared that the crowd is "that which acquires a collective presence as opposed to an individual one" and which "forms a single being, and is subjected to the law of mental unity of crowds" (2001 [1896]: 13), has largely been embraced by socialist revolutionaries and liberal or conservative democrats ever since. The crowd is thus anxiously understood as a discrete entity unto itself, occupying space, with a shape, movement, intent and force of its own (most elaborately in Canetti 1962); the crowd is defined as the other in relation to the individual, a de-individuated formation (a standardised academic phrase since Zimbardo 1969); the (protesting or revolutionary) crowd appears with distinctive class characteristics (Rudé 1981 [1964]; Thompson 1971); and the crowd then becomes a presence in the mediascape, a sociolinguistic signifier, a trope in social investigation, and so on, on the verge of disappearing into concept. And, of course, even the revolutionary or protesting crowd seems to disappear amidst the networked multitude that putatively resists the networked Empire in Michael Hardt and Antonio Negri's (2004) work. Very seldom (McPhail 1991 is one instance) has the ordinary individual found a coherent place in relation to the protesting crowd, although, paradoxically, the protesting crowd is generally regarded as composed of ordinary individuals.

However, ordinary individuals who have joined a protesting crowd do not consider that their individualities were suspended by doing so. Mostly, the individual convictions of participants appear to be confirmed through the materialisation of the crowd, and the individual experience seems to find affirmation in the crowd. This needs no analytical exegesis, nor any liberal valorisation of individuality. The sense of continuity between disaffected individual and protesting crowd is performed unthinkingly: in other words, it simply *is* so for the person in the crowd. Appointing Bouazizi as the spark that ignited the fire of protest was such an unplanned performative move. It was unusual in being so explicitly foregrounded, but was no more than an obvious signal of the unity of disaffected individual and protesting crowd. That appointment marked a speculation that was immediately confirmed by being acted upon, by being articulated in slogans, depicted on posters and evoked in discussions. By acting upon that speculation, the ordinary individual in the crowd appeared to stand out *as such* and *within* the crowd – without acknowledging the discrete organicity of the crowd and without concessions to manipulators of the crowd-mind (the prods of demagogues, the permissions of authority). It was, unthinkingly, a performed refusal of the analytical structuralism briefly outlined above, undermining some of the habitual predicates of analysis. Perhaps most reassuringly for those who were in (or at one with) the protesting crowds, the projection of Bouazizi made confident speculation – despite uncertain facts, and even using uncertain facts – work against the elision of the crowd into abstractions such as "social movement", "mediascape", "trope", "multitude". The protesting crowds were there, all too materially and physically. Of course, that couldn't last – and it didn't. It lasted only as long as the crowds were in evidence and until they fractured into many crowds and many more narratives. But it was there to begin with.

This performance of a continuous line from ordinary individual to protesting crowd had some characteristic features that cut across the initial suicide texts about Bouazizi. Tracking these in a scholarly text-by-text listing goes against their essential nature. These are perhaps best (and most expeditiously) articulated through an overview, adopting the perspective of an observer at the time, caught up in the flow of speculation turning into certainty and being performed as certainty. Here, the overview of initial suicide texts about Bouazizi is first outlined using this approach, before considering disaggregated dispersals and reversions with the usual scholarly apparatus.

The bare outline of somewhat shaky "facts" gleaned from numerous newspaper and broadcast reports, blogs, witness statements, on-the-ground accounts, expert explanations and so on produced at the time consisted in the following. Here is the ordinary individual: Mohamed (his first name was really Tarek) Bouazizi, a twenty-six-year-old who hadn't progressed beyond high school education (it was initially thought he was a university graduate), working as a fruit vendor in Sidi Bouzid. He had plied his trade from a cart for seven years, and was the sole breadwinner for a family of eight (not really sole, but certainly his family depended on his earnings). On 17 December 2010 he was accosted by a municipal official (rumoured at first to be a policewoman), Faida Hamdi, accompanied by several (not certain how many) policemen, who demanded to see his trading permit or licence (it is unclear whether a cart vendor needed one). Bouazizi didn't have one, but was well acquainted with police harassment and offered to pay a fine (or possibly a bribe). However, Hamdi confiscated his scales and allegedly assaulted him. According to some versions, she slapped him, spat at him, and shouted abuse about his deceased father; in others she did none of these things and it was her associates who beat him and upturned his cart. Naturally aggrieved, Bouazizi went to the Governor's office to complain (or perhaps simply to reclaim his confiscated scales). Here he was ignored although he threatened to kill himself if he wasn't heard. Bouazizi left and returned before the Governor's office within an hour with a can of gasoline (or petrol or paint thinner), shouted "How do you expect me to make a living?" (almost certainly), doused himself with the gasoline and set himself on fire. He was taken to hospital with third degree burns. Protesting crowds started gathering in Sidi Bouzid within a couple of hours after the incident, and these gatherings gradually spread across the country. The international media picked up the story in due course. Zine el Abidine Ben Ali, president since 1987, launched an investigation into these events and visited Bouazizi in hospital on

28 December 2010 amidst the growing and obdurate appearance of crowds demanding his immediate departure from office. Bouazizi died on 4 January 2011. Ben Ali had abandoned his post by 14 January 2011 and took refuge in Saudi Arabia, while an interim caretaker government was formed with Fouad Mebazaa as acting president (he had been president of the Chamber of Deputies since 1997). A pattern of protesting crowds gathering and demanding regime change and liberal government had evolved in the interim.

Of course, reporters tried to tease out the personality of the ordinary individual whose death had proved so momentous. Initially though, between 17 December 2010 and 14 January 2011, the personal story seemed to acquire little traction. Bouazizi remained the "street vendor" who "sparked" what came to be labelled as the "Jasmine Revolution" and then the "Arab Spring", a name to conjure with, a portrait image on placards borne by crowds. But the attempt was made immediately: homing in on personal stories when reporting large-scale conflict is a standard media frame – it courts a sentimental readership and sells news, and it tends to deflect critical attention from social contradictions. But every attempt at that time seemed to both multiply the uncertainty of facts and concretise the general drift of their import. Mohamed Bouazizi's mother and sister (usually photographed holding a picture of him) were quoted prolifically, and so were his acquaintances and neighbours. His educational qualifications were investigated, as were his working circumstances and previous encounters with the police. The possibilities of the life story – close up, individual – were told and retold in equivocal fragments. And each telling and retelling shifted the facts around a bit; each version contradicted the others, without disturbing the tenor of the speculative line drawn from Bouazizi to the protesting crowds. Bouazizi's individual circumstances were swept to the margins by ever wider agglomerations of protesting crowds, insisting "Ben Ali dégage". The reading of Bouazizi's "tipping point" of choosing death by fire – the moment when he chose to die protesting against injustice – became disinvested of his unique life and invested with something other than his individual existence.

That the personal story of the ordinary individual initially resisted the sought-after media frame owed something to circumstances. No person or organisation assumed responsibility for the appearance of protesting crowds, and none appeared credibly as their representatives or spokespersons in that period. With hindsight, the impetuses of the protests came to be understood differently – but more of that later. But in this early period, the national and global news media wheeled out numerous experts and intellectuals and activists, all of whom spoke to varying degrees as participants, sympathisers or observers. The "leaderless" or "spontaneous" character of the protesting crowds became part of their media brand and was adopted as a badge: a massing of multiple interests and sectors driven by a common moral imperative, a formation so ideologically diverse that it appeared to be free of ideology, that was simply expressing the moral outrage of ordinary individuals. The silent image of the dying and then posthumous Bouazizi, the name of Bouazizi, appeared as an ideology-free insignia of ordinariness, pure and simple. It seemed, then, that to give it flesh would be to court a political position rather than to project a politically diffuse disenchantment which is politics-by-negation or, perhaps, politics itself on the cusp of moral rediscovery.

But speculation-made-truth indubitably underpinned a collective imagining of the individual impulse that resonated with the protesting crowds and rendered individuality abstract. It was barely articulated, but then it barely needed articulation for its immediate affective power to be unleashed. If it had been articulated it might have presented a few speculative steps to be negotiated, like the following. There must have been a tipping point that led Mohamed Bouazizi from simmering discontent with his life and environment to an unbearable crisis and then to the precipitation of that crisis in suicide. Perhaps the pressures of straitened circumstances, the responsibility that burdens a breadwinner whose earnings are never enough, the frustration of great effort expended for too little return had been accruing in Bouazizi's sensibilities for a while. When he encountered Faida Hamdi and her associates and suffered humiliation at their hands, those dissatisfactions crystallised into a single point. Perhaps Hamdi and her associates ceased to be individuals in Bouazizi's eyes; at that moment they embodied the oppression of the prevailing social order. Possibly they reoriented Bouazizi's entire view of his surroundings. In the clear and cold day (it was around 11 degrees Celsius that morning), Bouazizi's mind was overwhelmed with the apprehension of an injustice that was larger than the particular agents and event. The familiar streets and houses and buzzing markets and people lost their usual enveloping comfort and became strange, a landscape tinted pervasively by oppressions and humiliations. Thus, as Bouazizi hurried through the town to the Governor's office to seek redress, he already had the recourse of suicide in his mind. In his mind he was giving this abstract force, the brutal and indifferent state, and himself a last chance by appealing to another agent: the upper echelon of power, the bureaucrat. So when he approached the guards and petty officers at the portal of the Governor's office he was close to a decision – he issued an ultimatum (something like, "If you don't listen to me, I'll burn myself"). Perhaps they sniggered and turned away, or shrugged and told him to go about his business, or shouted abuse or shook their heads impotently ("Who do you think you are?"). It was a moment of confirmation for Bouazizi, the confirmation of his individual nullity – the tipping point. The remaining flickers of hope and the possibility of justice faded, and the alienated contours of his familiar environment settled into grey permanence. But it was more than that. It was also a moment in which his individual resistance was rendered utterly lonely. In being turned away brusquely, despite his ultimatum, he was not merely denigrated. It seemed as if he were de-recognised as a person, his very presence was annulled. It didn't seem possible to seek help from friends and supporters or to organise some sort of protest, to press for justice. It seemed, rather, as if he had already ceased to exist and no one could see him – or, if he could be seen, it was only as belittled and insignificant. Injustice subsumed all around him. And so a final act of resistance that would also be a final assertion of his existence and simultaneously a final withdrawal inevitably took shape. A gesture that, it seemed to Bouazizi, would confirm his integrity against the conspiracy to erase it. In feverish anticipation of this final gesture, Bouazizi ran to the nearby petrol station to get hold of a can of gasoline (or petrol or paint thinner). When he returned and doused himself and stood before the Governor's office and shouted "How do you expect me to make a living?" and lit the match, he set fire to the order of things in Tunisia.

It may have happened that way; it was probably imagined that way. Such imagining can expand into certainty ("it must

have happened that way") by working through the possibilities
– not in order to ascertain which took place but to find that all
the possibilities were equally and disturbingly *possible*, equally
likely to have occurred. The actions of an ordinary individual
are usually fuzzy around the borders. Perhaps other factors and
motives interacted with that account of his movements; perhaps
quite another account is possible. A little alteration here or there
in the sequence of events might have made for a quite different
account. Trying to edge closer to Bouazizi's last hours on the
morning of 17 December 2010 entails asking questions. If he had
been harassed similarly by officials earlier, why did he react in
this way on this particular occasion? Why were Faida Hamdi
and her associates quite as brutal towards Bouazizi that morning? Was that their usual behaviour towards small tradesmen?
Was that symptomatic of the attitude of petty officials with a little
official power to a class of people with none? Or perhaps it was
motivated by something else – an accrual of little irritations, some
unregistered insecurity about officialdom, some gesture of resistance already. What were others on the scene doing? Perhaps
other vendors with their carts had a warning and quickly slipped
into a side alley, grateful that they had managed to evade Hamdi
and company. Shoppers and bystanders on the street may have
looked on the spectacle of Bouazizi being humiliated in various
ways: some with shock, some seething in silence, some with the
relish that such spectacles generate in certain hearts. To most,
it was probably another momentarily eye-catching but ultimately
unremarkable moment in the everyday life of the market. But in
their own way they became complicit in Bouazizi's humiliation,
and also silent agents of his alienation and loneliness. Possibly
Bouazizi's gesture was addressed as much to the callous violence

of the state as to the silent spectatorship of passers-by and onlookers. If anyone had objected to the treatment meted out to Bouazizi, would he have acted differently? What happened at the Governor's office? If some officer had given him a sympathetic hearing, had recognised his claim to some degree, would Bouazizi have paused? Would that have made any difference to the nature of the regime that such bureaucracies work within? Did someone add insult to injury instead? If there had happened to be a long queue at the petrol station, if Bouazizi had found that he didn't have enough money, if he had encountered a relative or friend on the way ... would any of that have made a difference? Bouazizi was evidently a person who took his family responsibilities seriously. Why didn't his position as breadwinner, a thought for his dependants, give him pause?

None of these questions can possibly be answered with any degree of certainty. More importantly, none of them need to be answered. They can be raised, and, in small ways, the range of speculative reach expands along the possibilities they suggest. That is why the individual Bouazizi slipped away in the immediate aftermath of self-immolation and death. The hypothetical account set out above of the events and consequences leading to the suicidal tipping point is of that moment, not because it was what Bouazizi must have experienced but because it was some such account – imagined or inferred – that resonated with other ordinary individuals. Others were roused to protest because some such account of Bouazizi's protest resonated with their individual lives. They understood Bouazizi's tipping point as a plausible experience within their own lives and as a synecdoche, symbol or symptom of malaise within their shared environment. Some recognised Bouazizi's tipping point as a culmination of other tipping points – the act that crystallises the unremarked suicides, failed protests, unobserved gestures of having reached an unbearable impasse, enacted already by other individuals. That other such suicides had taken place was observed by several sources (with few details given), and certainly Bouazizi-like suicides followed very soon afterwards and were widely reported. These became invested in Bouazizi's self-immolation, and, in that moment, Bouazizi the individual became an aggregate of all those other individuals. And as these perceptions took hold and became collectivised, another tipping point was enacted: a move from the implosive, where the ordinary individual tips over into self-destruction when faced by something unremittingly unbearable, to the explosive, where ordinary individuals are tipped over into the protesting crowds to confront that which is unbearable.

A conjunction of the various connotations of the phrase "tipping point" occurs here, in both idiomatic usage and more precise academic registers. On the latter, a quick note. I am using the phrase in the sense of a precipitate perceptual change. In sociology, it has been used since the 1950s largely to analyse racial segregation in urban housing – mainly the point at which white residents start moving out of a neighbourhood because they feel that there are too many black inhabitants (this sense of the phrase was coined in Grodzins (1957) and widely picked up soon afterwards). Journalist Malcolm Gladwell (2000) has given the phrase a more general and upbeat appeal as an explanation for various everyday social and marketing phenomena, which he understands as epidemics – the "tipping point" here is a kind of spontaneous moment when epidemics suddenly strengthen or subside. My emphasis in using the phrase, however, relates to the earlier sociological sense, though dislocated from the discourse of segregation. The phrase is used here roughly as described by Gregory Weiher: "The tipping point is the point at which a change takes place in the way people *think* about an objectively defined area, the point at which their sense of place changes" (1991: 61–2, emphasis in the original). As such, there are several tipping points that are relevant in the Bouazizi suicide archive. First, there is the speculative tipping point that collapses the frame of Bouazizi's tolerance and pushes him to suicide. Second, there is an imaginary replication of that breaking point in others who share something of Bouazizi's circumstances. Third, there is the perception that Bouazizi's act was not merely the culmination of his experience; it was a culmination of other such experiences and other such acts: a retrospective collectivisation or de-individuation of Bouazizi's suicidal act. Fourth, there is the shift that decisively turns the mode of protest from enactment upon one's own body to enactment upon the state itself, the prevailing social and political order. And fifth, there is the anticipation of comprehensive regime change that will also be a social transformation and a transformation of lives – a sought-after tipping point from the present regime to a future one, or a demand, in brief, for revolution.

Initially, the more the symbolic stakes of Bouazizi's suicide were upped, the less distinctly individual and characterisable he appeared to be. To render his personality vivid would have been to undermine his ordinariness. After all, the ordinary individual is always too diminutive against the scale of large social protests and mobilisation. And that is as it should be: the social movement was directed in principle towards erasing overdetermined individuals and making an appeal for the totality of the protesting demos. Perhaps this occurred most cogently in the rhetorical turn that announced Bouazizi as an "ordinary person", the "common Tunisian", the "man on the street", one of the "have-nots", "bullied", "unemployed youth". There are, of course, no aggregates or averages that can be condensed into the image of the ordinary individual; all aggregates or averages are arrived at by cancelling out particularities, by extrapolating common denominators from a complex of individual numerations. The image of the "ordinary individual" is no more than a metaphor – this aggregate and average person can have no personality. From a slightly different perspective, the ordinary individual is often not thought of so much in terms of denominators and numerations as in terms of the absence of these: the ordinary individual is simply *not* extraordinary. Where the extraordinary person – the powerful, the celebrated, the rich – can be imaged and recognised, the ordinary individual is unrecognised and uncharacterisable. The ordinary individual has only negative attributes; in contrast to the extraordinary person, she or he is of modest means, subject to larger forces and programmes, indistinguishable within the majority. From this perspective, too, there is no personality of the ordinary individual; it can only be a set of attributes that the viewer considers to be *not* noteworthy. So, the very use of Bouazizi's image and name in crowded protests as those of an ordinary person also courted a paradox. When Bouazizi's image became, albeit for only a short time, the image of the ordinary individual – distinct, recognisable, and agreed for a while as such – it was as a sign of resistance to the image of what is extraordinary now. It suggested the paradoxical rendering of the ordinary as extraordinary. Through Bouazizi's image, for a brief period, the ordinary individual assumed a definite face and person without becoming a leader, an icon, a hero, or even a martyr. Of course, that couldn't last – but more on that later.

Thus, the weight of social reality both foregrounded and erased the individual suffering and will of Bouazizi, and immediately filled the space. Mohamed Bouazizi was cleared of unique attributes so that his act could assume neutral social proportions. He immediately became a concrete designation with statistical magnitudes behind him. In 2010, the proportion of those unemployed in Tunisia was 14 per cent, but among the youth it was in the region of 30 per cent – and Bouazizi was in that group. In 2004–08, the literacy rate for male youth (aged fifteen to twenty-four) was 98 per cent, with a high proportion holding high school or university degrees – and Bouazizi was in that group too (various assertions about his level of education appeared in reports of the time). Bouazizi's act became their expression, a fire lit by the faceless population that embodied the neutral statistical figure. The statistical reckoning in such demographics is indifferent to the ideological attitudes of those to whom it applies. So no one enquired into Bouazizi's allegiances: the strength of his religious convictions and what they were, what sort of political convictions he held, what his attitudes were towards … anything. None of that mattered, because Bouazizi ceased to be a person when he committed suicide. Bouazizi's act could be used to unify all divisions and creases in the social fabric, just as the statistical aggregate or average can.

There was almost a design to the instrumentalisation of Bouazizi for anti-establishment mobilisation: a sort of design of the moment rather than of an alignment. It certainly wasn't Bouazizi's design; he lost possession of his act the moment he set himself alight.

Academic turns

With academic hindsight, the foregrounding of the posthumous Mohamed Bouazizi in 2011 as the face of the "revolution", the spark that set it off, seemed misconceived. A careful accounting of the causes of the uprising offered a more temperate and complex reckoning *against* the misleading focalisation of Bouazizi in the first instance. Precursors of Bouazizi-like acts were noted, earlier collective actions recalled (the ruthlessly suppressed uprisings in Gafsa in 2008, Fériana in 2009 and Ben Guerdéne in 2010), and existing organisational structures of resistance examined (especially the Union Générale Tunisienne du Travail, Ennahdha, the Progressive Democratic Party and a range of social movements); the neoliberal policies and corruption and repressions stemming from Habib Bourguiba's regime and continued under Ben Ali were charted. Histories with a longer view of the background to the 2011 uprising appeared. And, as the history of the aftermath of Ben Ali's abrupt departure from Tunisia unfolded, troubled and dramatic but still less fraught than in other "Arab Spring" contexts, the significance of Bouazizi's suicide seemed to become a momentary point of return – usually a sort of anomaly – in narrating the revolutionary moment of early 2011. It remained a momentary reference point in the narrative grid of a series of uprisings, a passing symptom of something larger than itself within Tunisia, within the Arab world; often not worth mentioning as the battleground of uprisings widened to Egypt, Syria, Libya and beyond. When Bouazizi's suicide was paused on in the accumulating historical record of the Tunisian uprising, it seemed, as Laryssa Chomiak observed, like a "creation myth" or an "origin story", where "no single point of origin" really existed, where "the revolution emerged from seemingly scattered activism in pre-revolutionary Tunisia and certain moments of resistance under dictatorship that were closely interconnected" (2014: 23).

That was certainly applicable in the long view of history, and yet Chomiak overstated the case in characterising Bouazizi's self-immolation as a misleading "origin story". Although Bouazizi's suicide allowed for a conceptual line to be drawn from the ordinary person to the protesting crowd, at no point had he been regarded as the *cause* of the uprisings. The metaphor of the "spark" presumed that there was plenty of ready tinder waiting to be set alight. The thrust of the speculative account above is that it made Bouazizi into a concrete and simultaneously emptied signifier of ordinariness. Bouazizi's image and name were held up to draw in all around him, at the expense of his unique individuality (projecting, so to speak, a generic individuality), and to become a rallying point for crowds; in appearing in this way, his singular experience and act were imbued with all that others endured and sought to resist – which naturally extended to all the precedent causes that historians have outlined since. This paradoxical quality of appearing, in December 2010 and January 2011, as a concrete and yet emptied signifier has kept certain kinds of academic interest alive. What Bouazizi's suicide meant may have receded into near oblivion in the historical narrative, but it has kept reappearing as a phenomenon unto itself, a juncture that lends itself to theorising. Such theorising, at its most productive, has focused on the mechanics of the posthumous Bouazizi's rise in that revolutionary period rather than his place in history, so that the initial suicide archive of Bouazizi offers a way into political and philosophical reflection. This is a matter of tracking through the relevant suicide texts the way in which the concrete–empty signifier Bouazizi could actuate political apprehension and praxis, thereby often turning reflexively upon contemporary political theorising itself. Various noteworthy academic reflections have thus become part of the Bouazizi suicide archive, illuminating the ideological present.

In one of the most perceptive early analyses of the Tunisian revolution, Mouldi Guessoumi noted the peculiarity of foregrounding Bouazizi's suicide at the head of a *revolutionary* movement:

> Prior to Bouazizi, it was nearly impossible to imagine such experiences [other similar suicides] crystallizing into a revolution, because there had been no clear indications in Tunisia of there being a general revolutionary tendency; moreover, revolutionaries never engage in self-immolation, as is well known, undertaking instead armed combat and resistance in order to conquer or be defeated. (Guessoumi 2012: 21)

That, in turn, led him to reflect on the character of this revolution itself – and, indeed, on its characterisation as a "revolution". Presciently, the concrete emptiness of Bouazizi as a signifier of protest radiated out, in Guessoumi's analysis, into the dramatic and yet unavoidably hollow echo of this "revolution":

> This is a revolution that has not affected Tunisia's mode of production, or the overall structure of its society, or even the political consciousness and reasoning. Rather, it has been a surgical intervention undertaken by the citizenry in the daily life-practices of society. Up until now, it has not been a political revolution because it has not changed the system, nor is it a social revolution because it has not eradicated the ruling classes. (Guessoumi 2012: 22)

This was a "revolution", then, that was on the cusp of becoming one or not becoming one, currently no more than morally charged with being a "Revolution of Dignity", open to becoming operationalised or undermined by various interest groups.

The theoretical horizon of what is conceived as a "revolution" had itself been thrown into relief. Briefly, the naming of "revolution" seemed aspirational rather than decisive (an "intervention" doesn't necessarily bring change); the agents of such a "revolution" seemed defined by what they already were ("citizenry") rather than by what they wanted to be; and the revolutionary stage seemed decidedly inchoate ("daily life-practices of society"). The received concept of "revolution" and the evident content of this "revolution" didn't quite gel. The many histories of the failure of and disappointed hopes in the so-called "Arab Spring" that have appeared tell their own story, and the very understanding – indeed possibility – of revolution has seemed elusive ever since. And that, perhaps more than anything else, has tacitly underscored the embarrassment with which Bouazizi is often mentioned now, as an eventual marker of another tipping point: from optimism to pessimism. Bouazizi, after all, had sparked this "revolution" through a contradiction: by self-annihilation rather than armed resistance. However, that observation is too pat. The development and cautious expression of that embarrassment has been a complex process, one that involves a putting into place of the ordinary individual – on which more in due course.

A few years later, contemplating the Bouazizi phenomenon has become a mode of testing conceptual horizons in other ways too – in ways that draw on some of the broader issues outlined in Chapter 1 (especially on suicide-as-protest). Nicholas Michelsen (2015), for instance, understood the political significance of protest suicides (sacrifice) as being assigned predominantly by subsequent narratives, as a matter of reception rather than intention, much as this book does. And, from this perspective (presented with a weightier theoretical toolbox than here), Michelsen articulated the emptiness of the politically effective signification of the individual committing suicide, with reference to Bouazizi, as follows:

> Mohammed Bouazizi, unlike Bobby Sands [Provisional IRA member who died on hunger strike in prison in 1981], did not even attempt to predetermine his mythic effects, strategically preframing his act within a poetic project of transcendent imagining. He articulated no identifiable ends. It is its radical negativity that gave his act fertility and force. Bouazizi is a political subject of divine violence; his self-burning was a pure means, without heroic ends or positive intentions, which as such opened a space for the subsequent proliferation of myth. This suggests the analytical value of the Benjaminian concept of a *suicidal political subject* [referring to Benjamin 1986 [1966]] … as one who needs no transcendent referent or connection to a sovereign semiosis to occupy political space. (Michelsen 2015: 95–6)

The point of interest here is that Michelsen uses the Bouazizi suicide archive to extend the concept of resistant political subjectivity within the process described by Banu Bargu, outlined in the previous chapter, as the "*biopoliticization of sovereignty* meet[ing] the *necropoliticization of resistance*" (Bargu 2014: 27). However, that extension involves a kind of inversion of Bargu's case studies of starvation suicides. Here, nullified political subjectivity is rendered effective despite the subject, in a way because the subject does not set an agenda, does not articulate, is annihilated. The necropoliticisation of resistance here is itself posthumous, and the biopoliticisation of sovereignty is inscribed more in the suicide archive than in the resistant suicidal act. However, elsewhere, the appointment of Bouazizi as a representative ordinary individual also invited reflection on the corporality of the individual. Bouazizi's body seemed to be the site of necropolitical resistance, even though that site could only be located in the suicide archive. It was in suicide texts that the corporeal experience of Bouazizi's self-immolation could be generalised as the node of biopolitics that is necropolitics. Didier Fassin was perhaps the first to comment on this, holding Bouazizi's act and its repercussions as demonstrating that "the relation between the state and violence takes two forms, which are linked in a specular way – in other words as mirror images. The body is not only the site where power is exerted or resisted, it is also the site where truth is sought or denied" (2011: 284). On a related but distinct note, which is relevant to the above account of the conceptual line from ordinary individual to protesting crowd, Andreja Zevnik considers the common ground between the somewhat different kinds of resistant self-erasure involved in Bouazizi's self-immolation and in *sans papiers* (migrants or refugees who destroy their identity papers) in order to reconsider anti-establishment political subjectivity:

> The shared experience of Bouazizi's powerlessness, *sans papiers* or mass political gatherings in the squares, Syntagma in Greece, Tahrir in Egypt or Pearl Square in Bahrain, displaces the initial subject–sovereign relation and instead (re)position the struggle for political recognition away from political action mobilised by the old narratives of the class, race, ethnicity or religion. In recent contestations, which consequently saw the birth of a new resistant political subject, space emerges as a key force of political action and a forum for political subjectivities. As a rather dispersed and horizontal political actor, space produces collectivised rather than individual logics of political subjectivation, such as the crowd and the multitude. (Zevnik 2014: 105)

Zevnik's emphasis on the spatiality of the protesting crowd as a bodily formation, and her emphasis on its appearance as a discrete political subjectivity, in many ways recalls the structuralist approach to crowd versus individual noted above, although with various nuances. In the above quotation, as in Zevnik's argument generally, the individuality (subjectivity) of Bouazizi is submerged to some extent by being conjoined with *sans papiers* and mass political gatherings.

But this summary of the manner in which the Bouazizi suicide archive gradually incorporated theoretical precepts and tested general conceptual horizons, principally in academic forums, has run ahead of itself. Other suicide texts intervened from well beyond those forums, and became grist to the academic mill. In fact, philosophical reflection via Bouazizi's self-immolation occurred after the fact of those extra-academic texts, which appeared mainly in the interim between the initial speculative line drawn above and considered theoretical formulations – preceding and informing such formulations. Three such areas of the Bouazizi suicide archive are discussed briefly in the remainder of this chapter: those relating to martyrdom, gender politics and news media. Each area entailed different ways of filling in or further evacuating the emptiness of the ordinary individual as a face of outraged ordinary collectivity. The net result was a gradual putting into place of Bouazizi's ordinary individuality; or rather, a putting into place of ordinariness in general, which is the same as returning the ordinary to the norm of becoming unnoticed and negligible.

MARTYRDOM

By the time the Ennahdha Party-led government settled in following the October 2011 Constituent Assembly elections in Tunisia, less than a year after his death by self-immolation, Mohamed Bouazizi was firmly recognised as a revolutionary martyr – a publicly embraced *shahid*. This circumstance of the posthumous Bouazizi's singular career has naturally attracted scholarly attention (for example, Khosrokhavar 2012; Halverson et al. 2013; Mittermaier 2015) and considerable media interest. Most have tended to stress the religious connotations and roots of *shahid*. Although it originates in Quranic Arabic and therefore has a religious meaning, the word *shahid* is currently used as much – and probably more often – in an areligious, state–nationalist sense in various languages from North Africa to South Asia (with slightly different inflections in, for instance, Swahili, Turkish, Farsi, Urdu, Hindi, Punjabi, Bengali and Malay), covering diverse religious and cultural formations. The word is particularly redolent of the myths and realities of postcolonial nation formation; it comes with an anti-imperialist (but not anti-establishment) nuance in habitual usage – including in Muslim-dominant contexts in the Maghreb. It was therefore a reductive move on the part of journalists and academics to take up the word as principally bearing religious connotations in the context of the uprisings in Tunisia and subsequently in Egypt. The recruitment and redefinition of the religious connotations of the word by Islamist organisations (which Khosrokhavar (2005) and Asad (2007) have analysed trenchantly) may possibly have overly coloured the vision of commentators. The easy translation of "martyr" to "*shahid*" also encourages an over-determination of the religious underpinnings.

Given its broader current connotations, then, firm recognition as *shahid* involves a confluence of two directions: evidence of a popular or collective (communal) consensus; and sanction by an authorising formation or an authority-bearing alignment (usually religious or governmental). Although an assessment of causes, intentions and effects seems critical to both directions for recognition as *shahid*, once so recognised all ambivalences and doubts surrounding the *shahid*'s life and death are replaced by a greater significance, an ineffable weight of confirmation that supersedes scepticism. All the circumstances of the *shahid* become imbued with a higher meaning, which is confirmed in advance by the popular consensus and the sanction of authority. The *shahid* is thus never really a historical figure but one filled with significance above historicity, crossing from historiography into hagiography, or perhaps nuancing historiography into hagiography. The narratives that perform recognition as *shahid* eschew contextual and consequential considerations and become static affirmations of collective consensus and established authority.

That such an ineffable significance was conferred on Bouazizi's image and name by popular consensus became evident almost as soon as a conceptual line was drawn from his ordinary individuality to those in the protesting crowds. The invocation of his name in slogans and his image on posters among the crowds before Ben Ali was ousted was synonymous with *shahid*-like status, and eulogistic songs and poetry started appearing about him accordingly. Nevertheless, he was not and could not be firmly established as *shahid* unless some kind of authorising sanction appeared. Until that appeared, the conferment of *shahid* status would merely be a confirmation of a desire of ordinary people, confined to a sphere of ordinary discourse that informally signals but cannot formally confer *status*. Having status and ordinariness are close to being antonyms: the granting of status would immediately break the conceptual line from ordinary individual to protesters; it would raise Bouazizi above ordinariness. Bouazizi was firmly confirmed as *shahid* by mid-2011, but complexities in the suicide texts in question need to be registered to grasp what that meant. These complexities also go some way towards explaining the gradual waning of Bouazizi's stature as *shahid* in subsequent years. Despite popular consensus, religious scholars initially balked at acknowledging Bouazizi as *shahid*. Khosrokhavar has given a detailed account of those initial deliberations, effectively of discord between the desire of ordinary people (protesters) and authority-bearing clerics who spoke for establishment religion:

> People called it martyrdom, but the Ulamas, with few exceptions, regarded the act as an infringement on God's commandment. According to that commandment, no one should take his or her own life, and one's death can only be decided by God. From the dominant Islamic perspective, Bouazizi's act could not be qualified as martyrdom but as a desecration of God's commandment stipulated in the Koran: "No person can ever die except by Allah's Leave at an appointed term" (Koran, Surat ImrÁn Family, verse 145), or more explicitly: "Don't kill yourself" (Surat The Women, verse 29) or "Don't throw yourself into destruction" (Surat The Cow, verse 195). In spite of misgiving and even condemnation by some of the Ulamas, people celebrated his heroic death, and songs and videos were created in his honor, calling him a martyr. (Khosrokhavar 2012: 172–3)

A few clerics and religious scholars demurred, Khosrokhavar notes, but generally confirmation from religious authority was withheld. However, the popular consensus that had grown around Bouazizi's suicide, the protesters' insistence on his *shahid* status, could nevertheless maintain a religious edge irrespective of establishment denial. The idea of *shahid* in Islamic terms is somewhat more fluid than its equivalent "martyr" in Christianity: the assessment of motives and intentions underlying the *shahid's* death, and of their relationship to effects, is arguably less rigorous than "martyrdom" suggests. Or, put otherwise, the Islamic concept of *shahid* is more accommodative of ordinary lives and deaths than "martyr" in the Christian sense, including deaths that are not ostentatiously motivated by faith or do not seem to explicitly confirm faith. Testament of Islamic faith through death has a broader purchase. The authoritative source that is often cited in this regard is the Hadith *Sahih Bukhari* (Volume 4, Book 52): "Allah's Apostle said, 'Five are regarded as martyrs: They are those who die because of plague, abdominal disease, drowning or a falling building etc., and the martyrs in Allah's Cause'" (Number 82); and, "The Prophet said, 'Plague is the cause of martyrdom of every Muslim (who dies because of it)'" (Number 83). Asad's (2007) examination of the nuances of *shahid* in Islamic terminology shows that further pathological or accidental causes of death have been added to the remit of *shahid* in various Islamic contexts. He consequently observes that *shahid* could then be understood as being "constituted as a sign of human finitude in the world created by an eternal deity" (ibid.: 49), irrespective of motives and perhaps even including "self-death", and differentiates *shahid* accordingly from "sacrifice" or *dahiyya*.

The weight of perceived significance – the importance of signification after the fact – and the relative inconsequence of motives and intentions allowed the popular consensus on Bouazizi's *shahid* status to be upheld with a kind of religious verve even without the confirmation of authority. What mattered, it seemed, was that the ordinary populace had signified Bouazizi as embodying their sense of impotence against power and their urge to protest, and that signification was not wholly inconsistent with Islamic interpretations of *shahid*. The popular consensus seemed to gain further momentum as another "revolution" gathered pace in January 2011, and contemplation of other *shuhada* sharpened the mechanics of signifying Bouazizi as *shahid*. At any rate, Bouazizi's status as popular *shahid* in Tunisia appeared to echo that of Khaled Said in Egypt, another point of mobilisation against the state, another signification and embodiment of protest – albeit murdered rather than committing suicide. The strong association that developed between Bouazizi's image in relation to the uprising in Tunisia and Said's in relation to that in Egypt concretised the popular consensus for the former, while retaining a vaguely confirmatory, but not emphatic or authoritatively endorsed, religious spirit.

After Mohamed Bouazizi died by self-immolation, others followed his example, but most failed to garner a similar popular consensus – they didn't even come close. Immediately after Bouazizi's death on 4 January 2011, self-immolation as a way of registering political protest spread beyond Tunisia. Between 12 and 25 January 2011, fourteen people set themselves on fire in different public spaces in Algeria, and twelve in Egypt. Attempted or successful self-immolations were also reported from Mauritania, Syria, Morocco, Yemen and Saudi Arabia, and they began to appear in European countries: more on the latter in subsequent chapters. Many of these were ordinary individuals expressing discontent, but their ordinary *individuality* failed to become *collectivised* in the way Bouazizi's had, let alone consecrated as *shahid*. They were all immediately dubbed copycat suicides in the news media, and all were seen as would-be Bouazizis. In fact, their suicides redounded to Bouazizi's credit and mainly served to confirm his status as *shahid*. The rest became shadows of Bouazizi, and Bouazizi became ever more emphatically *shahid*. To seal the diminishing returns of self-immolation as protest after Bouazizi, such suicides in Egypt (mainly in Cairo and Alexandria) up to 25 January 2011 flowed into something momentous that would effectively lead to a great proliferation of *shuhada*. With the so-called "Revolution of 25 January 2011" in Egypt, the ordinary individual as *shahid* was overtaken and erased by the collectivised revolutionary youth who died as *shuhada*. In the image of Khaled Said, and with the slogan "We are all Khaled Said", there was already a precursor for these *shuhada* in Egypt, predating Bouazizi's gesture. Khaled Said was a twenty-eight-year-old who was beaten to death by plainclothes policemen outside an internet café on 10 June 2010. He was an avid Facebook networker, and his death inspired the Facebook movement "We are all Khaled Said", moderated by Wael Ghonim. Ghonim's book (2012) detailed how, as a Google executive in Dubai, he coordinated the "We are all Khalid Said" network and the 25 January protests before being detained. For a brief period in January 2011 the significations of Bouazizi and Said seemed to resonate strongly with each other. In this period, the Tunisian uprising appeared to flow into a burgeoning Egyptian effervescence. Revolutionary *shahid* narratives gradually captured and fixed Bouazizi and Said in a mirroring manner, drawing on precedent narrative structures of hagiographic martyrdom stories (from Islamic, Coptic and secular traditions), as Halverson et al. (2013) argued.

Nevertheless, as revolutionary *shuhada*, the juxtaposition of Bouazizi and Said is indicative as much in terms of their differences as their similarities. The testimonies of their lives, and particularly their deaths, signified differently. Said lived in a middle-class suburb, was computer-literate and connected to the world (a wider virtual world than Egypt), and wasn't especially concerned with earning a livelihood; Bouazizi was of the working class, knew want, and was a harassed breadwinner for his family. If "ordinariness" evokes ground-level populations, acted upon and dominated, then Bouazizi was more likely to be regarded as such across a wider spectrum of social classes than Said. Bouazizi's death by self-immolation accentuated that ordinariness, as an act of both defiance and victimisation. Said's death by other hands foregrounded mainly the culmination of passive victimisation and the pervasiveness of oppression. Oppression, it seemed, took him *despite* his middle-class background and in a middle-class neighbourhood in Alexandria, so that his neighbour, Amro Ali (who wrote several articles on Said), observed:

> It was not just the manner of Khaled's death that had disturbed me, but the deep reach of President Hosni Mubarak's repressive police state into a neighborhood where I had grown up and idealized as a beacon of harmony. Up until then, I naively thought that such things happened to other people, in the slums, Islamist strongholds, in prisons, on the news, Alexandria's rural outskirts, or any "other area." My area became that "other area."
> (Ali 2012)

This much Said shared with Bouazizi: again in Ali's words, "the absence of any obvious ideological bent in his background enabled many to claim ownership of Khaled as 'their' everyday Egyptian" (ibid.). Between the ground level of working-class ordinary people and the everydayness of the middle-class internet citizens there is a narrow area of overlap, and both Bouazizi and Said fell within that overlap. This is the overlapping area where individual convictions are neither owned nor ascribable. Bouazizi's and

Said's deaths signified differently, but they shared their immediate emptiness of ideological commitments and their openness to multiple ascriptions. They weren't fitted into revolutionary *shahid* narratives because they preferred death to compromising their commitments, but because they suffered from injustice. Neither explicitly championed any broader cause or ideological vision, but that lack of explicit commitment meant that they could be recruited to exemplify all sorts of causes and visions whereby injustice can be articulated, however contrarily and contradictorily – they could be recruited as revolutionary *shahid*, with a vaguely religious and an unavoidably political turn.

Gradually through 2011, the popular consensus on Bouazizi as *shahid* found state authorisation, the authorisation of a new regime in (troubled and contested) power, instead of authorisation from the religious establishment – and, in a way, the religious qualms and nuances receded into silence. He was incorporated into *official* discourses of being *shahid*: memorials and statues were erected, postage stamps bearing his image were issued, squares and streets and an airport were named after him, posthumous honours awarded, films of his life planned, and so on. A state bureaucratic apparatus confirmed Bouazizi's *shahid* status, now meeting the popular consensus halfway, claiming its legitimacy through that consensus and courting it. The structures of religious narrative were not exactly done away with, but were merged with the structures that narrated national consolidation and state legitimacy and were submerged within them. The ineffable greater significance of being *shahid*, of being put beyond doubt and ambivalence, of becoming indelibly *extraordinary*, was enabled by a new political order feeling its way into doubtful sovereignty. The international regime, which is accustomed to undergirding state legitimacy in North Africa, also signalled its approbation of the emerging order via Bouazizi on occasion, by underlining his extraordinary status as national icon. Interestingly, that signalling of extrinsic legitimation also indicated that "revolution" and "status quo" have a counterintuitive way of gelling. Former colonial and reigning neo-colonial organisations and their observers appointed Bouazizi as not quite *shahid* but as a hero of democracy, which is close enough as a paternalistic thumbs-up to the post-"revolutionary" state in Tunisia. Indeed, it is a confirmatory nod and ideological co-optation of the so-called "Arab Spring" itself, a way of symbolically harnessing uprisings in Egypt, Syria and Libya into their self-affirmations. So, a Place Mohamed-Bouazizi appeared in the 16th arrondissement of Paris; the 2011 Sakharov Prize for Freedom of Thought was awarded in October to five "Arab Spring" protesters by the European Parliament, and Bouazizi was the only (posthumous) recipient from Tunisia; in December 2011, the British newspaper *The Times* named Bouazizi "person of the year"; and in the same month the American magazine *Time* named the "protester" as "person of the year", and naturally Bouazizi featured prominently as one such protester.

But if the state–national confirmation of Bouazizi as *shahid*, and the international recognition of Bouazizi as a hero of democracy, seemed to propel the ordinary individual through the protesting crowd into transcendent extraordinariness in 2011, moves towards pulling posthumous Bouazizi back into mundane ordinariness and forgetfulness were already under way. In the Bouazizi suicide archive, state hagiography and everyday farce were already jostling with each other as 2011 waned. In fact, even as the *Time* magazine named the "protester" as "person of the year" and gave space to Bouazizi as such, an article appeared entitled "Mohamed Bouazizi's Unexpected Sequel: A Tunisian Soap Opera" (Abouzeid 2011b). The title itself ran counter to the *shahid* narrative of Bouazizi and undermined it – and, already, it said nothing new. Gendered and domestic anxieties had cut into hagiography, and even amidst the posthumous Bouazizi's rise as *shahid*, there were portents of his fall back into trivial ordinariness.

THE GENDERED AND DOMESTIC

In the outline of shaky facts with which I began – the imagined account that enabled a conceptual line to be drawn from Bouazizi to the protesting crowd – the alleged role played by municipal official Faida Hamdi proved effective and discomfiting in equal measure. The story that circulated was explicitly that of a confrontation between the state agent and the ordinary individual; this story was also variously sharpened, given nuance, encouraged as a confrontation between an aggressive woman and a victimised man. Insofar as the latter shaped the issue, Bouazizi was not merely an ordinary *individual* but more accurately an ordinary *man*: his masculine strength was wounded in being beaten by a woman (in a 2014 Ahram Online interview, Hamdi observed, "Had a man hit him, none of this would have happened"); his male dignity was derided (Hamdi was said to have spat at him); and the entire patrilineal order was shown disrespect (Hamdi allegedly shouted abuse about Bouazizi's father). In that encounter, it appeared, ordinary masculinity had been emasculated, and perhaps it is not much of a stretch to feel that patriarchal ordinariness itself had become unmanned. There is a kind of symmetry here with accounts of the retribution that followed, of the "revolution": if the retribution of the protesting crowd for the repression of ordinary individuality was to extirpate state authoritarianism, bearing Bouazizi's humiliation in mind it could also be thought of as a re-masculation of ordinariness. In an unthinking way, that line was also pushed in accounts of the Tunisian uprising, from all sides: it always seemed worth mentioning particularly that *women* were participating too, that *women* had played a decisive role in the "revolution" – it was understood that ordinariness and protesting crowds carry a male norm within them.

The fissure in the overlapping narratives of the encounter between Hamdi and Bouazizi (state authority and ordinary individual/assertive woman and victimised man) gradually radiated out and cracked the democratic discourse of protest, of the "Arab Spring" itself. In a broad way, it accentuated preconceived fissures between East and West, religious conservatism and secular liberalism (or, more loosely, cultural conservatism and liberalism). More immediately, it had a bearing on a complex and ongoing debate on whether the focus of feminist activists working in Islamic societies should simply oppose the (often severe) limits placed on female agency or extend a liberated feminine space by capitalising on the different kinds of agency permitted in those societies. In other words, whether feminist activism should accommodate to some degree or simply militate against Islamic tenets on gender roles, which are in any case diverse (recent interventions in this debate appear, for instance, in Mahmood 2005; Badran 2009; Boucherine 2014). Cutting across these considerations, and complicating the debate, is the awareness that Muslim women have been consistently stereotyped most shrilly in Europe and North America (the so-called "West") to justify imperialist interventions under the guise of liberal equalitarianism (on this, recently, see Zayzafoon 2005; Abu-Lughod 2013). The gendered reading of Bouazizi's encounter with Hamdi seemed to taint the uprisings with a tinge of that stereotyping. Importantly, these broad ideological polarities had a particularly complicated purchase within Tunisia. The regimes of Habib Bourguiba and then Zine el Abidine Ben Ali had instituted a liberal judicial apparatus with regard to women: the Personal Status Code of 1956/1957, which had remained in force since then, abolished polygamy, gave women significant rights in marriage and divorce, set a minimum age for marriage and consent, discouraged the hijab, offered the right to abortion, and opened voting to women in municipal elections. The uprising of 2010–11 against the Ben Ali regime, with the participation of conservative and religious organisations (which certainly capitalised on the uprising later), prompted both firm support from and a degree of anxiety among women activists. The gendered account of the Bouazizi–Hamdi encounter served up a meaningful stew of contradictions for women, articulated well by Norma Claire Moruzzi (2013):

> The policewoman who slaps the hapless poor man was part of a state policy of incorporating some women into an authoritarian state; thus the vendor was persecuted by a corrupt and imperious security apparatus in which women could (as agents of this state) have positions of power. Precisely because Ben Ali's Tunisia was not a democratic society (the state did not empower its people, only its agents), women's individual empowerment as state agents did not necessarily contribute to more egalitarian social relations, and patriarchal norms could coexist with the individualized advancement of women. Hence the man was doubly humiliated by the state's repression, provided in the guise of a woman (as a formal state actor) belittling him in a social form (the slap).

As it happened, Hamdi was arrested several times thereafter, protested that she had not acted beyond her official capacity, and eventually, in April 2011, was released without charge when Bouazizi's mother (of whom more below) withdrew the family's legal complaint. Subsequently, Hamdi's story was seen in a somewhat different light. She came to be regarded as a more or less helpless cog in the state apparatus herself, more a scapegoat than a perpetrator, in many ways an ordinary *woman* to Bouazizi's ordinary *man*. Indeed, Hamdi told her own story in various interviews (for example, Davies 2011; Totten 2012; Ahram Online 2014); she professed herself a supporter of the "revolution" and regretful of her fateful encounter with Bouazizi, and yet also glad that it unravelled as it did. The above-quoted passage by Moruzzi leads to the following, keeping these developments in mind:

> But after the formal democratic transition, the vilified state agent is redeemed and reincorporated within the social polity by being recategorized as a modest woman. Her actions are reinterpreted: She is no longer seen to have acted as a (female) state agent, but as a proper (feminine) social subject. Just as Bouazizi asserted his compromised masculine dignity as the last signifier of his claim to respect from the state (as an appropriate political subject), Hamdi proffered her righteous feminine honor as her claim for inclusion within the new state as an appropriate social subject (and of her rejection of transgressive gender politics). Yet nothing in this shifting balance of gendered protest and obligation has much of anything to do with democratic agency, emancipation or equality. (Moruzzi 2013)

The anxiety that feminists felt about the transition, the mixed feelings, are apparent here. It was an anxiety that anticipated a deterioration in women's agency after the "revolution", despite the oft-noted decisive support that women had given it – with time, it seems, some scholars have found reason to feel reassured on this score (Labidi 2015).

If the gendered account of the Bouazizi–Hamdi encounter cast a shadow on the posthumous rise of Bouazizi from ordinary individual to *shahid*, redolent of the complexity of a clash of civilisations (Islam and the "West", conservatism versus liberalism), it remained nevertheless no more than a shadow. And yet the gendered dimension of the Bouazizi story was already taking another turn – and perhaps had done so from its inception – that came to dominate the suicide archive, and eventually to domesticate posthumous Bouazizi back into ordinary individuality. It spiralled into embarrassment about his *shahid* status and settled into farce, a "soap opera". The ineffable weight that the signification of *shahid* acquires between popular consensus and nation-state affirmation (with a hint of religious confirmation), as happened with Bouazizi, is not easily shifted by academic reasoning or historical documentation – *shuhada* and historical personae exist in different registers. Hagiography is not really countered by historiography; it can, however, be countered by focusing on the trivial, the mundane, the rumoured, and especially the farcical. An attitude of irreverence – simply performed repeatedly and bitterly, or dispensed tongue-in-cheek – is perhaps the most effective counter to what is presumptively constructed to be revered: the *shahid* (or, for that matter, the hero). The suicide archive here offers a shift of emphasis, gradually pushing the Bouazizi story into the realms of domesticity, as always gendered, and in this case feminised with patriarchal dismissiveness. This is a turn in the gendered dimension of the story that has been little noted, unlike the narrative of the Bouazizi–Hamdi encounter, perhaps because it did not chime immediately with those big ideological polarisations of East–West and conservative–liberal. Or rather, the deployment of patriarchal stereotypes in this shift was often at the behest of *this* side, the "liberal West" and its "international" or "global" media industry; at any rate, all sides participated in it without feeling compromised, in united recourse to gendered stereotypes and the habituated norms of patriarchy.

As observed above, the constitution of Bouazizi as the ordinary individual in collective protests involved an emptying out of his individuality, a reduction of the sequence of events culminating in suicide into a spare narrative, so that his name and image could be filled in with the ordinary individualities of all protesters, the crowd itself. That spare narrative circulated prolifically and repeatedly and became, for a while, a vehicle of protests; at the same time, and this is also mentioned above, news media demanded a distinctive personal account of Bouazizi, some affective dimension beyond the spare narrative to satisfy news consumers. To this end, testimonies and witnesses of Bouazizi's life and suicide were called upon (Who knew him? Who had seen him set himself on fire? What did they do? ... and so on), and broad social indicators were mined to interpret his life and suicide (How did Bouazizi fit into a pattern of authoritarian policing? How representative is Bouazizi of Tunisian youth? ... and so on). The former kind of framing soon called upon the testimonies of Bouazizi's immediate family. And, gradually, his mother Manoubia Bouazizi in particular and to some degree his sisters Basma and Samia were foregrounded. They were presented not merely as informants on Mohamed Bouazizi's life, but as interpreters of his suicide, proxies for articulating his intentions, carriers of his message, confirmers of his humanity, and embodiments of his legacy. As such, they were used to rescue Bouazizi from emptied signification as ordinary individual and affix Bouazizi as a distinctive male type: the dutiful or loving son and brother. Every affirmation of this turn by Manoubia, Samia and Basma also fixed them in the stereotyped role of mother and sisters; not ordinary individuals themselves, but recognisable only through their uncomplicatedly gendered relation to the ordinary *man* Bouazizi, as *women* playing their parts. The more reporters and broadcasters courted and highlighted their statements from December 2010 onwards – and this was particularly intensive among global news channels – the more Mohamed Bouazizi was fixed as son and brother, Manoubia as mother and Samia and Basma as sisters in an inextricable mutual bind.

This was a habitual media framing of personal stories, grounded in conventional family relations and domesticity – and it had a trajectory. The trajectory involved moving the site of contemplating posthumous Bouazizi from the streets and squares where protesters gathered to his domestic household, to small interiors and modest houses. Bouazizi's significance moved from being a signifier of ordinary individuality for protesting crowds to being the ordinary man who could be described though interpersonal relations. The domestic space within which the posthumous Bouazizi could now be found was conceived as a predominantly feminine space, as domestic spaces usually are. To this, Bouazizi had mainly brought a whiff of the masculine world outside, as his sisters' chaperone, as breadwinner, as the transient nightly presence in the bedroom. In this feminine domestic space, Bouazizi's significance remained fuzzy, a blur of the man of the house seen by affectionate dependants. That reallocation of posthumous presence for Bouazizi worked as a foil for his status as icon of ordinary individuality, as *shahid* and hero of democracy; his distinctive ordinariness gradually appeared to be closely linked to specific persons, embroiled in small-scale anxieties, involved with the minutiae of everyday domestic politics rather than the enormity of "revolutionary" politics. Step by step, the trajectory of the media narrative tracking posthumous Bouazizi's career moved further away from public domains; the rhetorical turn and the suggestive phrase gradually decentred Bouazizi altogether so that his mother and sisters become the protagonists of the story. This trajectory is most economically presented through the following set of quotations – a small selection – from news reports in mainly global media channels, from December 2010 to December 2011. The nuances of media framing and the shifts of narrativisation are self-evident and need no commentary.

31 December 2010, *Gulf News*
Samia Bouazizi, Mohammad's sister, told the daily [...] "My brother is 26 years old and did not succeed in getting the high school diploma, so he took up selling fruits and vegetables in order to make some money for himself and the family" [...]
"On December 17, he left home and went about his small business, selling fruits and vegetables when a municipality agent, a woman, put pressure on him on the grounds that he did not have a licence [...] The standoff degenerated and she confiscated the weighing scales, slapped him on the face and threw away the fruits and vegetables he was selling," Samia told *Assabah*, an independent daily as it carried a field investigation of the incident [...] Mannoubia, the mother, said that she was in an olive grove when she was told about the tragedy. "The doctors told me that he should be fine, and I keep praying. I am burning inside and I hope that he will recover [...] I am confident that the authorities will uphold my son's rights," she said.
(Toumi 2010)

13 January 2011, *The National*
"He was my soul, my life, my heart," said his mother, Mannoubia Bouazizi. "Now he's a symbol." […]
"We don't agree with protesters resorting to violence," said Samia Bouazizi. "But we're with the people peacefully demanding their rights." (Thorne 2011)

20 January 2011, *The Guardian*
"He was funny," says Basma, "and generous." She stops for a moment to recall the elder brother who once walked her to school. "When he would get angry with me he always came afterwards and asked me to forgive him."
His mother, Manoubia, points to where her late son slept in the tiny white-walled bedroom he shared with his younger brother, Karim. It is picture-less and stacked with a few cushions and bedclothes. (Beaumont 2011)

20 January 2011, *Al Jazeera*
"My sister was the one in university and he would pay for her," Samya Bouazizi, one of his sisters, said. "And I am still a student and he would spend money on me." […]
Menobia Bouazizi said the former president was wrong not to meet with her son sooner, and that when Ben Ali finally did reach out to her family, it was too late – both to save her son, and to save his presidency […]
"The invite to the presidential palace came very late," she said. "We are sure that the president only made the invitation to try to derail the revolution."
"I went there as a mother and a citizen to ask for justice for my son." (Ryan 2011a)

21 January 2011, *The New York Times*
"She [Faida Hamdi] humiliated him," said his sister, Samia Bouazizi. "Everyone was watching." […]

And as the story has traveled past the olive groves and cactus that surround Sidi Bouzid, others saw a tale of oppression, despair and recovered dignity. In the last few weeks, people in other impoverished countries have started mimicking Mr. Bouazizi's act.

"I'm sad for their families," said Samia Bouazizi, his sister, as she hurried from interview to interview, sharing a family's personal tragedy with the world. "I know what they go through." (Fahim 2011a)

21 January 2011, *Time*
Though proud of the consequences of Bouazizi's self-immolation, his family is still indescribably sad. "Mohammed did what he did for the sake of his dignity," says his mother, Mannoubia, standing in the room he shared with his brother Karim, 14. It's one of four in her small but well-kept home. She points to the two thin olive-green foam mattresses on the floor where her two sons slept. The only other piece of furniture in the room is a large cabinet. Weeping, his mother pulls out a black-and-grey jacket, lovingly clutching it before burying her face in it. "It smells of him," she says. Her teenage daughter Basma rushes to comfort her. (Abouzeid 2011a)

21 January 2011, *The Independent*
Sitting at the family home, a three roomed house, surrounded by her children, 48-year-old Mannoubia talked about how her son's death has politicised her: "I now know how Ben Ali had been stealing from the country. How the relations of Leila Trabelsi have been stealing" […] She continued: "I have a lot of people who come up to me now to say it is not just me who has lost a son, but the whole village that has lost a son. I am proud of what he did. I would like to go up to Tunis and take a look at these demonstrations. It is good to know that my son had played a part in changing things." (Sengupta 2011)

18 March **2011,** *Der Spiegel*
Manoubia Bouazizi, the mother of a hero, is sitting on a bench,
warming her hands with a pot, in the inner courtyard of her narrow three-room house, which includes a kitchen and an entry
hall. She says no one gave her money. A new computer with an
Internet connection is visible in one of the rooms. Basma, the
15-year-old sister of Mohamed Bouazizi, is sitting in front of the
computer. She is now a member of Facebook. (Rohr 2011)

20 April **2011,** *BBC News*
The case against Faida Hamdi was dropped at the start of her
trial in Sidi Bouzid after his mother withdrew her complaint,
Tunisian media report.

Mannoubiya Bouazizi said she wanted to promote reconciliation […]

Hundreds of people outside the court cheered as the charges
were dropped, shouting "freedom, freedom", and saying Ms
Hamdi had been used as a scapegoat. (BBC 2011)

17 June **2011,** *BBC News*
It has emerged his mother and stepfather accepted several thou-
sand dollars in "compensation" from President Ben Ali, as he
struggled to hang on to power.

The family has since moved from their modest home in Sidi
Bouzid to a much bigger house in the upmarket Tunis suburb
of La Marsa. Frustrated, even jealous, detractors accuse them of
cashing in. (Davies 2011)

5 August **2011,** *The New York Times*
[The Bouazizis' neighbours'] anger stemmed from rumors that
the family had accepted large sums of money to move to a fancy
villa in Tunis. But more than that, they said they were furious
at being left behind, in a place with no jobs, money or hope,
without the famous Bouazizis to give voice to their despair.
"She abandoned us, and nothing here changed," said Seif Amri,

18, a neighbor, speaking of Mr. Bouazizi's mother, Mannoubia Bouazizi [...]

The Bouazizi family did not move to a fancy villa, though their one-story home, tucked in an alleyway in the Tunis neighborhood of La Marsa, is bigger than their cramped house in Sidi Bouzid [...] Their journey, from a poor inland town to the more prosperous coast, is repeated by thousands of people every year. [Samia Bouazizi, Mohamed's sister] said that claims that the family had received money were "lies." So was the contention that the Bouazizis had forgotten their roots. "We speak up for the town every chance we get," she said. She had no explanation for the wild rumors that had followed her family, except one. "Envy," she said. (Fahim 2011b)

14 December 2011, *Time*
A lengthy interview with Manoubia is followed by an article by the interviewer (entitled "Mohamed Bouazizi's Unexpected Sequel: A Tunisian Soap Opera") with the following observations, in Time *magazine's 14 December 2011 edition, which declares "the protester" as the "person of the year":*

But in the months since the crush of foreign and local media crews, dignitaries and well-wishers has subsided, a quiet backlash has developed against the Bouazizis in some parts of their impoverished town. "As the days went on, the talk increased, and the attempt to smear us started," says Bouazizi's mother Mannoubia [...]

Mannoubia blames one particular neighbor, Haniya Dawi, for much of the gossip. The two women had frosty ties even before Mohamed's death. Their dislike appears to stem from the neighbor's alleged 10-meter encroachment on the Bouazizi property. It descended into physical violence in early November, on the Muslim Eid al-Adha holiday. The Bouazizis had returned to their old home to spend the day and, as is customary, visit the graves of relatives, principally Mohamed. "Yes, she came here on Eid, and we had a fight. I hit her and she hit me. I opened up her head," says Dawi, a woman with piercing blue eyes and brown tartar on her teeth, as she stands at the gate of her property. She is proud of the stitches Bouazizi's mother had to get in her scalp. "We don't like each other. Mohamed's not a martyr, and she's not the mother of a martyr. He burned himself and used to drink. She has 4 billion dinars, you know, from Europe, America and [United Nations Secretary-General] Ban Ki-moon." (Abouzeid 2011b)

Curiously, as the carefully mediatised story developed along the lines sketched above, the posthumous Mohamed Bouazizi somehow became culpable – although it remained unclear what he was guilty of. In a way, he became guilty for everything that had gone wrong: for slow or no change in the lives of ordinary people in Tunisia, for the disappointments following the "Arab Spring" more widely, for the undermined principles of "revolution", for the material compromises made by his family, for the compensation culture of big media and governments, for the indifferent realpolitik of multiparty democracy and international power play. He simply became culpable; to try to articulate what he was culpable of is to miss the point – he had become guilty really of his own ordinariness, he had been put into place as a particular ordinary individual whose appearance on posters and banners and in slogans from December 2010 to February 2011 now seemed an overweening pretence. So, by the end of 2014, it seemed quite natural for a comment in *Al Araby Al Jadeed* to state the obvious in its title: "Why Mohamed Bouazizi is Blameless" (Hamid 2014): "Many believe his death brought about revolutions, uprisings, demonstrations and even civil war. They blame Bouazizi and no longer consider it offensive to swear whenever his name is mentioned, or when people speak of what he did."

NEWS MEDIA

The sources that feed the Bouazizi suicide archive determine what threads are woven into it and become traceable. This chapter so far has followed those threads. The suicide archive here is dominated to a great degree by texts in print or online newspapers, magazines, broadcast reports, blogs – or broadly in news media. The suicide archive also consists of research reports and analyses, and various more or less analytical publications. The latter are grounded to a significant degree in news media texts too, referring to their evidence and information-providing commentary (alongside further fieldwork, witness accounts, interviews, statistical analyses, historical reckonings and the like). Thus, news media texts constitute a kind of moving front line for the suicide archive. Further, news media texts often reflect upon their own construction of the news, on the mechanics of their own generation of news stories: that is, the operations of news media are often themselves news covered in the media. Similarly, critical investigation of the news media is a salient dimension of the analytical publications mentioned above: that is, news media are as much the objects of research as the sources. Researchers find that what the news is and how the news appears are usually inextricably enmeshed in each other and need to be explored in a correlated fashion. Insofar as the news in question concerns large-scale protests and social mobilisations, since roughly the late 1990s research and analysis have tended to break the media field into two broad sections: one that is structured along formal industrial lines, organised into public or private firms, producing print, broadcast or online news texts for local or global constituencies; and a second that is loosely structured to enable the circulation of information from informal and dispersed sources (such as posters and leaflets, and overwhelmingly of late through the internet, especially social networking resources such as Twitter and Facebook). With regard to social mobilisations and large-scale protests, the structuring of informal and dispersed flows of information has dominated scholarly attention: on the one hand, these appear to express or reveal a bottom-up view, which mainstream media also capitalises on; on the other, they seem to be complicit in mobilisations and protests, and even allegedly actuate them.

In print, the various uprisings of the so-called "Arab Spring" have often been accounted for in terms of the role played by social networks and "new" media. Naturally, the sequence of events following Bouazizi's suicide and the appearance of protesting crowds have focalised this too – both within news media and in scholarly accounts. One of the first mainstream media outlets to give sustained attention to the role played by social networks was, unsurprisingly, Al Jazeera at the end of January 2011 (Ryan 2011b). That brought to the fore another Bouazizi, Mohamed's cousin Ali, an anti-government activist since at least 2008. He had recorded Mohamed's self-immolation on his mobile device and, with the help of Rochdi Horchani, another relative, had placed it on Facebook, encouraged its circulation with assistance from a lawyer, Dhafer Salhi, and gave the first interview on the incident to Al Jazeera on 17 December 2010 itself. The Al Jazeera article recounted the story of the Tunisian "revolution" as a media triumph, a struggle between government attempts to block internet activists and the tenacity with which this was opposed, so that Bouazizi's suicide reached beyond local precincts into international coverage. Ali Bouazizi, it was later observed, had deployed some calculated misinformation ("white lies") in putting out the

Facebook video which maximised its popular purchase. Sustained analysis of the manner in which Bouazizi's suicide was instrumentalised by various social network and media savvy activists has followed (for example, Stokel-Walker 2011: Chapter 3; Hill 2013: Chapter 4; Howard and Hussain 2013: especially Chapter 1; Lim 2013; Collins and Sari 2015–16). The more recent of these studies present summative observations from such investigations that are relevant to understanding how the Bouazizi suicide archive is constituted. A usefully brief overview by Merlyna Lim outlines the process through which mediatisation of the Bouazizi story bridged various geographical and class divides:

> This was possible through the employment of three key mechanisms [...] First, the availability of the archetypal image that had iconic value – Bouazizi's burning body – elevated the non-event of the poor to the public spectacle [...] Second, frame alignment with a master frame that culturally and politically resonated with the entire society successfully fostered a sense of injustice and identity that united the people of Tunisia. This master frame revolved around Ali Bouazizi's "white lies" that rendered Muhamed's burning body political and turned him into a revolutionary symbol of the fight for justice, freedom, and dignity. Third, the activation of a hybrid network that reflects the cultural and technological logic of media convergence to facilitate connective structures that became a platform to generate *collective action* among Tunisians who shared collective identities and collective frames, and *connective action* among individuals who sought more personalized paths to contribute to the movement through digital media. (Lim 2013: 937–8, emphasis in the original)

Noteworthy too are the conclusions reached by Catherine Collins and Miles Sari in their study of framing strategies in media narratives of Bouazizi's self-immolation. Their paper explores both mainstream media and "citizen journalists" (the informal flow of information mentioned above), and finds little difference between their framing strategies. However, in a general way they observed:

> when all four [mainstream] news sources constantly refine the story of Bouazizi's self-immolation they lose sight of the purpose of the Arab Spring, and thus, we lose sight of why Bouazizi lit himself on fire, why this revolution is occurring, and the consequences of widespread social unrest. One of the specific problems with citizen journalism in this case is that it mirrors the problematic framing of mainstream media in largely ignoring the purpose of Bouazizi's desperate act and the population's response to their shared desperation living under authoritarian regimes. (Collins and Sari 2015–16: 15)

That the news media that had enabled the Bouazizi suicide archive to grow into an international event was also designed to lose sight of the significance of his act and the protests that followed complies, within a narrow perspective, with observations in the previous section.

Collins and Sari, in fact, gesture tangentially towards a troubling tendency in much current analysis of media – especially of social networks and "new" media – in relation to mass protests and social mobilisation: that is, a tendency to regard the *means of production* of information about protests as the *agents* of protests. Arguably, Facebook, Twitter and other social networking resources provide greater speed and wider reach in communications than heretofore and are difficult to censor, so they can be used as instruments of anti-establishment mobilisations. But that is quite different from considering them as constituting or structuring protests. It is difficult to argue, for instance, that despite the advantages these present as instruments of activism they have in fact generated activism in themselves. Throughout the nineteenth and twentieth centuries, much larger-scale and more effective protests and revolutions have been enacted across wider geopolitical areas without these advantages. And yet, it now seems rhetorically expedient to think of post-2000 protests and mobilisations as undertaken not by ideologically described or politically organised peoples but by technological savviness: in terms of the "Facebook generation", "Twitter revolutionaries", "connected social movements", "socially networked youth", and so on. This rhetorical expediency seems to have two kinds of thrust. First, it appears to confer some of the agency of the demos – the normative weight of "democracy" loosely understood – to the technology and its users. It is taken for granted that the dispersed and variously sourced information flows in this technological infrastructure effectively give a voice to the "people" itself and materialise "ordinary individuals" in collectivised form (or are a form of "crowd sourcing", "citizenship journalism", and so on). There is a moral allure of democratisation in this thrust, although it constantly runs into difficulty when the limited and generally affluent social strata that have unlimited access and the knowhow to capitalise on this infrastructure are factored in. Their representativeness always seems in doubt. Second, focusing on the means of communication as if they constitute the agents of anti-establishment action helps elide the ideological drives of protests and social mobilisation. It becomes possible to talk about protests in an upbeat or downbeat manner as if they should spring from a spontaneous well of moral and humane values embedded in technological facilities, without asking difficult questions about political choices and principles. Or rather, this studiedly depoliticising thrust tacitly carries its preferred ideological choice as the only possible and natural one: one in which global media conglomerates and networking service providers seek to co-opt and manage all levels of communications by way of facilitating consumers. These considerations play meaningfully within the suicide archive of Bouazizi. The conceptual line in appointing Bouazizi as the face of the ordinary individual for the protesting crowds could, in due course, be deflected by putatively giving ordinary individuals a voice as the Facebook generation, as "citizen journalists". The significations of the posthumous Bouazizi amidst protesting crowds could be slowly diluted by claims that the voice of the living crowd itself could be heard through Facebook, Twitter, Al Jazeera and Al Araby, among others. Moreover, the desire for change that was fuzzily grasped with the appearance of protesting crowds, that was vaguely signalled in the interstices of a "revolution" without ideological clarity, could be manoeuvred towards a moral order of democracy and dignity *at the behest* of technocrats and media savviness. In short, the means through which the posthumous Bouazizi was briefly raised to public eminence were structured so that the significance of his rise would be gradually neutered and diminished.

No tragic figure

The interlocking rationales outlined above of the rise and fall of the posthumous Bouazizi offer no pat recommendations, conclusions or prescriptions. If some sense of the shape and form of Bouazizi's suicide archive is conveyed here, of the ideological system that it records, then the work of this chapter is done.

By way of drawing this chapter to a close, a perhaps unnecessary reminder: nothing in the discussion above is about the person that was Mohamed Bouazizi. Nothing has been said about his personality or disposition, only about the significations attached to his name and image after his self-immolation and consequent death, in a collection of suicide texts.

Where attempts have been made elsewhere to attach a distinctive personality to Bouazizi after his death, to confer on him the shape of a tragic figure (if not quite *shahid* or hero of democracy or guilty party), those too have not been about the person that was Bouazizi. A depiction of Bouazizi as a person has been attempted occasionally. The texts that do this have firmly turned aside from the Bouazizi suicide archive and have mainly foregrounded the imperatives of authorship. Tahar Ben Jelloun's "By Fire" (2013; originally published in 2011 as *Par le feu*) is a fictional text that deliberately draws on accounts of Bouazizi's self-immolation. The interview with Ben Jelloun that appeared with its first publication in English (Treisman 2013) drew a clear web of significances *away* from the Bouazizi suicide archive and towards considerations of textual artifice: as "literature", as the imaginary work of a novelist, as part of the author's oeuvre, as an achievement of style ("the style had to be simple, direct, dry. The subject didn't allow for adjectives and flowers!"). Along quite different lines, and with a claim to recovering a historical personality, an article in the *Foreign Policy* magazine by Hernando de Soto (2011, entitled "The Real Mohamed Bouazizi") concluded, after "three months [of] painstakingly reconstructing Bouazizi's life and world", that: "Above all, he was a repressed entrepreneur [...] Bouazizi's talent was for buying and selling." This leads de Soto into a panegyric on free enterprise, and it becomes evident that this characterisation of Bouazizi is as an allegorical personification masquerading as the "real" person. Such texts appear in the hinterland of the suicide archive that this chapter examines, noted here merely to clarify its current boundaries. Other and more relevant turns in the archive may yet appear.

References

Abouzeid, Rania (2011a) "Bouazizi: The Man Who Set Himself and Tunisia on Fire". *Time*, 21 January. http://content.time.com/time/magazine/article/0,9171,2044723,00.html.

Abouzeid, Rania (2011b) "Mohamed Bouazizi's Unexpected Sequel: A Tunisian Soap Opera". *Time*, 14 December. http://content.time.com/time/specials/packages/article/0,28804,2101745_2102138_2102235,00.html.

Abu-Lughod, Lila (2013) *Do Muslim Women Need Saving?* Cambridge MA: Harvard University Press.

Ahram Online (2014) "Four Years On, Who Is Woman that Slapped Mohamed Bouazizi, Paving Way for the Arab Spring?" *Al Bawaba News*, 17 December. http://www.albawaba.com/news/mohamed-bouazizi-slap-arab-spring-633788.

Ali, Amro (2012) "Saeeds of Revolution: De-Mythologizing Khaled Saeed". *Jadaliyya*, 5 June. http://www.jadaliyya.com/pages/index/5845/saeeds-of-revolution_de-mythologizing-khaled-saeed.

Asad, Talal (2007) *On Suicide Bombing*. New York NY: Columbia University Press.

Badran, Margot (2009) *Feminism in Islam: Secular and Religious Convergences*. London: OneWorld.

Bargu, Banu (2014) *Starve and Immolate: The Politics of Human Weapons*. New York NY: Columbia University Press.

BBC (2011) "Tunisia Revolt: Mohamed Bouazizi Police Suspect Freed". BBC News, 20 April. http://www.bbc.co.uk/news/world-africa-13138301.

Beaumont, Peter (2011) "Mohammed Bouazizi: The Dutiful Son Whose Death Changed Tunisia's Fate". *The Guardian*, 20 January. http://www.theguardian.com/world/2011/jan/20/tunisian-fruit-seller-mohammed-bouazizi.

Benjamin, Walter (1986 [1966]) *Critique of Violence: Essays, Aphorisms, Autobiographical Writings*. New York NY: Schocken.

Boucherine, Ibtissam (2014) *Women and Islam: Myths, Apologies, and the Limits of Feminist Critique*. Lanham MD: Lexington Books.

Canetti, Elias (1962) *Crowds and Power*. Translated by Carol Stewart. Harmondsworth: Penguin.

Chomiak, Laryssa (2014) "Architecture of Resistance in Tunisia" in Lina Khatib and Ellen Lust (eds) *Taking to the Streets: The Transformation of Arab Activism*. Baltimore MD: Johns Hopkins University Press, pp. 22–51.

Collins, Catherine Ann and Miles Sari (2015–16) "Sparking the Arab Spring: A Pentadic Framing Analysis of Bouazizi's Self-Immolation by Media and Citizen Journalists". *Global Media Journal* (Arabian edition) 4 (1–2): 3–18.

Davies, Wyre (2011) "Doubt Over Tunisian 'Martyr' Who Triggered Revolution". BBC News, 17 June. http://www.bbc.co.uk/news/world-middle-east-13800493.

de Soto, Hernando (2011) "The Real Mohamed Bouazizi". *Foreign Policy*, 16 December. http://foreignpolicy.com/2011/12/16/the-real-mohamed-bouazizi/.

Fahim, Kareem (2011a) "Slap to a Man's Pride Set Off Tumult in Tunisia". *The New York Times*, 21 January. http://www.nytimes.com/2011/01/22/world/africa/22sidi.html?_r=2&pagewanted=2&src=twrhp.

Fahim, Kareem (2011b) "In Tunisian Town of Arab Spring Martyr, Disillusionment Seeps In". *New York Times*, 5 August. http://www.nytimes.com/2011/08/06/world/africa/06tunisia.html?rref=collection%2Ftimestopic%2FBouazizi%2C%20Mohamed&action=click&contentCollection=timestopics&region=stream&module=stream_unit&version=latest&contentPlacement=8&pgtype=collection.

Fassin, Didier (2011) "The Trace: Violence, Truth and the Politics of the Body". *Social Research* 78 (2): 281–98.

Ghonim, Wael (2012) *Revolution 2.0*. New York NY: Houghton Mifflin.

Gladwell, Malcolm (2000) *The Tipping Point: How Little Things Can Make a Big Difference*. New York NY: Little, Brown and Co.

Grodzins, Morton (1957) "Metropolitan Segregation". *Scientific American* 197: 33–47.

Guessoumi, Mouldi (2012) "The Grammars of the Tunisian Revolution". Translated by R. A. Judy. *boundary 2* 39 (1): 17–42.

Hadith *Sahih Bukhari* (Volume 4, Book 52). Available at http://www.sahih-bukhari.com/Pages/Bukhari_4_52.php.

Halverson, Jeffry R., Scott W. Ruston and Angela Trethewey (2013) "Mediated Martyrs of the Arab Spring: New Media, Civil Religion, and Narrative in Tunisia and Egypt". *Journal of Communication* 63 (2): 312–32.

Hamid, Salama Abdul (2014) "Why Mohamed Bouazizi Is Blameless". Translated from the Arabic edition of *Al Araby Al Jadeed*. *The New Arab*, 17 December. https://www.alaraby.co.uk/english/comment/2014/12/17/why-mohamed-bouazizi-is-blameless.

Hardt, Michael and Antonio Negri (2004) *Multitude: War and Democracy in the Age of Empire*. New York NY: Penguin.

Hill, Symon (2013) *Digital Revolutions: Activism in the Internet Age*. Oxford: New Internationalist.

Howard, Philip N. and Muzammil M. Hussain (2013) *Democracy's Fourth Wave?: Digital Media and the Arab Spring*. Oxford: Oxford University Press.

Jelloun, Tahar Ben (2013) "By Fire". Translated by Rita S. Nezami. *The New Yorker*, 16 September. http://www.newyorker.com/magazine/2013/09/16/by-fire. Originally published in 2011 as *Par le feu*.

Khosrokhavar, Farhad (2005) *Suicide Bombers: Allah's New Martyrs*. Translated by David Macey. London: Pluto.

Khosrokhavar, Farhad (2012) "The Arab Revolutions and Self-Immolation". *Revue d'Études Tibétaines* 25: 169–79.

Labidi, Lilia (2015) "The Arab Uprisings in Tunisia: Parity, Elections and the Struggle for Women's Rights" in Fahed Al-Sumait, Nele Lenze and Michael C. Hudson (eds) *The Arab Uprisings: Catalysts, Dynamics, and Trajectories*. Lanham MD: Rowman and Littlefield, pp. 175–203.

Le Bon, Gustave (2001 [1896]) *The Crowd: A Study of the Popular Mind*. Kitchener: Batoshe Books. Available at http://socserv2.mcmaster.ca/~econ/ugcm/3ll3/lebon/Crowds.pdf.

Lim, Merlyna (2013) "Framing Bouazizi: 'White Lies', Hybrid Network, and Collective/Connective Action in the 2010–11 Tunisian Uprising". *Journalism* 14 (7): 921–41.

Mahmood, Saba (2005) *Politics of Piety: The Islamic Revival and the Feminist Subject*. Princeton NJ: Princeton University Press.

McPhail, Clark (1991) *The Myth of the Madding Crowd*. Piscataway NJ: Aldine Transactions.

Michelsen, Nicholas (2015) "The Political Subject of Self-Immolation". *Globalizations* 12 (1): 83–100.

Mittermaier, Amira (2015) "Death and Martyrdom in the Arab Uprisings: An Introduction". *Ethnos* 80 (5): 583–604.

Moruzzi, Norma Claire (2013) "Gender and the Revolutions: Critique Interrupted". *Middle East Report* 268 (43). http://www.merip.org/mer/mer268/gender-revolutions.

Rohr, Mathieu von (2011) "The Fruits of Mohamed: The Small Tunisian Town that Sparked the Arab Revolution". Translated by Christopher Sultan. *Der Spiegel* (Spiegel Online), 18 March. http://www.spiegel.de/international/world/the-fruits-of-mohamed-the-small-tunisian-town-that-sparked-the-arab-revolution-a-751278.html.

Rudé, George E. E. (1981 [1964]) *The Crowd in History: A Study of Popular Disturbances in France and England, 1730-1848*. London: Lawrence and Wishart.

Ryan, Yasmine (2011a) "The Tragic Life of a Street Vendor". *Al Jazeera*, 20 January. http://www.aljazeera.com/indepth/features/2011/01/2011116 84242518839.html.

Ryan, Yasmine (2011b) "How Tunisia's Revolution Began". *Al Jazeera*, 26 January. http://www.aljazeera.com/indepth/features/2011/01/2011126121 815985483.html.

Sengupta, Kim (2011) "Tunisia: 'I Have Lost My Son, But I Am Proud of What He Did'". *The Independent*, 21 January. http://www.independent. co.uk/news/world/africa/tunisia-i-have-lost-my-son-but-i-am-proud-of-what-he-did-2190331.html.

Stokel-Walker, Chris (2011) *The Revolution Will Be Tweeted?* Raleigh NC: Lulu.

Thompson, E. P. (1971) "The Moral Economy of the English Crowd in the Eighteenth Century". *Past and Present* 50: 76-136.

Thorne, John (2011) "Bouazizi Has Become a Tunisian Protest 'Symbol'". *The National*, 13 January. http://www.thenational.ae/world/tunisia/ bouazizi-has-become-a-tunisian-protest-symbol.

Totten, Michael J. (2012) "The Woman Who Blew Up the Arab World". *World Affairs*, 17 May. http://www.worldaffairsjournal.org/blog/ michael-j-totten/woman-who-blew-arab-world.

Toumi, Habib (2010) "Man at the Centre of Tunisia Unrest Recuperating, Doctors Say". *Gulf News*, 31 December. http://gulfnews.com/news/ mena/tunisia/man-at-the-centre-of-tunisia-unrest-recuperating-doctors-say-1.738967.

Treisman, Deborah (2013) "This Week in Fiction: Tahar Ben Jelloun" (interview). *The New Yorker*, 6 September. http://www.newyorker. com/books/page-turner/this-week-in-fiction-tahar-ben-jelloun.

Weiher, Gregory R. (1991) *The Fractured Metropolis: Political Fragmentation and Metropolitan Segregation*. Albany NY: State University of New York Press.

Zayzafoon, Lamia Ben Youssef (2005) *The Production of Muslim Women: Negotiating Text, History and Ideology*. Lanham MD: Lexington Books.

Zevnik, Andreja (2014) "Maze of Resistance: Crowd, Space and the Politics of Resisting Subjectivity". *Globalizations* 12 (1): 101-15.

Zimbardo, P. G. (1969) "The Human Choice: Individuation, Reason and Order Versus Deindividuation, Impulse and Chaos" in W. J. Arnold and D. Levine (eds) *Nebraska Symposium on Motivation*. Lincoln NE: University of Nebraska Press.

THREE | Austerity annuls the individual:
Dimitris Christoulas and the Greek
financial crisis

Theodoros A. Spyros and Mike Hajimichael

Breaking news

Dimitris Christoulas, a seventy-seven-year-old pensioner, shot himself in Syntagma Square in front of the Greek parliament in Athens on 4 April 2012. This was explicitly performed and recognised as a protest suicide against the escalation of austerity measures in Greece. This chapter focuses on a relatively narrow set of suicide texts in the Christoulas suicide archive: those that appeared in the form of "breaking news" in print and online news forums immediately after the event.

Our relatively narrow purchase on the Christoulas suicide archive is deliberate. It seems reductive to us to speak of the case-specific suicide archive as a distinctive and especially indicative one in this context. In fact, for Greece, in the midst of a prolonged financial crisis, there was a wider and dense suicide archive already in the making, and the one that relates to Christoulas fitted immediately into this larger gathering of suicide texts. We may think of this larger context-specific suicide archive as a crisis-struck Greek suicide archive. The contours of this larger archive are cogently outlined by anthropologist Elizabeth Davies, who summarises her investigations as follows:

> I explore different accounts of suicide in Greece that construe
> these economic and social conditions as causes. I examine

statistical studies and press reports on the suicide "epidemic" since the crisis, notes written by people who committed or attempted suicide in public during the crisis, and narratives of suicidality from psychiatric patients I knew before the crisis, in dialogue with the psychiatric epidemiologies saturating their clinical environment. These accounts summon three axes of comparison around suicide in Greece. The first is that of historical difference, defined by the economic crisis in relation to the time before it. Another is the axis of locale, contrasting the public sphere of media coverage and consumption with the northeastern region of Greek Thrace [...] Finally, I work along the axis of evidence, moving from the public discourse on suicide [...] to clinical ethnographic research that I conducted almost a decade ago in psychiatric clinics in Thrace. (Davies 2015: 1009)

The spatial, temporal and discursive traversals of this research seem to articulate the nation-state integrity of the suicide archive in Davies's paper. That indeed is a prevalent way of thinking about protest suicides and other suicides that are putatively caused by austerity (see also, for example, Mantzari 2016).

In focusing on "breaking news" suicide texts that are specifically addressed to Christoulas, we avoid presuming that the integrity of nation-state boundaries underpins a more or less coherent suicide archive. Instead, through this narrower focus, we obtain a view of the larger picture beyond, one that overlaps with some of the material examined by Davies but is underpinned by a stronger sense of news media rationales and practices than of national boundaries. In our view, the construction of the crisis-struck Greek suicide archive is thoroughly mediated through news media discourse, and is best understood accordingly. These media rationales and practices are woven together with a range of political, commercial and expert agencies and public perceptions and responses that are pertinent here and are discussed below. We choose to focus on Christoulas's suicide because it has been the most highlighted in news media, both national and international, out of a range of public suicides and suicide attempts (six are discussed in Davies 2015: 1015–23). That circumstance also enables us to consider intra-media dynamics by juxtaposing coverage in international (in this case British) English-language news media and reporting in the Greek language and addressed to local constituencies. This distinction between international ("outside") and local ("inside") is often made in media studies, and is apt to be overdetermined either in the direction of constructing polarities (e.g. international news misrepresents where local news is authentic) or erasing difference (e.g. international and local news is much the same – in fact, the latter often derives from the former). Our account is, we hope, more nuanced – the similarities and distinctions we find below relate to the ways in which news texts address their readerships. The Christoulas suicide archive contains both studiedly intrinsic and carefully extrinsic perspectives.

Unless indicated otherwise, all translations from Greek texts are by the authors.

In the British media

Mike Hajimichael

Politicians often make rhetorical statements which we know they do not really mean or intend to act upon. Citizens, however, especially when faced with harsh everyday realities and circumstances beyond their control, do not expect to be heard and are forced to act. We may imagine this as an axis between tactical political rhetoric and grounded experience and action. On the one hand, we have Eleni Theocharous, a Cypriot Member of the European Parliament, expostulating against a federal solution to the Cyprus problem at an event in a bookstore in Athens. The politician proclaims: "If setting oneself on fire at [Athens'] Syntagma Square is what it takes to push for a union of Cyprus and Greece, then I will strive to be the first to do it" (Christou 2016). On the other, there is Dimitris Christoulas, a Greek citizen completely disillusioned with austerity, holding a gun to his head on a spring morning in 2012 outside the Greek parliament, pulling the trigger and committing suicide. In his pocket there is a suicide note. Clearly, politicians say and citizens do.

Christoulas's suicide could be classified in Emile Durkheim's (1979 [1897]) terms as both "altruistic" and "anomic". However, Durkheim's positivist approach to the subject of suicide is not equal to engaging with the reception of actual acts of suicide, by individuals, and their political interpretations and implications. In many ways, post-Durkheim societies have changed drastically in the intervening century. Even our use of terminology such as "reception" belongs to a meta-narrative that reflects completely different societal conjunctures and assumptions. Reception, however, is an important consideration in contemporary societies of the European Union in the grip of austerity policies, where suicide rates have clearly risen due to those policies. This is all too evident from studies on the Greek debt crisis, which, as researcher George Rachiotis observed in an interview, caused a 35 per cent increase in suicides: "Our main finding was that after 2010, when harsh austerity measures were implemented in Greece, we noted a significant increase in suicide rates for the years 2011 and 2012 in comparison to the period between 2003 and 2010" (Harrison 2015; the research is found in Rachiotis et al. 2015). Similar increases were noted in Cyprus, where, following the bailout/bail-in of 2013, suicides hit their highest mark (Christou 2015). Research showing such increases after the 2007–08 financial crisis and consequent adoption of austerity measures across a wide range of countries has been cited in Chapter 1.

Given this wider context, then, our main concern in this section is the reception of Dimitris Christoulas's suicide through a sample of British and Greek news media. We examine what the action itself suggests and what its aftermath was, how it was interpreted and understood, by using a combination of critical (van Dijk 2001; 2008) and contextual discourse analysis (Song 2010), with grounded textual analysis (Cho 2014). Such a project reveals the manner in which power, control and media representations work from "within" and "outside" Greece. As we show, the Christoulas "story" as a mediated narrative differs at times from what happened and what he seemingly intended, as reflected through the performance of his suicide and the note he left behind. This section explores three media texts from "outside" Greece, in British newspapers, and the next two parts discuss four from "inside".

The news texts from "outside" Greece that we have chosen for analysis appeared in *The Guardian* (Smith 2012), *The Telegraph* (Anast and Squires 2012) and *Daily Mail* (McDermott and Martin 2012). These were all "breaking news" reports that appeared in the British media, in the newspapers and on their widely read websites. These newspapers cater to distinct readerships: *The Telegraph* and *The Guardian* are broadsheets, respectively received as leaning towards a conservative and liberal-left line; *Daily Mail* is a tabloid, largely regarded as emphatically

conservative. According to figures from the Press Gazette (http://
www.pressgazette.co.uk), their average print circulations in 2015
were: *The Telegraph* 494,675; *The Guardian* 185,429; and *Daily
Mail* 1,688,727. However, that is only moderately indicative of
their reach: their online versions, Telegraph.co.uk, Guardian.
co.uk and Mail Online, reportedly had, in that order, daily unique
users of 1.5 to 2.5 million in 2010 (see Kiss 2010). Our analysis
of the breaking-news reports that appeared in these newspapers
focuses on qualitative observations which take into account a
number of key themes: How was he depicted?; How accurate
was the reporting?; What sort of language was used? The sources
included in the coverage enable observations on "who speaks"
and who is given a "voice", so that is another key question here:
Who is included and, in some instances, what was their relationship to Christoulas? Further, the extent to which these media
reports were cognisant of his suicide note will be considered:
Was the note referred to or not?; And, where referred to, was it
quoted and to what effect?

Appearing as an explicitly political act, Christoulas's suicide
represented and was understood as a gesture against power, corruption and inequality. There are many examples of political
suicides in history, and while their initial import may have been
variously distorted or re-signified in subsequent years, the his-
toric character of such acts as symbolic moments in struggles
should not be forgotten. Thus, the political significance of
Mohamed Bouazizi's self-immolation in Tunisia in 2010, discussed at length in Chapter 2, was first and foremost an immediate one; and although that significance seemed diminished later,
its initial impact remains undeniable. Soon after its enactment,
Didier Fassin, in a scholarly analysis of such suicides, understood

Bouazizi's self-immolation as squarely grounded in the corrupt state and its agents:

> The Tunisian case is exemplary in that the violence of the state and the resistance of the individual are embodied in one person. Mohamed Bouazizi is a victim of both the structural and the political violence of the state: his dire living conditions are intricately linked to the corruption of the regime and the massive theft of public goods organized by the state, and his harassment is the expression of the unlimited possibility of police officers and public officials to abuse with impunity. Facing this intolerable excess of violence, the powerless young man still had the power to expose his life and exhibit his suicide as a desperate act to save his dignity. (Fassin 2011: 282)

So Bouazizi came to be viewed as the opening symbol of resistance in what is often referred to as the "Arab Spring". In a parallel way for the Greek crisis, Christoulas's suicide immediately spurred a moment of "we-have-had-enoughness"; it was an individual act that mobilised thousands of people onto the streets. However, a "Greek Spring" did not materialise. Christoulas was forgotten quickly. Even on 5 April, a *Guardian* opinion piece observed: "Dimitris Christoulas has already vanished under a swarm of platitudes and slogans, another martyr in a country that already has too many" (Margaronis 2012). And if something in that direction eventually seemed to be in the offing, through the election of the first Syriza government in 2015, then it was decidedly more temperate and tame and fizzled out soon enough – indeed, it was reversed after a year, with hopes of promised resistance to austerity measures dashed.

Nevertheless, at least for a brief interlude, parallels were drawn between Bouazizi and Christoulas. The opinion piece just quoted also wondered: "Will this be the start of a bigger uprising, the 'Greek spring' some observers have been waiting for? Some are saying Europe now has its Mohammed Bouazizi, the man whose suicide sparked the uprising in Tunisia" (ibid.). A *Daily Mail* report observed: "In Greece they speak of him becoming the country's very own Mohammed Bouazizi, the Tunisian fruit and veg seller who started the Arab Spring by setting fire to himself" (McDermott and Martin 2012). And an account in *Time* magazine caught the mood of that immediately made connection thus:

> [Mourners] encircled the tree where Christoulas had taken his life. They left bouquets of roses, tulips and gardenias. They burned incense and candles.
>
> "When I heard the news this morning, I immediately thought of Tunisia," said one mourner, a man in his 50s who gave his name as Michalis and said he worked in nutrition science. He was referring to Mohamed Bouazizi, the 26-year-old street vendor who set himself on fire in the Tunisian town of Sidi Bouzid last year, sparking the Arab Spring revolutions. Michalis wondered what the death of a retired Greek pharmacist would mean in a country paralyzed by fear, debt and uncertainty. He watched as mourners pinned sympathy notes to the trunk of the tree. Some notes were tinged with sadness, saying that he didn't die in vain. Some were angry, beseeching Greeks to take up arms against the government. A few people in the crowd broke into spontaneous chants. "This was not a suicide!" they yelled. "It was a state-perpetrated murder!" Later, the protest turned violent. Young men in hoods threw Molotov cocktails at riot police, who responded with tear gas. (Kakissis 2012)

That was a much-reported rallying call by protesters after Christoulas's death: "This was not a suicide, it was murder." It appears in live video coverage of his funeral by Zafeiris Haitidis

(2012), which was followed by a march of thousands to Syntagma Square, the place where he died. To understand the indignation and defiance of this statement, the note Dimitris Christoulas left behind, following his suicide, needs to be considered – we have a few comments on this later in this section.

In terms of the reception of the suicide generally, a key theme found in our sample of British print coverage is how Christoulas was depicted: how the question "Who was this person?" was answered. In our sample, this is how he was, so to speak, announced to readers.

The Telegraph (Anast and Squires 2012) article, under the heading "Austerity suicide: Greek pensioner shoots himself in Athens" began with the sentence: "A cash strapped Greek pensioner who said he feared having to 'scrounge for food' shot himself dead in Athens' main square". *The Guardian* (Smith 2012) differed slightly with the headline "Greek suicide seen as an act of fortitude as much as one of despair", coupled with the subheading: "Pensioner Dimitris Christoulas wanted to 'send a political message' about the inequities of Greece's crushing debt crisis". Finally, the *Daily Mail* led with the headline "Riots erupt in Greece after 'martyr' shoots himself over debt crisis", and Christoulas is referred to in a subheading as "a retired pharmacist" (McDermott and Martin 2012). Christoulas was announced, then, as a retired pharmacist, a pensioner – in Britain, as indeed in many other contexts, that circumstance evokes an image of passive vulnerability and dependence on the state, a remainder of the past (and a virtuous past, to do with healing). Arguably, this characterisation worked against recognising Christoulas as a political *agent*, as someone who could take an active and uncompromisingly defiant political stand in the present.

By way of bolstering this characterisation, Christoulas's suicide note was selectively cited. At this point it is useful to have the text of the suicide note in view (the translation below by Kostas Kallergis appears with a facsimile of the note in Kallergis 2012):

> The collaborationist Tsolakoglou government has annihilated my ability for my survival, which was based on a very dignified pension that *I alone* (without any state sponsoring) paid for 35 years.
>
> Since my advanced age does not allow me a way of a dynamic reaction (although if a fellow Greek was to grab a Kalashnikov, I would be the second after him), I see no other solution than this dignified end to my life, so I don't find myself fishing through garbage cans for my sustenance.
>
> I believe that young people with no future, will one day take up arms and hang the traitors of this country at Syntagma Square, just like the Italians did to Mussolini in 1945 (Piazza Loreto in Milan).

The opening sentence equates the then government of Greece, led by Lucas Papadimas, with "Tsolakoglou" – Georgios Tsolakoglou was the military officer who became the first prime minister of the Greek collaborationist government during the Axis occupation in 1941–42. This association with Second World War collaborationists is extended one step further by ending the note with a desire to see the current "traitors" in power hanged just as Mussolini was. However this note is read, on the face of it, the content presented an active call to arms and a defiant claim of right rather more emphatically than striking a note of passive victimisation and despair.

Returning to how this note was cited in the newspaper reports in question in order to characterise – or present an image of – Christoulas, we find the following:

The Guardian
The 77-year-old had written in his one-page, three-paragraph
suicide note that it would be better to have a "decent end" than
be forced to scavenge in the "rubbish to feed myself". (Smith
2012)

The Telegraph
A suicide note found in his coat pocket blamed politicians and
the country's acute financial crisis for driving him to take his life,
police said.
   The government had "annihilated any hope for my survival and
I could not get any justice. I cannot find any other form of struggle
except a dignified end before I have to start scrounging for food
from rubbish bins," the note said. (Anast and Squires 2012)

Daily Mail
The divorced father-of-one, who had lived alone in a flat,
declared "I cannot find any other form of struggle except a dignified end" which was preferable to scavenging through "rubbish
to feed myself".
   The suicide note also blamed "the occupation government of
Tsolakoglou" for forcing him to end his life. Georgios Tsolakoglou was Greece's first collaborationist prime minister during
Germany's occupation of his country in the Second World War.
The reference appears to be a veiled criticism of Germany's role
in enforcing Greece's current austerity measures. (McDermott
and Martin 2012)

Significantly, all three reports prime the "scavenging in garbage"
theme in referring to the suicide note, the phrase most suggestive of being victimised, most likely to garner sympathy for the
vulnerable. The terms of the accuser are diluted to "blaming
the government" (*Telegraph*) and "wanting to send a political
message" (*Guardian*) about austerity – most could sympathise

easily with that understatement, many would want to do that much. So the second paragraph of the suicide note was highlighted. The opening statement about a collaborationist government was mentioned only in the *Daily Mail* report. However, this was followed by an explanation, that it was an apparently "veiled criticism of Germany's role in enforcing Greece's current austerity measures". This is a weak reinterpretation, as the term "veiled criticism" is a very mild way of describing an act of treason, which is what Christoulas's note actually said. Most importantly, none mentioned the call to arms: that he would follow his fellow Greeks in taking up arms against the government, that young people with no future will take up arms and hang the traitors in the government. These are more confrontational statements; they suggest a strength of defiance and resistance and a conviction that cannot be reconciled easily with the image of a passive, elderly, deprived victim. It was redolent of powerful rage and uncompromising opposition to the established order, which may make news consumers uneasy. So it was entirely elided. Between how the suicide note itself may be read and how what was reported of it may be read, there is an immense gulf that swallowed up Christoulas's last testament – at least as far as the British, the international, news consumers were concerned.

Thus, Christoulas's voice – his text – was massaged out of recognition in the news reports. Let us turn then to the issue of who was given a voice in these breaking-news reports, who were invited to mediate, and, in some cases, what was their relationship to Christoulas. Table 3.1 is a content analysis table showing who is included in the articles.

Only the *Daily Mail* report quoted a family member, Christoulas's daughter Emy Christoulas. However, all the newspaper

TABLE 3.1 Who speaks/sources

Newspaper	Family	Neighbour/friend/ acquaintance	Official/ government/ politician	Witnesses	Protesters	"Note on tree" theme
Guardian	0	2 (same source as *Daily Mail*: Mr Skarmoutsos)	0	0	0	0
Telegraph	0	1 (Mr Lourantos, president of Pharmaceutical Society of Athens)	0	2 (secondary sources not specified)	0	3 notes referred to
Daily Mail	2 (daughter)	4	1 (prime minister)	1 (anonymous witness)	0	2 notes referred to

reports referred to friends and neighbours, especially a friend called Skourmatsos (quoted in both the *Daily Mail* and *The Guardian*), and a professional acquaintance, Lourantos, the president of the Pharmaceutical Society of Athens (*The Telegraph*). Where the voice of the reporter emphasised the austerity-struck pensioner's plight in characterising Christoulas, it was left to brief quotations from his daughter and friends to underline his political agency – to give a sense of his political convictions and to suggest that his suicide was an act of political assertion. His daughter was quoted thus:

> "My father's note leaves no room for misinterpretation. His whole life was spent as a leftist fighter, a selfless visionary," said his only daughter, Emy Christoulas, 43. "This final act was a conscious political act, entirely consistent with what he believed and did in his life."
>
> She added that, for some, "committing suicide is not an escape but a cry of awakening". (McDermott and Martin 2012)

And his friend's observation was reported as follows in *The Guardian*:

> "With his suicide he wanted to send a political message," Antonis Skarmoutsos, a friend and neighbour was quoted as saying in the mass-selling Ta Nea newspaper. "He was deeply politicised but also enraged."
>
> Until 1994 Christoulas was a local chemist in the central Athens neighbourhood of Ambelokipoi. A committed leftist, he was active in citizens' groups such as "I won't pay", which started as a one-off protest against toll fees but quickly turned into an anti-austerity movement. (Smith 2012)

The observations of family and friends in news reports are generally expected to accentuate the personal dimension of a person in the limelight, and may be read as imbued with more sentiment than balanced observation (balance is the reporter's prerogative). Nevertheless, these appeared as firm affirmations of Christoulas's political convictions – and Emy Christoulas's view of the suicide note as a "cry of awakening" is the nearest these reports came to acknowledging, at third person, the explicit call to arms in the note.

Actual witnesses to Christoulas's suicide are a grey area in all the articles, and the various statements attributed to them are of doubtful interest. The *Daily Mail* reported: "Witnesses to the death said the pharmacist declared 'I don't want to leave my debts to my children' before producing a gun and shooting himself in the head at 9am" (McDermott and Martin 2012). *The Telegraph* report had two similar references: "Witnesses said he put a gun to his head and pulled the trigger after yelling 'I have debts, I can't stand this anymore'." And, also: "A passer-by told Greek television the man said 'I don't want to leave my debts to my children'" (Anast and Squires 2012). The sources for these witness statements are difficult to locate and confirm. More interesting are references to the multitude of notes placed on the tree beside which Dimitris Christoulas took his life. The *Daily Mail* quoted notes saying "His blood is on your hands, traitors" and "A government of murderers" (McDermott and Martin 2012). The report also included a photographic image directly above these quotations, entitled: "Tragic: Mourners gather at the spot where Dimitris Christoulas committed suicide in front of the Greek Parliament". *The Telegraph* report noted:

> Within hours of his death, an impromptu shrine with candles, flowers and handwritten notes sprung up in the tree-lined square in the heart of the city. One note nailed to a tree said "Enough is

enough", another asked "Who will be the next victim?" while a
third said "It was a murder, not a suicide." (Anast and Squires
2012)

These appeared as textual evidence of a public mood, a response,
which was akin to that found in Christoulas's note. It seemed that
Christoulas's rage was shared and there were others like him – a
gathering force.

But, with hindsight, we know that this force didn't quite gather,
at least not as any effective movement. In a way, these reports
both registered the appearance of this force and laid its impetus
to rest.

Two of the articles analysed here extended the scope of their
observations beyond Greece. The *Daily Mail* article ended with
a brief general section on indicators of deepening economic woes
and hardships in Spain, Portugal and Italy. The report from *The
Telegraph* first offered an overview of the situation in Greece at
the time:

> Greece's fifth consecutive year of recession has been worsened
> by drastic cuts to public services, pensions and salaries and
> higher taxes, which were introduced in response to the demands
> of the International Monetary Fund and the European Union in
> exchange for financial bail-outs.
>
> One in five Greeks are unemployed, depression is on the rise
> and there is a growing feeling of despair across the country.
>
> The government said last year that suicides had increased
> 40 per cent over the previous two years. (Anast and Squires
> 2012)

The report then made the interesting move of citing particular
cases of suicide and attempted suicide in Italy that could also
be linked to austerity: a seventy-eight-year-old woman in Gela,

Sicily, who jumped from the balcony of her third-floor apartment because her monthly pension had been cut; a fifty-eight-year-old businessman in Bologna who set himself on fire outside a tax office; a twenty-seven-year-old Moroccan immigrant in Verona who also set himself on fire after not being paid for four months (see Chapter 5).

The thrust of the political act and immediate response that centred on Dimitris Christoulas at Syntagma Square, Athens, on 4 April 2012 was set to be dispersed beyond Greece and into a larger condition of austerity in other countries too and other suicides – all victims of that condition.

In the Greek media

Theodoros A. Spyros

In Greece, the suicide of Dimitris Christoulas emerged as emblematic amidst a public debate on the relation between "augmented suicide rates" and "austerity policies" following the signing of the First Economic Adjustment Programme for Greece (the First Memorandum) in May 2010, and then the second in March 2012. As is well known, these consisted of bailouts for Greece (suffering from a severe debt crisis) from the European Commission, European Central Bank and International Monetary Fund (the so-called Troika). The bailouts were given on the condition that the Greek government would reduce its deficit, which entailed the adoption of strict austerity measures – a reduction in public spending. Those arguing against these measures (anti-Memorandum) cited the growing suicide rate as evidence of the disaffection and despair the measures were generating; those defending the measures (pro-Memorandum) felt that the suicide rates had been inflated and misunderstood. Amidst these debates, the ways in which "statistical (un)truth" was claimed on both sides and "concrete statistics" were tacitly evoked and incorporated in various texts on Christoulas's suicide are matters of considerable interest (see Davies 2015: 1010–15; Mantzari 2016: 10–13). Such statistics played a significant role in the various texts that composed and recomposed the Christoulas suicide archive.

With that background in mind, this section analyses four Greek texts published in the printed press or posted on the internet as breaking news on Christoulas's suicide. The analysis addresses three issues: first, how perceptions of the suicide were sieved through a bipolar discourse on "political protest" and "personal despair" via different *voices* emerging from the texts; second, how the views of "experts" were integrated into the different narratives; and third, how the presence or absence of what we think of as the "political world" is registered in these texts. Two of the texts under analysis were published in two "institutional" newspapers that are among those with the highest circulations in Greece: by Eleftheria Kollia (2012) in *To Vima* (*The Step*), and by Vivian Benecou (2012) in *To Etnos* (*The Nation*). The other two articles were posted on two widely read information websites: *TVXS* and *ISKRA* – no authorship was attributed to these, so they are referred to below by the website names as *TVXS* (2012) and *ISKRA* (2012).

Some background information on these news outlets may serve to contextualise the chosen articles. The newspapers *To Vima* and *To Etnos* are constantly on the front line of the "pro-Memorandum camp", having supported the implementation of austerity policies according to the Troika's neoliberal directions from the beginning, advocating throughout "the necessity of reforms" in the Greek economy and society. Historically, both newspapers have been an integral part of the "liberal-democratic" and "modernistic" bourgeois camp, which, through various ideological and institutional transformations and phases, constitutes a stable reference point for the Greek imaginary political geography (for a historical perspective, see Meynaud et al. 1965, and on political geography Lyritzis 2011). Moreover, both newspapers are parts of larger business groups whose products include a range of printed and electronic media, alongside other entrepreneurial activities, such as public constructions or cultural projects. All the media resources owned by these business groups have supported the Memorandum policies in Greece, adopting the discourse of "bourgeois modernisation" and "reformation" (on Greek "modernisation projects", see Featherstone 2013). The Mega Channel, one of the largest TV channels in Greece, has been and continues to be the communication flagship of the pro-Memorandum camp – two of its three main shareholders, the Lambrakis Press Group (under the direction of Stavros Psycharis) and Pegasus Publishing S.A. (under the direction of the Bobolas family), are also the owners of the two newspapers in question.

The two information websites mentioned above, *TVXS* and *ISKRA*, represent the anti-Memorandum camp in different ways. *TVXS* is a site founded and administered by the journalist Stelios Kouloglou, ostensibly representing "the left wing". During the 1980s, Kouloglou was a journalist for publications of the "reformist left" – the magazine *Anti* and the newspaper *Avgi* – and then became a correspondent for a private "bourgeois" media corporation in Moscow during the downfall of the Soviet Union (1989–92) and in Yugoslavia during the civil war (1992–95). Between 1996 and 2008 he worked in ERT (the National Radio-

Television Foundation of Greece). In 2015 he replaced Giorgos Katrouggalos, who became deputy minister, as member of the European Parliament for Syriza. At the time of Christoulas's suicide he was an active media spokesperson for anti-Memorandum policies promoted by Syriza. The other website, *ISKRA*, was the semi-official organ of the "Left Trend" at the time, the largest "radical" (according to its members) or "leftist" (according to its enemies) group of intra-party opposition within Syriza. It is worth noting that after the vote on the Third Memorandum (August 2015) by Syriza's government, almost the entire membership of this group left Syriza and established a new left-wing anti-Memorandum party, Laiki Enotita (Popular Unity), supporting a rupture with and, if necessary, exit from the Eurozone. At the time of Christoulas's suicide, this intra-party group was in silent conflict with Syriza's leading group, mainly because of the latter's "obsession with the currency", or its promotion of a policy based on simultaneously abolishing Memorandum-led austerity policies and making Greece's continuing membership in the Eurozone a non-negotiable commitment.

The titles of the chosen texts are indicative of the ways in which Christoulas's suicide was perceived and interpreted by the media and thereby transmitted into public deliberation. Although these titles didn't quite correspond to the content of the articles, each offered a point of departure for the following narrative, thereby setting interpretive horizons for the given "facts".

The *To Vima* article (Kollia 2012) announced Christoulas's suicide under the heading "Political message, personal deadlock", followed by the subtitle "How the experts explain the escalation of suicides because of the crisis". It was therefore immediately evident that this account would be woven around two axes: the conjunction of the personal and the political, and the concern with growing suicide rates due to the crisis. Insofar as Christoulas's suicide was presented at the conjunction of the political and the personal, he represented an individual (like many others) who was deeply affected by his powerlessness in the face of the financial crisis and felt abandoned by Greece's political representatives, and therefore sought and found an "exit" through his dramatic self-erasure. To reinforce the political dimension of the suicide, Kollia (ibid.) cited the statement by Christoulas's daughter Emy (also quoted in the *Daily Mail* article discussed in the previous section), where she maintained that her father's "final act was a conscious political act, entirely consistent with what he believed and did in his life" as "a leftist fighter, a selfless visionary".

Although the author thus recognises the political dimension of Christoulas's suicide, she separates it emphatically from the personal, in much the same way as in the British media reports discussed. Moreover, Kollia doesn't link Christoulas's sharply defined political position to the manner in which the Greek government's spokesman, Pantelis Kapsis, also quoted, commented on it in a press conference, saying that, "like any suicide", that of Christoulas is "a complex and unique action [...] the political message [of which] obscures the limits of his personal deadlock". Kapsis's statement effectively served to deflect attention away from, at least to some extent, the political stance that was found in his suicide note, in the mode and location of the act. The emphasis of the statement, and the article, was on the "shock" that Christoulas's suicide had been to "the collective unconscious" (probably of Greek society). Although Kollia made reference to "the clear political symbolism" of his suicide, the "tragic personal circumstances" were foregrounded. Insofar as the article placed the individual act within the context of increased suicide rates in Memorandum-driven Greece, Christoulas's suicide was classified as potentially belonging to the category of "suicides because of the crisis" and interpreted through "sociological" or "suicidological" explanations (see Chapter 1 on these), as arising from a decomposition of social order. Accordingly, the author gave the floor to a number of "experts" and their interpretations in the article – I comment on those later in this chapter.

The *To Ethnos* report (Benecou 2012) bore the title: "Dimitris Christoulas, the person who shocked Greece". Centring "Dimitris Christoulas" by name thus, the author began by outlining his personal profile: his age ("the 77-year-old"), the qualities of his personality ("uncompromising and stubborn"), and his political attitude ("deeply politicised"). Benecou went on to present Christoulas's personality as the principal motivating factor for the decision to commit suicide and the public enactment of his action – as a particular type of personality which responded to the context of austerity in an almost predetermined way. As Benecou put it: "He couldn't endure the humiliation of his life and those of others because of poverty, and by his action he wanted to send a message to the government and to society." This was because, the author explained, Christoulas was "one of those who don't leave decisions to destiny ... Throughout his life he wanted to hold his destiny in his own hands. Accordingly, he had planned his end, in the same place where he had passed his afternoons wounded by hard reality, watching citizens hastening to keep up with the time that was slipping away." So, it seemed, Christoulas's suicide was a kind of chronicle of a death foretold, inevitably driven by personality and circumstance. Also of interest in Benecou's report is how the political character of Christoulas's suicide was recounted. Rather than being obviously owned by Christoulas, the political dimension was distributed in the report across different voices. Christoulas's daughter, first of all, was quoted (in the same statement referred to above) observing that: "My father's note leaves no room for misinterpretation [...] the suicide of my father is a political act. He wanted to send a message to the government and to the society which suffers and he has done that" (ibid.). The author then focuses on Christoulas's reported allusion to some lines from a poem, "As Much As You Can", by C. F. Cavafy:

> Even if you can't shape your life the way you want,
> at least try as much as you can
> not to cheapen it totally. (Cavafy 1972: 24)

According to Benecou (2012), "as Cavafy had seen that near the obligatory end of life there's a risk of being degraded by humiliation, misery and persiflage, so did the pensioner. He showed the morality of uncompromising dignity, accompanied by strong will and calmness of soul even in front of a tragic end." Besides his daughter, Christoulas's friends and neighbours also gestured towards the political thrust of his suicide, describing him as "an active citizen [...] someone who always participated in the social movements", whose past "had empowered him and made him deeply aware of solidarity and humanism", as a "democrat, fighter", as someone who was "deeply concerned about what happened to the people". Quoting the suicide note, a neighbour said that "he had spoken these words of Cavafy in our last meeting [...] Finally he found the courage to act upon them." So, the political dimension of Christoulas's suicide was positioned apropos of the crisis as both a personal and, inextricably, a social condition of existence. It was presented here as more the result of an explosion of the social consciousness of an active citizen than as caused by a personal financial deadlock of a passive victim. To that end, Benecou referred to the "unanimous" view of "his friends" that "it was not merely financial reasons that drove him to his action, he wouldn't permit himself to die for such a reason". Further, with the suicide note in view, he concluded that "the humiliation of his own life and those of his fellow people, in whom he was always interested, due to financial poverty was a fact that he could not endure".

The inextricable interweaving of political commitment with human aspects and personal biography in reading Christoulas's suicide opens up a more general perspective: one in which the social field appears as an intermediate space linking *faceless politics* – almost metaphysically perceived – to the concrete life of *identifiable and differentiable individuals*. In this perspective, various social fields emerge as different versions of a civil society mediating and matching personal experience and collective action. A reference to Christoulas's service as administrator for a women's volleyball team seemed to acquire significance as another aspect of his life between faceless crowd and socially conscientious individual. Team spirit was inserted into the suicide archive of Christoulas. The team appears to symbolise a civil society of active individuals, more in the sense of a network of intimate inter-subjective worlds of life experience and human solidarity than of a collective body for political struggle. In a similar vein, the article made reference to the homage paid to Christoulas by Panathinaikos fans during the match of their basketball team against Maccabi Tel Aviv for the EuroLeague. They posted a banner for him with the words: "I will go to build a shelter in the sky, to come down when I want to laugh. Dimitris, we will meet again" (Benecou 2012). This reference to the fans' sentiments and desires, and to their farewell addressed affectionately to a specific person, confers on them the character of an inter-subjective multi-faced entity, composed of everyday human beings like Christoulas, rather than of a faceless crowd.

Turning now to the information websites with an anti-Memorandum inclination, let me begin with the *TVXS* (2012) report entitled "In Syntagma Square again the Indignants after the suicide", with the subtitle "suicide shock". The title emphasised the location of the suicide (Syntagma Square), and the Indignants (*Aganaktismeni*) Movement, which emerged in Greece, and especially in Athens, during the first years (2010–11) of implementation of the First Memorandum's agreements (on this movement, see Tambakaki 2011, and, with hindsight, Simiti 2014). The location presents an obvious connection between Christoulas's suicide and the Indignants Movement, both of which were, so to speak, performed at Syntagma Square, in front of the Greek parliament. Moreover, a symbolic connection was thereby established between this personal act and the collective action of citizens, as the choice of this performance space was made for the same reason: as a message to the Greek people to resist and seek change. Further, the subtitle links "the shock" of Christoulas's suicide to the revival of collective resistance against austerity policies. In what followed, "dignity" emerged as the element that connects personal rage to the revival of collective protest. The article quoted Lourantos, president of the Pharmaceutical Society of Athens and an acquaintance of Christoulas (and also quoted in the *Telegraph* article in the previous section): "I remember him as a most dignified man […] I consider that because of his sense of dignity he couldn't permit himself to live under conditions that undermine that sense and was driven to this action, which saddens and also shocks us" (*TVXS* 2012).

The *TVXS* author understood the hoped-for passage from the revolting subject to the protesting crowd by focusing on two factors. The first was precisely that sense of shock that was felt by the public, expressed in "public opinion", at "the suicide of the 77-year-old man" – and, moreover, at the mode of suicide "by a bullet to his head", like a self-assassination or execution. The trigger that killed Christoulas could be thought of as the trigger that drove the crowd to Syntagma Square to demonstrate or, as the article noted, to "put a flower and to leave notes with messages like 'It's enough' and 'Assassin Memorandum'". The second factor was, predictably, Christoulas's suicide note. The *TVXS* author quoted two parts of it: "The collaborationist Tsolakoglou government has annihilated my ability for my survival" and "I see no other solution than this dignified end to my life, so I don't find myself fishing through garbage cans for my sustenance" – and added to the latter, perhaps for enhanced sentimental effect, "and becoming a burden for my children" (ibid.). Interestingly, the thrust of both factors was accentuated by a photograph of a poster hanging on the tree under which Christoulas had shot himself. This poster referred to the suicide note's phrase "Tsolakoglou government" and foresaw that "any who were guilty [of Christoulas's suicide] would be hanged one day on this tree by the people", and called on people to participate in the protests organised in Syntagma Square. There was an indirect reference here to the six political and military leaders who were condemned and executed in 1922 as "responsible" for the "Asia Minor catastrophe" by the military "revolutionary" regime that

had emerged after the Greek defeat. This was possibly one of the
more direct gestures towards the call to arms in Christoulas's suicide note.

The other website article (*ISKRA* 2012) announced Christoulas's suicide thus: "Society is shocked by the suicide of a 77-year-
old man." As in the title of the *Ethnos* report, here the shock was
expressed feelingly, likened to "a punch in the stomach" of Greek
society. Unlike the *Ethnos* report, though, Dimitris Christoulas
wasn't named and appeared as an unnamed "77-year-old man".
Christoulas appeared here not as an individual person, but as
a category of individuals who share a common vulnerability to
the crisis because of their advanced age. And so the article pro-
ceeded to relate Christoulas's suicide to "the thousands of suicides and attempted suicides that are recorded [...] in Greece
during the last two years of implementing the Memorandum". All
these suicides were perceived by the author as "political murders
[...] Even if most of those actions occur privately and cannot be
directly conferred the political symbolism of yesterday's tragedy,
all those who planned, supported and executed these policies
are morally responsible." The author of the *ISKRA* article then
emphasised the political dimensions of this act of suicide as a call
to arousing Greek society, a gesture designed to shake citizens
into action against perpetrators – thus echoing Christoulas's suicide note instead of simply repeating it, in a way speaking as and
on behalf of Christoulas:

> [The suicide sends a] clear political message to all those who by
> their Memorandum policies drive the Greek people to humilia-
> tion and despair. The choice of the place of his death, but also
> his shattering [suicide] note doesn't leave any doubt that this is a
> political murder with morally responsible abettors.

And here a statement from the much-quoted president of the Pharmaceutical Society of Athens, Lourantos, is given as confirmation of this political position rather than as a kind of character reference for Christoulas – Lourantos is quoted as saying: "There are moral abettors [...] It doesn't matter who the person that committed suicide was but why he did it. No one has the right to take another life, even if without actually shooting the gun. In fact, there are morally responsible culprits." That Christoulas's message, assumed and reiterated by the *ISKRA* author, was also already being taken to heart by a protesting crowd was naturally a part of the message of the article itself. The author thus wrote of "thousands of people" having come "to the place where the man died to leave a flower, a note, to light a candle in his memory", and of their having organised "spontaneous demonstrations" through the internet "in the memory of the 77-year-old man" in Athens and Salonika. Citizens' collectives were also mentioned, such as the "Indignant Motorcyclists of Greece", who organised a motor march to denounce "all those who have trampled on the constitution of Greece and butchered the structures of the democracy that they allegedly serve [and] have armed the hand of our suicide-brother today". The *ISKRA* article concluded with a timeline of demonstrations and conflicts between protesting crowds and the police.

So far, then, the four texts I have been examining present different voices speaking on Christoulas's suicide. First of all, there are the texts' authors: named journalists in some cases (*To Vima* and *To Ethnos*), anonymous or "collective" discourse producers in others (*TVXS* and *ISKRA*). The authors incline or exhort their readers one way or another on their own account at times, but more often they do so by weaving their own voices with those of others – by a selective and eclectic use of other voices, mainly of "witnesses" to the act, speaking for the crowd, for Christoulas's personality, and so on. In a way, they produce a ventriloquist discourse on the subject, dispersing their own voices through those of others. Notably, two of the texts being discussed here (*TVXS* and *ISKRA*) made explicit reference to the political thrust of the protests following Christoulas's suicide. Another (*To Ethnos*) spoke of the shocked people who "leave flowers, light a candle or leave a note" where Christoulas died; although the crowd was not absent from the narrative there, emphasis was given to its ceremonial and human presence rather than to its politically resistant tendency. In the *To Vima* article, the protesting crowd was almost totally absent. Further, only the *TVXS* and *ISKRA* articles made direct references to and gave the floor to the political world, to representatives of political parties and organisations.

At this juncture another voice enters the picture: the disembodied voice of "facts" that have political import, especially in relation to the increasing suicide rates in Greece since the Memorandum agreements started being implemented. This was already being hotly debated by the pro- and anti-Memorandum camps. In fact, the apparently disembodied voice of "facts" was not disembodied at all; this voice could only be heard through or silenced by political party representatives. The fundamental agents in the production of the Christoulas suicide archive were the political party representatives, both through their presence and, often, through their absence. They worked through accounts such as those that are being examined here. It is not coincidental that the two texts giving the floor to oppositional political party spokespersons and their ideological readings were those belonging to the anti-Memorandum camp, for whom the increasing suicide rates had political import. In contrast, the pro-Memorandum camp, represented by the other two articles, refused or at least diluted the implications of suicide rates by making out that each suicide is "a personal drama". Instead of party representatives contemplating suicide rates, one of these articles (*To Vima*) offered a privileged role to "experts" to interpret Christoulas's suicide.

The triangulation between "facts", party representatives and experts is a complex business, and is also traceable through the chosen articles.

EXPERTS AND PARTY REPRESENTATIVES

All the reports mentioned above referred explicitly or implicitly to the increase in suicide rates in Greece during the Memorandum period. Two of them (*To Vima* and *ISKRA*) referred to statistical figures by giving the floor to "experts" (on expertise as a "performance of authority", see Evetts et al. 2006). At the same time, it is worth noting that these two texts represent different political camps and adopt different points of view regarding the political interpretation of Christoulas's suicide.

The *To Vima* article (Kollia 2012) laid the greater emphasis on expert views, calling upon three authorities. The first was Gerasimos Moschonas, an associate professor of comparative politics at the Panteion University of Social and Political Sciences of Athens. He offered a Durkheimian approach and considered this suicide, like any suicide under crisis, as "anomic", relating it to "the economic disaster and to the ruptures provoked by unemployment and bankruptcy". But he also spoke of its complementary "altruistic" dimension since Christoulas had claimed the "advocacy of society". The second "expert" was Antonis Politis, Assistant Professor of Psychiatry at the University of Athens. Although he started by saying that "we can only evaluate what happens today after five years", he didn't hesitate to note that "there is an intensification of the phenomenon of suicides and it is expected to become bigger, unprecedented by Greek standards". Although he didn't propose a direct "explanation" for the current rise in suicide rates, his "expectation" of a further intensification of the phenomenon suggested a connection between suicide rates and austerity (for a statistical and "medical" approach to the relation between austerity policies and suicide rates in Greece, see Branas et al. 2015). The third "expert" was "the police". The author cited statistical data given by police departments, according to which suicide rates were strongly influenced by crisis-ridden Greece (they increased by 45 per cent between 2010 and 2011, giving a total number of 1,730 suicides between 2009 and 2011). The police were the only "expert" source referred to in *ISKRA* (2012) as proof that suicide rates were increasing. The *ISKRA* author observed that "according to police data, since the beginning of 2009 till December of 2011, the suicides and attempted suicides numbered at least 1,750". The report also referred to other "frightening data", according to which, "since 2010 the number of suicides in Greece has increased at a rate of 45%, mainly because of the financial crisis [...] it's estimated that during 2011 alone 450 have committed suicide. The larger number is due to problems arising from the crisis." These references suggest a positivistic approach to the issue, combining the logics of suicidology and of structural-functionalistic sociology (discussed in Chapter 1). In this context, the observations of the psychiatrist, Politis, are of particular interest for two reasons. The first concerns the definition of statistical categories that are at "high risk" of committing suicide. According to him, "men of 50 years and above, we always consider to be a high-risk group"

(Kollia 2012). The second reason is related to the "prevention" of suicides, through the detection of individuals in high-risk categories (lonely men, people who have lost their jobs, people suffering from disabilities), and the implementation of practices that "can resolve their problems", such as social networking and raising social awareness (for the psychiatric-epidemiological approach to suicides in Greece, see Davies 2015: especially pp. 1023–8; Mantzari 2016: 18–23).

As I have already mentioned above, two of the reports (*TVXS* and *ISKRA*) integrated into their narratives the voices of political spokespersons and alignments, commenting on Christoulas's suicide. This integration was made in two different ways. One strategy was to directly quote statements by politicians and political parties. The other was to criticise selected extrapolations from existing statements by such spokespersons and alignments. Both are found in the report in *ISKRA* (2012) and are presented in two correlated moves: on the one hand, it detailed the official announcements of three major political organisations of the left (Communist Party of Greece, Antarsya or Anticapitalistic Left Collaboration for Subversion, an extra-parliamentary coalition of the radical left, and Youth of Synaspismos, the core party in Syriza); on the other, it denounced the statements of the government's representatives.

The announcement of the Communist Party of Greece began with the familiar Homeric phrase of Ajax: "Shame on you Argos" (*Iliad*, Rhapsody O, line 502). According to the *ISKRA* article, the shame is on:

> those who are accomplices and jointly responsible for the suffering and the despair of the Greek people, those who make attacks by using lies and slanders against all working peoples' fights

against poverty, they should at least fall silent before the abominable results of the capitalistic crisis and their politics instead of pretending to be saviours.

The Youth of Synaspismos also denounced Memorandum policies as responsible for Christoulas's suicide:

The suicide today of a 77-year-old man is a tragic fact by itself. The dramatic end that our fellow human being chose brings out in the most painful way the impasse that a great part of society is at. The many burdens that the working people, the unemployed, and pensioners experience due to Memorandum policies, and their connection to the increase of suicide rates, have for long been exposed in various specialist researches. It is time to stop the barbaric policy which condemns the people in our country, and also other European people, to poverty and despair. We must promote collective struggles and solidarity as a shield of protection for all against the violence of poverty and wretchedness. (*ISKRA* 2012)

Finally, the announcement of Antarsya was particularly severe on the Troika; all those who were regarded as pillars of Memorandum policies were denounced as "murderers". ISKRA (ibid.) presented only excerpts from this announcement:

Rage and unspeakable sorrow provoked the suicide of an elderly fellow human in the centre of Athens. Having been condemned to an unbearable life without a crack of light for a better future, he ended his life just in front of the Greek parliament – there where the executioners of the economic occupation-plan every day murder millions [...]

In such moments, struggle, solidarity and subversion are matters of survival. We must send them away before they exhaust us [...]

Let's transform rage into collective struggle.

In terms of denouncing representatives of the Memorandum policies, the author of the *ISKRA* report referred to the "immoral statements that blemish the dead man by Beglitis and Koukoulopoulos", two leading Pasok members. The report continued: "At a time when the entire country is paralysed by shock at the suicide of a 77-year-old pensioner in Syntagma Square, eminent members of the governments that drove us here make cynical and provocative statements that blemish the memory of the dead man." To substantiate this censure, phrases attributed to Panos Beglitis and Paris Koukoulopoulos were cited. Regarding Beglitis, it was alleged that:

> the former spokesman of Pasok and former minister of defence in the Papandreou government, P. B., said on Sky Television [...] a few hours after the tragic incident: "... if he had or had not debts, if his children or he have eaten the money, has a bearing on this case ...", leaving obscene hints about the moral character of the dead man. Then, he tried to correct the irreparable.

Regarding Koukoulopoulos, the author of the *ISKRA* article observed: "The sub-minister of internal affairs, P. K., was hosted by Sky at 7 o'clock with Nikos Evangellatos [a famous TV journalist]. He felt that it is appropriate to relate the suicide of a 77-year-old pensioner to the explosive rise in pharmaceutical costs!" After this exclamation of disgust, the offending words of the politician were quoted: "If Christoulas had a different approach, he could have helped us very well to understand how the pharmaceutical expenditure [of the health system] had increased in a few years from 4 to 9 billion euro ..." Reportedly, this statement had provoked tensions, probably between the participants in the programme. After that:

[Koukoulopoulos] didn't hesitate to respond that "I didn't come to a psychoanalysis programme." Earlier, after he had spoken of his anguish and reflections, he tried to … interpret the last words of the man who committed suicide: "He speaks in the name of many people, though it is evident that the retired pharmacist, no matter how many years have passed since his retirement, has never searched in the garbage."

The *ISKRA* author comments that "any comment is unnecessary", then extends his ire more generally to the government under Prime Minister Lucas Papademos at the time, based on the support of New Democracy, Pasok and Laos. He also decries the fact that:

> On being asked about the tragic incident, the government spokesman confined himself to saying that it is a human tragedy, and adding provocatively that it offered no scope for political discussion (!) and "We all must respect it". Responding to a journalist's remark that the subject is related to "concrete politics" which has driven the 77-year-old man to this "moment of despair", Mr Kapsis said that he doesn't know the precise conditions under which [Christoulas] was driven to this action, and emphasised that "We all must have composure and respect the real facts, which we don't yet know to the full extent."

The *TVXS* (2012) article was less denunciatory and more polyphonic in this respect. The author referred to the corresponding statements and announcements in a "neutral" way. Specifically, he quoted the announcements of the Communist Party and the Youth of Synaspismos mentioned already; and he cited the statements of the government spokesman, as well as of the three leaders of parties supporting Papademos's government. He also reported the statements of two small parties of the opposition, one

(Democratic Alliance) belonging to the pro-Memorandum and the other (Panellinio Arma Politon) to the anti-Memorandum camp.

Regarding the official government statement, the author emphasised that "[it] advises [citizens] to be calm", adding that, on "being questioned about the tragic incident, the government spokesman Pantelis Kapsis said only that it consists of a human tragedy that is not offered for political discussion". Similarly "non-political" perceptions of "the fact", in different shades, were adopted by the leaders of the three parties that supported the government: Evangelos Venizelos (Pasok), Antonis Samaras (New Democracy) and Giorgos Karatzaferis (Laos). Venizelos stated: "The fact is so shocking that any political comment is jarring and cheap. Let's reflect on the situation of our country and society in terms of national solidarity and cohesion." Samaras, according to the *TVXS* author:

> declared himself shocked [...] by the suicide of the pensioner this morning in Syntagma. In his statement the President of New Democracy underlines that this is not the first such death, as we now know from the suicide record [...] "I have spoken of national depression [...] death is not only about bankruptcy, but also about living without hope [...] This makes it our urgent goal to take Greeks out the swamp and the despair."

And Karatzaferis stated that:

> the bullet [that was shot] this morning in Syntagma Square must have hit the consciousness of the political world directly, and we all must feel [as if we were] beside the trigger. Someone who commits suicide is not simply a dead person. What had this person seen from the politicians? He had seen no one among them stealing his money for many years being imprisoned. He had

seen that they didn't facilitate him with his loans. He had seen cuts in his pension, although they have said that they didn't make those cuts.

Karatzaferis ended with an interesting play on time: "I have said before, when people start to commit suicide in Syntagma, then we have reached the ultimate stage of social incoherence." In a single sentence, he struck a note of alarm about a dystopian future, recalled an anxious forecast he had made in the past, and thereby sought vindication in the fraught present.

The *TVXS* article also, as already noted, gave voice to two small opposition parties with contrary ideological views. The Democratic Alliance, a small neoliberal party, was founded by Dora Bakoyannis, former Minister of Foreign Affairs and a leading member in New Democracy governments. She founded the party in 2010 after she failed to be elected as president of New Democracy. The spokesman of the party reportedly offered his condolences on Christoulas's suicide, and observed: "Instead of investing in the despair and arousing the reasonable anger of citizens, the political sphere of the country must come up with a concrete plan so that the country can overcome this crisis and ensure that those who have most need are effectively supported." The other statement came from Yiannis Dimaras, president of the Panellinio Arma Politon (Pan-Hellenic Chariot of Citizens), founded by Dimaras and another former deputy of Pasok (Vassilis Economou) in 2011, after both were expelled from Pasok for refusing to vote in favour of the second Memorandum of Understanding. The *TVXS* author quoted Dimaras's statement without comment: "The shocking and at the same time tragically symbolic suicide of a pensioner in Syntagma Square indicates where Greek society has been driven to. All those who voted to undermine our country and our dignity are guilty of shedding the blood of the Greek pensioner."

On the whole, despite its fluidity and fragmentariness, Christoulas's suicide archive from Greece was essentially grounded in public debate about rising suicide rates during the financial crisis and in the face of austerity measures. Irrespective of whether the correlation between suicide rates and austerity measures was aptly made, it provided the preponderant frame for engaging with and accounting for suicide in the Memorandum period. Further, the two oppositional left-wing texts discussed here decisively understood the "increase of suicide rates" as generally a form of political protest, as a symptom of the "necropoliticization of resistance" that Banu Bargu (2014: 27) theorised – that is, resistance against the neoliberal order and its political representatives. In contrast, the two establishment texts of the time argued against any correlation between suicide rates and austerity, and maintained that suicides are an apolitical matter, to do with "personal drama" and the "despair" of social actors. Although they conceded the deleterious impact of the financial crisis, they did so in an abstract – even metaphysical – vein that seemed disinvested from concrete political agents and particular policies.

Whether received as an act of resistance or of despair, Christoulas's suicide was an emblematic moment for the public management of suicide in austerity-struck Greece. The convergent and divergent perspectives that coalesced into the corresponding suicide archive contained a number of culturally specific assumptions and categories that formed a "structured conjuncture" (Sahlins 1981: 35), as shown above, around the incidental facts of the performance of Christoulas's suicide and the note he left to explain it. Such incidental facts can potentially play an important role in the continuous recomposition, reconciliation or alteration of the dominant semantic universe (ibid.: 67).

UNAMBIGUOUSLY POLITICAL

In retrospect, we can say that Christoulas's suicide did not become a catalyst for a general "revolt and resistance" against Memorandum policies. Nevertheless, Christoulas's suicide offered a point of reference that immediately sharpened and restructured a previously diffuse debate on austerity and suicide rates. More importantly, although its impact was gradually overtaken by larger and more urgent political dramas in Greece, it remains a disturbing memory that simmers in a quiet and constantly guilt-inducing manner.

Two years and nine months later, Syriza won the January 2015 legislative elections with a campaign promise of rolling back austerity measures and opposing further bailout conditions being imposed by the Troika. The campaign preceding this featured various emotive and advocatory appeals citing rising suicide rates, and Christoulas's suicide was often recalled among others. Concern about suicide rates in relation to austerity took a back seat amidst resurgent optimism as Syriza formed the government after reaching a coalition agreement with the right-wing party ANEL (Anexartitoi Ellines). However, in the following months, negotiations between the Greek government – represented by Prime Minister Alexis Tsipras and Minister of Finance Yanis Varoufakis – and the European Commission, International Monetary Fund and European Central Bank about conditions for a further bailout grew increasingly fraught. An agreement that could enable the Syriza government to keep its anti-austerity campaign promises was unforthcoming. In a period of desperation, Tsipras called a referendum to determine whether Greek citizens felt that the bailout conditions were acceptable, and recommended that they vote against the conditions. In the referendum of 5 July 2015, Greek citizens voted firmly against accepting the bailout conditions (by 61.3 per cent against 38.7 per cent). However, three days later the Greek government, under intense pressure, capitulated and accepted the bailout conditions, agreeing to the implementation of further austerity measures. Although various technical reasons have since been cited to disregard the referendum result, this capitulation appeared as a defeat of democratic process in Greece – a kind of suicidal juncture for Greek self-determination. In the dispirited months that followed, there was little stomach for mulling suicide rates and incidences in relation to continuing austerity in Greece. But that doesn't mean that the issue disappeared, or that, in particular, Christoulas's suicide was forgotten – although it has been relegated to occasional, incidental, increasingly fleeting references in the media and other public deliberations.

Even the hush that surrounds the memory now is an uncomfortable one, a kind of unwillingness to address something because it causes guilt and is a kind of aching scar. Four years after Christoulas's suicide there was little to identify the spot in Syntagma Square where it was enacted, but in the interim anniversaries of the day were marked in low-key events. Unlike Mohamed Bouazizi's suicide in Tunisia discussed in Chapter 2, or those of Plamen Goranov and others in Bulgaria in the next chapter, Christoulas's couldn't be trivialised, easily fitted into suicidological discourses, or otherwise diffused into ambiguity. The unmentionable fact is that it was enacted with a suicide note prophesying recourse to armed struggle if austerity and neoliberal governance continued:

a call to arms that could not be depoliticised, only uncomfortably silenced. Even in the international media, the political effect of Christoulas's suicide has continued to be registered as unambiguously political. A BBC article of 1 August 2016, reminding its audience of "[s]even times [when] ordinary people shook up political debate", included in its upbeat and Anglocentric account of such interventions the uncharacteristically dark impact of the suicide of Christoulas, "who shot himself dead outside the Greek parliament in April 2012 in response to strict austerity measures" (BBC 2016).

References

Anast, Paul and Nick Squires (2012) "Austerity Suicide: Greek Pensioner Shoots Himself in Athens". *The Telegraph*, 4 April. http://www.telegraph.co.uk/news/worldnews/europe/greece/9186568/Austerity-suicide-Greek-pensioner-shoots-himself-in-Athens.html.

Bargu, Banu (2014) *Starve and Immolate: The Politics of Human Weapons.* New York NY: Columbia University Press.

BBC (2016) "Seven Times Ordinary People Shook Up Political Debate". BBC News, 1 August. http://www.bbc.co.uk/news/world-europe-36942401.

Benecou, Vivian (2012) "Dimitris Christoulas. The Person who Shocked Greece". *To Ethnos*, 8 April. http://www.ethnos.gr/koinonia/arthro/o_anthropos_pou_sygklonise_tin_ellada-63641453/.

Branas, Charles C., Anastasia E. Kastanaki, Manolis Michalodimitrakis, John Tzougas, Elena F. Kranioti, Pavlos N. Theodorakis, Brendan G. Carr and Douglas J. Wiebe1 (2015) "The Impact of Economic Austerity and Prosperity Events on Suicide in Greece: A 30-Year Interrupted Time-Series Analysis". *BMJ Open* 5 (1): e005619. doi: 10.1136/bmjopen-2014-005619.

Cavafy, Constantinos P. (1972) *Selected Poems.* Translated by Edmund Keeley and Philip Sherrard. Princeton NJ: Princeton University Press.

Cho, Ji Young (2014) "Reducing Confusion about Grounded Theory and Qualitative Content Analysis: Similarities and Differences". *The Qualitative Report 2014* 19 (64): 1–20.

Christou, Jean (2015) "Nearly 200 Suicides Recorded in Cyprus in Five Years". *Cyprus Mail*, 6 December. http://cyprus-mail.com/2015/12/06/nearly-200-sui-in-five-years/.

Christou, Jean (2016) "Theocharous Prepared to Set Herself on Fire for Cyprus–Greece Union". *Cyprus Mail*, 28 January. http://cyprus-mail.com/2016/01/28/theocharous-prepared-to-set-herself-on-fire-for-cyprus-greece-union/.

Davies, Elizabeth (2015) "'We've Toiled Without End': Publicity, Crisis, and the Suicide 'Epidemic' in Greece". *Comparative Studies in Society and History* 57 (4): 1007–36.

Durkheim, Emile (1979 [1897]) *Suicide*. London: Macmillan.

Evetts, Julia, Harald A. Mieg and Ulrike Felt (2006) "Professionalization, Scientific Expertise, and Elitism: A Sociological Perspective" in K. Anders Ericsson, Neil Charness, Paul J. Feltovich and Robert R. Hoffman (eds) *The Cambridge Handbook of Expertise and Expert Performance*. Cambridge: Cambridge University Press, pp. 105–24.

Fassin, Didier (2011) "The Trace: Violence, Truth and the Politics of the Body". *Social Research* 78 (2): 281–98.

Featherstone, Kevin (2013) *Politics and Policy in Greece: The Challenge of "Modernization"*. London: Routledge.

Haitidis, Zafeiris (2012) *It Wasn't Suicide: D. Christola's Funeral (Athens, Greece)*. *YouTube*, 7 April. https://www.youtube.com/watch?v=Ex6mCuHH47k.

Harrison, Pam (2015) "Greek Debt Crisis: Tragic Spike in Suicide Rates". *Medscape*, 23 June. http://www.medscape.com/viewarticle/846904.

ISKRA (2012) "The Society Is Shocked by the Suicide of the 77-year-old Man". *ISKRA*, 5 April. http://www.iskra.gr/index.php?option=com_content&view=article&id=7302:syntagma-aftoktonia&catid=80:koin-dikaiomata&Itemid=180.

Kakissis, Joanna (2012) "As Hope Fades in Greece, an Elderly Pensioner Is Driven to Suicide". *Time*, 5 April. http://content.time.com/time/world/article/0,8599,2111267,00.html.

Kallergis, Kostas (2012) "Dispatch from Greece: Translation of Austerity Suicide Note Left by Pensioner Dimitris Christoulas". *Exile Online*, 10 April. http://exiledonline.com/dispatch-from-greece-translation-of-austerity-suicide-note-left-by-pensioner-dimitris-christoulas/.

Kiss, Jemima (2010) "ABCes: Mail Online Presses Ahead as Rivals See Post-World Cup Dip". *The Guardian*, 26 August. http://www.theguardian.com/media/2010/aug/26/abces-july-2010.

Kollia, Eleftheria (2012) "Political Message, Personal Deadlock. How the Experts Explain the Increase of Suicide-Rates Because of the Crisis". *To Vima*, 8 April. http://www.tovima.gr/society/article/?aid=452433&h1=true#commentForm.

Lyritzis, Christos (2011) *Greek Politics in the Era of Economic Crisis*. London: Hellenic Observatory, London School of Economics and Political Science.

Mantzari, Dimitra (2016) "Constructing Suicide during the Economic Crisis in Greece". Unpublished master's thesis. Athens: Panteion University of Social and Political Sciences, Department of Social Anthropology.

Margaronis, Maria (2012) "Dimitris Christoulas and the Legacy of his Suicide for Greece". *The Guardian*, 5 April. http://www.theguardian.com/commentisfree/2012/apr/05/dimitris-christoulas-legacy-suicide-greece.

McDermott, Nick and Daniel Martin (2012) "Riots Erupt in Greece after 'Martyr' Shoots Himself over Debt Crisis". *Daily Mail*, 5 April. http://www.dailymail.co.uk/news/article-2125686/Riots-erupt-Greece-martyr-Dimitris-Christoulas-shoots-debt-crisis.html#ixzz44SwwgjuV.

Meynaud, Jean, with Panagiotis Merlopoulos and Gerasimos Notaras (1965) *Les forces politiques en Grèce*. Lausanne: Études des Sciences Politiques.

Rachiotis, George, David Stuckler, Martin McKee and Christos Hadjichristodoulou (2015) "What Has Happened to Suicides during the Greek Economic Crisis? Findings from an Ecological Study of Suicides and Their Determinants (2003–2012)". *BMJ Open* 5 (3): e007295. http://bmjopen.bmj.com/content/5/3/e007295.full.

Sahlins, Marshal (1981) *Historical Metaphors and Mythical Realities: Structure in the Early History of Sandwich Islands Kingdom*. Ann Arbor MI: University of Michigan Press.

Simiti, Marilena (2014) *Rage and Protest: The Case of the Greek Indignant Movement*. GreeSE Paper 82. London: Hellenic Observatory Papers on Greece and Southeast Europe, London School of Economics and Political Science.

Smith, Helena (2012) "Greek Suicide Seen as an Act of Fortitude as Much as One of Despair". *The Guardian*, 5 April. http://www.theguardian.com/world/2012/apr/05/greek-suicide-dimitris-christoulas-protest.

Song, Lichao (2010) "The Role of Context in Discourse Analysis". *Journal of Language Teaching and Research* 1 (6): 876–9.

Tambakaki, Paulina (2011) "Greek Protest in Syntagma Square: In Between Post-Politics and Real Democracy". *OpenDemocracy*, 28 June.

https://www.opendemocracy.net/paulina-tambakaki/greek-protest-in-syntagma-square-in-between-post-politics-and-real-democracy.

TVXS (2012) "In Syntagma Square again the Indignants after the Suicide: Suicide Shock". *TVXS*, 4 April. http://tvxs.gr/news/ellada/ ilikiomenos-aytoktonise-stin-plateia-syntagmatos.

van Dijk, Teun A. (2001) "Critical Discourse Analysis" in D. Sciffrin, D. Tannen and H. E. Hamilton (eds) *The Handbook of Discourse Analysis*. Malden MA and Oxford: Blackwell Publishers, pp. 352–71.

van Dijk, Teun A. (2008) *Discourse and Power*. Basingstoke: Palgrave Macmillan.

FOUR | Self-immolations in Bulgaria:
a quietly accumulating record

Milena Katsarska

An interview

This chapter explores the rather large and sprawling archive of a series of suicides in Bulgaria that were performed or at least regarded as acts of protest. These started on 18 February 2013 with the self-immolation of twenty-six-year-old Trayan Marechkov in the town of Veliko Turnovo, followed soon after by that of thirty-six-year-old Plamen Goranov on 20 February 2013 in front of the municipal building in Varna (he died a few days later). Since January 2013, crowds had been demonstrating against the government in various Bulgarian cities, for reasons which I outline later – these suicides were naturally understood as coeval with those protests. Subsequently, as many as thirty-five further suicides and attempted suicides were reported and associated – albeit to varying degrees and in different ways – with political disaffection (see Table 4.1 at the end of the chapter).

Let me begin my explorations from a tangent. Incidentally, all translations from the Bulgarian in the following are by the author, unless indicated otherwise.

Here is a snippet from an exchange between cultural theorists Kamelia Spasova and Darin Tenev during an interview with journalist Irina Nedeva on Bulgarian National Radio on 11 June 2015:

Spasova: There are swift and slow gestures of revolt; of course, the swift ones are effective, but they cut short the opportunity for dialogue ...

Tenev: ... and the opportunity for reflection.

Spasova: ... so self-immolation is such a swift, visible gesture, we can think of it as a metaphor.

Tenev: A very radical gesture which is a refusal, really, that's it. There's no conversation there ...

The occasion was the launch of a special issue of the journal *Piron* (*Nail*), entitled "Julia Kristeva: Form and Meaning of Revolt". This exchange took place towards the end of the segment and might misleadingly suggest that the special issue offered scholarly analyses of self-immolations as a form of revolt in Bulgaria and elsewhere. In fact, the contents of the issue revolved around Kristeva's lecture, "New Forms of Revolt", delivered at the Sofia Literary Theory seminar at Sofia University (26 September 2014). A Bulgarian translation of Chapter 1 from her *La révolte intime* (1997, English translation 2002) and some of her subsequent work were published in the journal, and various reflections and discussions by local literary and cultural theorists – such as Spasova and Tenev – were included. The questions addressed, as stated in the announcement of the journal, were about the conceptual apparatus of Kristeva's oeuvre, and they were debated at a fitting level of abstraction:

What is the relation between the revolution in poetic language and the intimate revolt that Kristeva's psychoanalytical perspective calls for? To what extent is a psychoanalytical reworking of the problems of youth applicable as a way of responding to grave social cataclysms? Who, from what position, where and when, has the right to pronounce on revolt and judge what true revolt is? In what way should we transform the very form in which revolt and the act of revolting are being thought of in post-socialist countries, and in the case of Bulgaria? Should we compare different types of social revolt even when both their form and their matter differ so radically? What is the role of language, of different codes – religious, social, enforced by the media and conspiracy theories – when resurrecting old and engendering new forms of revolt? (Spasova and Tenev 2015)

The level of abstraction that these questions and their answers occupied rarely allowed consideration of concrete instances or particular enactments of revolt – although revolt had been in the air recently, especially in Bulgaria throughout 2013 and well into 2014. There was hardly any public forum or everyday space where revolt wasn't being contemplated; the air had buzzed with talk of revolt.

Of course, the scholarly discussions in the journal's special issue were imbued with a sense of the currency of the issues in question, though in a more global than local vein. It was not fortuitous that these questions were posed at that juncture, and that a critical fervour to engage with Kristeva's work was discovered accordingly. It is nevertheless significant that this critical fervour was more comfortable with sticking to the abstract at the expense of the concrete, with global generalities rather than local realities. In fact, even that snippet of an exchange about a particular and particularly disturbing form of protest in Bulgaria – one that was very much on the public mind – was due to an emphatic push. After ten minutes or so of on-air conversation on the journal's contents in abstract terms, the interviewer Nedeva posed the following questions, with a comment:

Do you have analyses of the self-immolating people in this issue?
Because, to my surprise, when I rewound to what's left from the
history of 1990, there was a warning about a self-immolation then
too. Also by a man named Plamen, Plamen Stanchev … […]
He warns that he will set himself on fire if the communist star
is not taken down from the Party Building [Communist Party
headquarters] […] When we talk about these different forms of
revolt, can we enumerate them … occupation, sit-in, civic dis-
obedience. Where is the end point? Is there an ultimate form?
(Nedeva 2015)

Spasova and Tenev's responses effectively answered the question by not quite answering it, by putting this particular form of
revolt – self-immolation – outside debate, as too fast to take in,
intrinsically a refusal of conversation and reflection (metaphori-
cally). And they managed to do so without making any reference
to the local context or to the social and historical grounding that
Nedeva had pushed for.

A couple of features that were indicative of the manner in
which these suicides were discussed in Bulgaria are found in
the above. First, as is apparent from Nedeva's questions, any
informed discussion of "new forms and meanings of revolt" in
Bulgaria now makes the habitual move of appointing a horizon
in terms of which all that is new can be understood: the protests
of 1990, which gave birth to post-socialist Bulgaria. After 1990,
social and political history in Bulgaria, especially in relation to
crises and protests, has been firmly framed by that defining horizon. It has provided a paradigmatic line against which subsequent
events can be mapped and normative judgements pronounced,
irrespective of that horizon's receding distance – fading gradually
into oblivion. Further, it is of some interest that a name seems

to have a particular resonance here: "Plamen", linking Plamen Stanchev in 1990 to Plamen Goranov in 2013. In fact, the latter's self-immolation has been centre stage in such discussion of these suicides as has taken place in Bulgaria. I discuss why that was so, and what the connection projected between it and an unfulfilled threat in 1990 amounted to, in the following pages.

Second, Spasova and Tenev's responses to Nedeva's questions effectively evaded them by striking notes of certainty and hesitation in equal measure. The latter transpired as a sort of critical distancing from engagement with particular acts – understandably so, given the tenor of the interview. At the same time, both confidently suggested that their hesitation wasn't because the critic needs or seeks distance but because the act itself – self-immolation – doesn't allow critical distance; it was the character of the act rather than their responsibility as critics that they were referring to: hence those categorical pronouncements on self-immolation per se as a "radical gesture", "cutting short the opportunity for dialogue", and "a refusal" that makes "conversation" impossible. For the person committing suicide that may well be so, but it is difficult to see why the critic should be deterred from analysing the act afterwards. At any rate, this study takes a contrary view, in which suicide texts accrue as a dialogic formation in the suicide archive, and this process unfolds mostly (though not exclusively) after the fact of specific acts of suicide. Suicide texts accrue and influence each other through resonances and responses that shape and shift – sometimes confirming, at other times contradicting or challenging – received expectations and dominant predispositions. This chapter therefore is an attempt at continuing a conversation amid many self-immolation suicide texts in the context of Bulgaria, in an expanding suicide archive since 2013, without evading their social or political grounding or withdrawing into evasive critical distance.

Bulgaria in 2013: protests and self-immolations

The year 2013 in Bulgaria appears to be marked both as one of continuous social upheaval and anti-establishment protests and as one in which a series of self-immolations garnered ongoing media attention.

The anti-establishment protests started in late January with a spontaneous outburst of indignation at exorbitant electricity bills, and spread across the country. Numerous rallies, marches, riots, demonstrations and manifestos, articulating a diverse repertoire of grievances – socio-economic and political – followed in subsequent months, continuing through the year and well into December, when protests by students (with occupations of universities) and academics became the more "localised" venue of social tension (Bigg 2013). All of these generated extensive media coverage, both within and outside Bulgaria. At the same time, and again continuously through the year, there unfolded cumulative news reports of cases of self-immolations; these began on 18 February with, as mentioned above, Trayan Marechkov setting himself on fire in one of the main streets in Veliko Turnovo, and ended with the case of twenty-one-year-old Sabin Sabinov setting himself alight in a small park in Varna on 9 December. Relying on initial Bulgarian media reports, there were ten self-immolation fatalities, seven self-immolation survivors and six prevented attempts at self-immolation during that year: for details, see Table 4.1 at the end of the chapter, which includes further cases to 2015. Irrespective of whether the act was completed or threatened, the ages varied from twenty-one (the youngest) to seventy-four (the oldest), with – where information is available – four people in their thirties, eight in their forties, and five in their fifties. Their geographical spread involved large and small towns alike, as well as villages across the country. The locations also varied in terms of public (streets, proximity to government buildings, stadia, town parks, etc.) and relatively private spaces (cars, homes and backyards). Especially with the latter in view, where enactment of suicide appears to be secluded and private, one may well ask whether some should not be excluded from the present discussion. That is not the approach taken here. My purpose here is to provide a general outline of the contexts which linked (or delinked) protests and self-immolations in Bulgaria. From this perspective, there is an obvious temporal association: a number of protests as well as a number of self-immolations occurred in tandem throughout the year. Also, further grounds for association were offered at the very least in terms of their overall spread across the country and their diversity. Moreover, it was not only that protests and self-immolations occurred in tandem as "events"; it is also the case that from their immediate to their more considered framing in reports, commentaries, analyses and so on, more or less stable narratives emerged through a complex process of different categories feeding each other. Therefore, Table 4.1 at the end of the chapter captures in minimal detail the cases of prevented, attempted and accomplished acts of self-immolation for the year 2013. These will form the primary focus of my subsequent discussion. Relying on further media reports, however, the record continues beyond the time frame of the calendar year that initially consolidated acts of self-immolation "as a form of protest". That initial consolidation in turn generated a centre of gravity in relation to which subsequent enactments were positioned – be that to reaffirm, diffuse or deny the association.

Returning to the "year of protest" in Bulgaria, the protests began with an explicit economic grievance. They were spurred by a dramatic hike in electricity bills at a time when households were faced with accumulating debts, and in a context of high poverty levels and unemployment rates (see Lessenski 2013; Bechev 2013). Protesters started demonstratively burning their electricity bills (Petkova 2013). The protesters' anger initially targeted major players in the Bulgarian energy sector, which involves national and foreign private electricity producers and carriers as well as government regulatory bodies in a sprawling web of relationships. These had emerged through privatisation and liberalisation from the 1990s onwards, enabled and approved by a succession of governments with different majority party constituencies. The protests immediately raised questions about current economic interests and their political underpinnings. On the one hand, doubts about the effectiveness of twenty years of transitioning from centralised state socialism to global liberal democracy were mooted, with calls for revisionism (for a "restart" of the process). On the other, unease was expressed, to put it mildly, about the prolonged period of everyday financial pressures and struggles arising from EU-driven and home-made austerity policies (Bulgaria became a member of the EU in 2007), especially following the financial crisis of 2007–08.

A revealing policy paper, "Bulgaria's Leaderless Protests", written early on by Marin Lessenski (2013), recalled that within the first few weeks of protests, the media took to highlighting experts pushing the former line (a failure of transition from state socialism) at the expense of the latter (a failure of the current neoliberal order). Explanations were sought in Bulgarian history ("What is wrong within the country?") rather than in the Bulgarian and austerity-struck EU's present (whereby links to anti-austerity protests in, for example, Greece, Spain and Ireland might have been suggested). Political commentators, especially of Bulgarian background, were at pains to remind readers of the "more complex" nature of this former socialist country of the Eastern bloc. Indicative in this respect are "Bulgaria's Anger, the Real Source" in *OpenDemocracy* (Bechev 2013) or some of the comments following "Bulgaria's Crisis: Poverty Protests" in *The Economist* (2013). Even in relation to extortionist utility bills, demands followed diverse and contradictory paths from "anti-monopolist" stances to calls for the "nationalisation of the energy sector". Prime Minister Boiko Borisov of the centre-right government of the GERB party (Citizens for European Development of Bulgaria) reacted by announcing the resignation of the Minister of Finance and Vice Prime Minister Simeon Djankov (on 18 February).

By that time, however, the state itself was being perceived as an active agent in the "energy arena" or, more broadly, in implementing EU policies at the local level. So the protests gathered momentum by expanding the scope of their disaffections and political demands – by questioning party politics, ties between party elites and big businesses, and oligarchic power and corruption, as well as by advocating more direct "citizen participation" as a corrective (through citizen quotas in local or national governing bodies, changes in electoral laws, etc.). In Varna, for instance, the protesters called for the resignation of the GERB-supported mayor who had ties to the economic structures of the TIM holding company (TIM is the Bulgarian equivalent of the word "team", written in capital letters), which is an alleged leader of organised crime in the country. In Sofia, protesters rallied at the official memorial ceremony marking the death of national liberation hero Vasil Levski on 19 February, which resulted in violent clashes with the police. The next day Prime Minister Borisov announced the resignation of the government.

The obviously diverse demands noted in Lessenski's (2013) policy brief were echoed in slogans, some against monopolies or corruption, some for the "future for the young" and a "dignified and strong Bulgaria", and others going in contradictory directions such as "All members of parliament – out" and "Parliament should finish its job and not abdicate". President Rosen Plevneliev appointed a caretaker government on 13 March, headed by Marin Raykov, and early elections were scheduled for 12 May. However, protests continued throughout March, voicing diverse grievances and providing a motley picture of associations and fragmentations. Local and national citizens' councils were formed with bids to participate in decision-making processes, non-mainstream nationalist parties came out with xenophobic sentiments, and further calls for nationalisation and against more privatisation of still publicly owned companies (the railways, for example) were heard (Tsolova 2013). A number of groups continued to demand decisive state measures to improve living conditions, and unions organised demonstrations of medical professionals, among other groups. Social unrest subsided to a degree in the weeks leading to the election in April. At the election, GERB received the highest number of votes but failed to obtain a clear majority, and refused to form the government. The party with the second largest number of votes, the centre-left Bulgarian Socialist Party (BSP), entered a coalition with the

Movement for Rights and Freedoms (DPS) and formed the new government under Prime Minister Plamen Oresharski. Oresharski had been Minister of Finance in the tripartite coalition government (which also included the National Movement of Simeon the Second) under which Bulgaria had joined the EU in 2007.

On 14 June 2013, the new government announced the appointment of Delyan Peevski, a media tycoon associated with oligarchic structures and the interests of major financial groups, to head the State Agency for National Security. This immediately provoked a public reaction that led to protests demanding that the appointment be revoked. That happened by a unanimous parliamentary decision five days later but failed to appease protesters. Protests with contradictory demands continued throughout the summer, some calling for the resignation of the new government and others supporting it while seeking responsible decision making and socially oriented policies. However, these protests were primarily focused in the capital and in some large towns, such as Varna and Plovdiv, while there also emerged counter-protests (protests against the protests). A schism rather than continuity now appeared between the earlier winter protests and these summer protests, although the underlying economic order remained unchanged. Whereas the former were now regarded as socio-economic protests, the latter were understood as "civic protests with moral concerns"; the former were associated with the unemployed and the poor, older age groups, the countryside, and violent methods, and the latter with "educated professionals with jobs", younger generations, the capital and large towns, and peaceful gestures. Even an "aesthetics" of protest and protesters appeared: the former were "the ugly ones" and the latter beautiful. Alongside these fissures, the events unfolding in the summer were cast as exceptional, as they seemed to be "increasing public support for democracy and the European Union" and in turn commanded the approval of EU officials and institutions (Krastev 2013). Moreover, if a line of continuity was sought at all between the earlier months of the year and the later period, this was found predominantly in relation to "anti-corruption" and "civic participation" in a political process, with a pronounced emphasis on condemning the legacy of "Communist Party apparatchiks" from before 1989 as the source of current oligarchic power.

These turns were of the moment, emerging within media discourse in 2013 and hardening as frames through reiteration (Gupta 2014; Katsarska 2015; 2016), irrespective of critical voices to the contrary (see, for instance, Ivancheva 2013a; 2013b). Thus, in the naming of the continuous protests of 2013, fragmented designations appeared: "anti-monopolist protests", "February protests", "winter protests", "protests leading to the resignation of the Borisov-1 cabinet", "June protests", "summer protests", "protests against Oresharski's government", "students' protests", and so on. In a similar vein, scholarly engagement with this year of protest tends to concentrate on a segment of the continuum and to predominantly focus on the peaceful civic democratic process. In retrospective analyses too, the divergences before and after the early elections in May are emphasised rather than the convergences (see, for instance, Ganev 2014).

Against this background of diverse and often contradictory protests, and their ongoing media and political framing and reframing, the series of self-immolations unfolded in February and continued throughout the year. They generated considerable interest both in the country and abroad, at least initially. On 18 February, Trayan Marechkov walked out of his home after dinner with his family, his older brother (who had just returned from abroad) and his girlfriend, carrying a two-litre can of petrol (which his father thought contained *rakia*). He walked the distance from the residential area of Kvartala to one of the main boulevards in the centre of the town, and set himself alight at about 9 pm. Passers-by called the emergency line and tried to extinguish the flames. The initial report in the district newspaper *Borba* (2013), entitled "A 26-year-old Person from Turnovo Set Himself on Fire Because of Poverty", alleged a mental condition and a previous record of hospitalisation, observed that Marechkov had been unemployed, and reported that no suicide note had been found. Trayan died in hospital and reportedly said: "I've had enough of this life." Protesters in Veliko Turnovo, who had been gathering regularly in front of the electricity company building for several days at that point, commemorated him (allegedly without being able to name him yet) together with national hero Vasil Levski with a moment of silence the next day – the anniversary of Levski's execution by Ottoman authorities on 19 February 1873. Nowadays, if one searches the suicide archive of self-immolations in Bulgaria, one discovers that the burnt remains of Marechkov's jacket had assumed the shape of a dove (*Trud* 2013a). One also comes upon Marechkov's mother saying in an interview on the programme "Let Them Speak … With Rosen Petrov" (bTV 2013) that in January he had asked her what Levski's words "A life must be laid for the revival of the state" meant. She notes that he was "only two months without a job", but "had taken part in Sofia protests against forest cutting" (possibly in 2012) and "together with other people from Veliko Turnovo protested against high electricity bills in front of the Ministry of Energy". Additionally, Marechkov's suicide note had allegedly been found and made public. It said: "I give my life for the people, the family and Bulgaria in the hope that politics and the government will improve the standard [of living] of the people." I haven't been able to discover where and when exactly this note appeared, but it is currently part of his suicide archive irrespective of its authenticity. It seems that within a month after being commemorated on the anniversary of Levski's death by a protesting crowd in Veliko Turnovo, a complex web of associations had developed. Marechkov had been conferred heroic and symbolic attributes, with national ideals at stake and historical references, and a voice that denounced the government and politicians for the economic hardships of the people. Something akin to "mutual adoption" had occurred: the protesters had recognised Trayan Marechkov as "one of their own" and, in turn, the young man had acquired the features of his "adoptive family".

In the interim there were three more fatalities and one survivor of public self-immolations, the GERB government had resigned, there was a national holiday (3 March, Liberation Day), and a national day of mourning (6 March) following the death of Plamen Goranov (who set himself on fire on 20 February and died on 3 March). The latter (6 March) was also the day when the GERB-supported mayor of Varna with TIM Holding ties eventually resigned and the interim caretaker government was appointed. Plamen Goranov, the second self-immolation victim, was among protesters in Varna who rallied spontaneously around oppressive utility (electricity and heating) bills and gradually became concerned about the TIM conglomerate's hold on the local economy; O'Brennan (2013) cites estimates of a 70 per cent hold facilitated by docile municipal government officials. Within a week, Varna's protesting citizens were demanding the resignation of the mayor,

Kiril Yordanov, and of the entire municipal council. Thirty-six-year-old Goranov was single, a keen climber, and had an interest in photography. At various points in his life he had held jobs in a photographic studio and on a cruise ship; latterly, he had worked with temporary contracts to install heat insulation on buildings, using his climbing skills. On the morning of 20 February, Goranov walked up the steps of the municipal building at 7.24 am carrying a backpack (containing spray cans, a thermos, etc.) and a written sign that read "Resignation of Kiro and the entire municipal council by 5 pm on 20.02.2013". After he had doused himself with petrol, he was noticed by officials inside the building and two police officers came out. There followed a brief verbal altercation and one of the officers took a plastic container from his left hand. This was the moment when Goranov caught fire and fell down the steps. The policemen extinguished the flames by 7.30 am and emergency services arrived. A guard from the building opposite who had run out to help heard him saying "Kiro, Kiro …" and "I just wanted to protest peacefully, now I should have been on holiday in Antalya and I didn't want to kill myself." In the aftermath, Goranov's suicide archive became especially weighty in a number of ways. This was largely because a national day of mourning was announced three days after his death, and because the regional prosecutor's office released a formal statement following investigations after eight months (I will return to this in due course). Goranov's suicide acquired a kind of official recognition, almost a sanction of authority.

On 26 February at around 3.30 pm, fifty-three-year-old Ventsislav Vasilev walked into the municipal building in Radnevo, Stara Zagora region, reportedly announced that "I will set myself on fire now" to the official in the entrance hall, and did so. Vasilev was taken to hospital and died on 10 March 2013. He was a father of five; both he and his wife were unemployed. He had held a temporary job on local archaeological excavations under municipal schemes for temporary employment. The family were on welfare, which had been stopped due to a small inheritance (reportedly 200 BGN, or €100), and had accumulated utility debts (the media cited sums for cumulative unpaid water or electricity bills). An article in the newspaper *Sega* (2013a) following Vasilev's death reported an interview with the mayor of Radnevo, who claimed that the man had never asked him for help or made demands or raised slogans against the municipality. The article noted that this was the third victim of self-immolation and detailed the previous two deaths, describing Plamen Goranov as "a symbol of the protests". Numerous comments appeared under the article, variously castigating the morally corrupt government of Borisov that had led the country to ruin, calling on the mayor to support the family, remarking that "those not carrying slogans" also deserve mourning, and describing Vasilev as "an ordinary man and father with dignity, crushed by misery and the impasse of democracy". There unfolded discussions on finding work abroad (in EU member states that allowed Bulgarians job permits) as an alternative to suicide, or simple statements were made to the effect of "God rest his soul". Needless to say, these were isolated sentiments. Reports and soul-searching observations proliferated as the numbers of self-immolation victims grew and reinforced the notion that self-immolation was a form of protest. Shortly thereafter, a woman joined the ranks of the self-immolated, when the body of Daniela Nakova, a forty-five-year-old cosmetician working from her home, was found burnt on Youth Hill in Plovdiv.

The policy brief "Bulgaria's Leaderless Protests", referred to earlier, was published in March and echoed the consensus that was beginning to emerge:

> Three persons have self-immolated in the course of two weeks as an outcry against the political and social situation in the country. One of them reportedly did it as a clear political demonstration in the name of a collective and public cause rather than out of social or financial depression. The tragic death of Plamen Goranov in Varna on the national holiday has evoked references to Jan Palach, but in the Bulgarian case this has been a last-ditch act against oligarchic abuse of political power. (Lessenski 2013: 2)

At the time, self-immolations were regarded *as articulating something about the situation in the country*, and subsequently discussions and disputes would develop as to what exactly they were voicing, what they meant and what had to be done. Then, in a rather obvious manner, a numerical preoccupation emerged – a focus on the headcount of suicides, which grew as the weeks went by. Numbers were cited as if they were significant and could be evoked to manage or take stock of something that was just beyond comprehension. With the self-immolation of one of the survivors, fifty-one-year-old blacksmith Dimitar Dimitrov in front of the presidency building in Sofia (the first one in the capital), this kind of accounting made it to the headlines in Bulgaria and into reports in the global media.

Perhaps one of the earliest international reports referencing self-immolations was published in *Al Jazeera* on 21 February, where the leading focus was still on protest demonstrations and establishment reactions. The two self-immolation cases were mentioned to illustrate that protests were escalating (Petkova 2013). A month later a CNN report would follow the headline

"Six in Bulgaria Die by Self-Immolation" (22 March) with a more revealing approach to the "phenomenon" (more on this below). This shift of emphasis had to do with registering the alarming tendency of a "wave" or "spate" of suicides that activated frames of suicidology and suicide prevention (Toshkov 2013a). At this stage, however, citing numbers often meant attributing something to a group *in toto* or as a shorthand to make a particular political, social or cultural point, or simply being unable to keep up with individual narratives. In other words, that meant entering a sort of reductionist and "manageable" mode of narrativising and dealing with the "phenomenon".

However, there are two other nuances that appeared in the above. With reference to public suicides by self-immolation, there appeared signs of cracks within the fabric of protests. At that point, intentions underlying these suicides were presented as being "a clear political demonstration" for "a collective and public cause" made by one person ("reportedly"), while the others were thought of as arising from "social or financial depression". So, a *suspension of the emphasis on the idea of a collective and public cause, due to socio-economic reasons,* seeped out from there – it seemed to imply that individual or private motives might have played a part in most cases. What began as a subtle implication in that direction would become more pronounced and explicit, almost a certainty, over the course of the year. The second nuance is more direct. Plamen Goranov's suicide had already been highlighted in social media and in Bulgarian-language media by the time the English-language media picked up the story. Goranov's suicide acquired an *exceptional character* that would serve to stabilise the self-immolation archive in Bulgaria for the year. In a curious way, the exceptional character of Goranov's act resonated with – fed into and fed off – the *avowedly exceptional character of the Bulgarian context* itself.

At home and abroad

Protests and self-immolations mark a state of exception. This is especially so if they appear to have the potential to effect significant political and socio-economic changes. The protests that had started over electricity bills seemed to have such a momentous political potential. An opinion piece published in *Al Jazeera* on 21 February 2013 captured that potential along two lines:

> On the economic side, the demands are: scrapping of contracts with the electricity companies and nationalising them; putting those who signed them on trial; revision of electricity bills with citizen participation; declassification of the contracts for all privatisation deals in the last 24 years; revision of all concession contracts for the past 24 years; and ceasing privatisation processes. On the political side, demands have gone even further to seek an overhaul of the political system in Bulgaria. They have made clear that the system has to be changed in such a way that when the next party comes to power, it can no longer behave the way all governments in Bulgaria have for the past 24 years. There have to be checks on political power and mechanisms to prevent collusion between politicians, private economic interests and organised crime. (Petkova 2013)

At a glance, a revolutionary spirit seemed to be in circulation, speaking of nationalisation and revision and possibly revoking past privatisation and concession deals, and putting a stop to further liberalisation policies. "Taking apart" an established political system was mooted, and, as other publications at the time suggested, there was "talk of" direct control on behalf of "the people" over governing institutions. Further, when the initial self-immolations were "inserted" into this picture and were regarded as an extreme form of the revolutionary spirit of the already numerous protests that were under way, old "spectres" were roused – ominous possibilities seemed in the offing – and assuaging moves seemed to be called for. However, it is only at a rather superficial level that such revolutionary spectres stirred. The *Al Jazeera* report also captured an inward turn; it was suggested that the "explanation" for these demands was contained within Bulgaria's twenty-four years of post-socialist transition, perhaps a lingering remnant of its socialist past. That suggestion gave a specific import to radical gestures (including self-immolations) even while announcing them: *that they came more emphatically from the past, and were not really emanations of the present.* Following this, a number of references to the past suggested that self-immolations as a gesture of protest were a peculiarity of such post-socialist contexts with their troubled socialist histories. Jan Palach, the Czechoslovakian student who registered his protest at the end of the Prague Spring in 1969 by self-immolation, was frequently recalled – aptly located in Eastern Europe and the former Soviet bloc – as a sort of symbolic token of context-specific behaviour. Any possible link between an authoritarian regime and a pervasive economic order that might have resonated with present forms of oppression was elided.

Another comment in the international media, *The Guardian* (Siderov 2013), began with the words: "Plamen Goranov set himself alight in a country desperate to reform itself. Emigration is not at the forefront of Bulgarian minds." This linked self-immolation to "reform" without any whiff of revolution, and that too with a characteristic Western European obsession with – anxiety about – immigration from the East, which was especially topical then:

For Bulgaria, 6 March is a day of national mourning, after Plamen Goranov, a 36-year-old man, set himself alight in protest
against corruption in his home city, Varna. Three days earlier,
inadvertently anticipating Plamen's demise by a mere 24 hours,
the German interior minister Hans-Peter Friedrich had told
Spiegel magazine that should the need arise, his country would
veto Bulgaria and Romania's entry into the EU's Schengen
free movement zone. Membership had been keenly desired by
government officials in both Sofia and Bucharest, which have
long since fulfilled the technical criteria for admission. Many in
Bulgaria find symbolic value in the near coincidence of the two
events. What is more, spurred by a European Central Bank operating in crisis mode, Bulgaria's centre-right government imposed
a strict regime of austerity that all but choked the economy, fed
unemployment and caused people's disposable incomes to plum-
met. All the while Bulgarians were being told that it was a point
of pride they had one of Europe's lowest debt-to-GDP ratios and
that fiscal health was a pan-EU priority of the first order. Plamen
Goranov's sacrifice may not resonate in the west as loudly as Jan
Palach's did during the Prague spring 40-odd years earlier, but
to Bulgarians it is just as cathartic. (Siderov 2013)

Despite gestures towards the shadowy pressure of EU
policies, Bulgaria's circumstances and Bulgarian desires are presented as a closed-in, internal matter; and Goranov's act seems
a localised event – a protest against corruption in his home city
(an isolated niche of political corruption). On 6 March 2013,
Bulgaria was refused entry into the Schengen zone. This might
have been prompted by raising another context-specific spectre
altogether – the Balkans as a "powder keg" – and associating
self-immolations with that, as in this quotation:

Of the many popular responses to the European economic crisis
– which includes Italy's recent election elevating a political party

run by comedian Beppe Grillo – Bulgaria's self-immolations
are clearly on the more extreme side. Though the protests have
brought about instant, visible change, the political deadlock facing the country is not likely to alleviate grievances any time soon,
leaving the door open for further escalation. While not quite at
the level of a "Balkan Spring" just yet, the extreme tactics of protesters in a region already known as a powder keg risk not only
heightening political tensions in-country but possibly adding fuel
(so to speak) to conflicts in neighboring Greece and Romania,
also grappling with the volatile popular response to the economic
crisis. (Moftah 2013)

The more of-the-moment frame for positioning protest at the
time was that of anti-austerity movements across and beyond
Europe in the aftermath of the financial crisis of 2007–08. This
frame appeared only fleetingly in international media, and was
neglected in the Bulgarian media. The BBC (2013a), for instance,
featured the photo caption "There have been two months of protests against austerity" in reporting the fourth case of self-immolation, but the act itself was termed "an incident" with "motives
unknown", following "weeks of protests against poverty, high
fuel bills and corruption". Within Bulgaria (as Lessenski (2013),
Ivancheva (2013a; 2013b) and others have observed) "anti-austerity connections" were not mentioned; no framing of self-immolations in terms of anti-austerity protests around Europe was
mooted. Instead, they were framed at times through the different terminology of "anti-monopolist" protests, thus allowing for
a separation from the wider EU protests. Again, a peculiarity of
"domestic arrangements" was effectively carved out, apparently
delinked from and indifferent to global concerns that were nevertheless very much on the doorstep – and indeed were inside the
domestic domain.

All media outlets, Bulgarian and international, were comfortable with placing self-immolations as protest in terms of "economic depression" and "poverty". These terms sound sympathetic and at the same time serve to obscure political causes and agencies, merely registering an unfortunate "condition" of vague provenance. The quotations below usefully capture the media discourse in which "protest" and a vaguely endemic "condition" are articulated in the same breath, in a sequence that is firmly affirmed with each subsequent suicide:

10 March 2013
Early on Sunday a 53-year old father of five who set himself on fire last month in desperation from poverty in the central town of Radnevo died from his burns, becoming the third victim of self-immolation since the protests started. (Tsolova 2013)

14 March 2013
Bulgaria was shaken over the past month by massive street rallies against growing poverty and unemployment that exacerbated people's perceptions of corruption and cronyism of the political elite. Four men had set themselves on fire in the first self-immolations in Bulgaria in decades [...] The severely burned body of a 45-year-old woman was also found on Thursday in a park in the central city of Plovdiv with the initial probe again pointing to suicide, local prosecutors said. Psychologists said poverty and despair were the reasons behind the self-immolations and an increasing number of suicides in the country. Only one of the men who burned themselves – 36-year-old Plamen Goranov – had voiced any political demands before setting himself on fire in the Black Sea city of Varna on February 20. Goranov's death turned him into a symbol of the weeks of anti-corruption rallies in the EU's poorest country that prompted the right-wing government to resign last month. (AFP 2013)

20 March 2013

A Bulgarian man set himself on fire Wednesday to protest poverty in his country, becoming the sixth citizen to do that in a month. The dramatic self-immolations have continued, despite an appeal by Bulgaria's influential Orthodox Church that such desperate actions must stop. They also have been part of nationwide protests that recently brought down the country's center-right government as punishment for its inability to fight poverty and injustice. On Wednesday morning, in the northern village of Sitovo, a 40-year-old unemployed man doused himself with gasoline and tried to commit suicide, said Dr. Daniela Kostadinova, head of the hospital where the victim was taken in critical condition. The unidentified man said he could no longer afford to even buy bread for his one child and that he "could not stand it anymore," the doctor said on Bulgarian National Radio. (Toshkov 2013b)

Amidst these kinds of accounts, self-immolations as protests were gradually reduced to being meaningful in a local way and targeted towards the local political elite. Within the country that meant the entire political class, but elsewhere it seemed contained within a (not especially large or influential) nation-state. An obvious association connecting self-immolations and protests at the time could have been made between Mohamed Bouazizi's suicide in Tunisia and the "Arab Spring" that followed. Even if it fleetingly appeared, it was eschewed by all sides.

The following brief dialogue between the anchor woman and the local correspondent Diana Radeva, broadcast on CNN on 22 March, exemplifies the main points made above:

> *Radeva:* Bulgaria is one of the poorest countries in Europe, so the answer will be really simple – in the winter the price of heating is extreme; after crisis measures people have become

even more poor now and this is their way to say, "Hey, I am here, I want to live in a better way." And their sacrifice is not in vain – we have seen the government resigning and the mayor of one of the biggest cities also left office. But the real change is yet to come, because the politicians don't have a choice now anymore and they are obliged to listen to the people. Otherwise nobody knows what is going to happen here in Bulgaria and when these cruel forms of suicide will stop.

Anchor: … when we see people setting themselves on fire like this and all this anger, especially economic and political, with the government, could there be a wave of revolution in Bulgaria, like we saw in Tunisia?

Radeva: I … I … don't know. Nobody knows *that* for now, because also, you know, in Eastern Europe, we have a history of self-immolations, dating back to communist regimes. This is how people protested against Soviet Union rule and the most vivid example is the Czech Jan Palach who became a hero. Actually, I believe that now in Bulgaria we should solve the problem and everything will be peaceful and quiet, because you know that we have elections here at the beginning of May. (CNN 2013)

The socialist past and Bulgarian exceptionality served to soothe anxieties about and pacify the radical potential of protests and self-immolations.

Exceptional individuals and ordinary people

As the above quotations show, initially the stories of individual self-immolators were recounted in public – they had names, ages, occupations, families, friends, personalities, circumstances, and so on. They were momentarily rendered exceptional by the fatal means of protest they had chosen. They, so to speak, made an intervention in the "national conversation" by committing suicide. In turn, the national conversation shaped their particular interventions in the accumulating self-immolation archive. In due course, these individuals seemed to coalesce into an exceptional collective, and self-immolation acquired the force of a collectivised intervention.

However, Plamen Goranov – the second to set himself on fire – both remained an exceptional individual in the above sense and, to some degree, later absorbed the collective force of self-immolations as protest.

Goranov's political commitments and the timing and performance of his suicide played their part in this. National and international media noted very soon that he had been active in demonstrations in Varna, and there was no gainsaying the significance of where he set himself alight – in front of the municipal building. For a brief moment, mainstream media hesitantly referred to the psychological problems of an unspecified individual, but the social media exploded in loud disagreement and emphatically demanded that the act be recognised as a political protest. As Biserka Anderson recalled:

> The mainstream Bulgarian media's coverage of Plamen's act has "ranged from deafening silence to attempts at character assassination", as his friends wrote in a manifesto which was shared in social media days before he died, in a bid to tell the truth about Plamen's personality and the motives behind his sacrificial protest act. (Anderson 2013)

In general, the immediate response simultaneously asserted that this self-immolation had unmistakably been an act of political protest and opened bids for interpretively framing *who* the self-immolators were and *against whom* they were protesting. The kinds of divergent accounts, revisions and further revisions that followed are discussed in the previous section.

The manner in which the story of Goranov's protest suicide was to be juxtaposed in relation to "the others" was anticipated in this *New York Times* blog a few weeks after he died:

> A 36-year-old man who set himself alight in the Black Sea city of Varna, hours before the government quit, has emerged as a symbol of the protest movement. Plamen Goranov, a photographer and rock climber, has been compared to Jan Palach, the Czech student who set himself alight in the center of Prague in 1969 in protest of the Soviet invasion of his country.
>
> Mr. Goranov, who lingered for 12 days before dying of his wounds, had told 30,000 demonstrators in Varna that corrupt local officials linked to organized crime were responsible for the country's plight.
>
> The self-immolations also recall the protests of Buddhist monks during the Vietnam War and, more recently, the suicide of Mohamed Bouazizi, the Tunisian street vendor whose death in December 2010 is regarded as the catalyst for the Arab Awakening.
>
> Other, more anonymous suicides in Bulgaria have been linked to economic desperation in a country where the average monthly wage is just $480, the lowest in the European Union, which Bulgaria joined in 2007. (Morris 2013)

In a number of ways this is indicative of how the dynamics of self-immolation-as-protest developed with time. Some self-immolations became increasingly anonymous, while one among them was gradually vested with symbolic weight and filled with unique individual characteristics. The other "symptoms of economic depression" were delegated to statistical value (numbers); in contrast, an exceptional individual stood out as an activist, with a public conscience that he could express lucidly. However, at the onset of self-immolation protests it appeared that Goranov's suicide text could "elevate" the others to a similar status of articulacy, especially since Marechkov's earlier suicide only came to be constructed similarly after Goranov's.

Only the connection with Jan Palach stuck in later narratives; the others didn't. Within the grand narrative of Bulgaria as a former socialist country, self-immolation-as-protest drew upon Jan Palach's act against the Soviet army invasion, only initially noting the political discrepancy between that and protests against a centre-right government. In any case, that discrepancy could be explained away in terms of the meandering path Bulgaria took to arrive at the present: the motto "restart of the transition" could make the present appear as a past distortion (Hristov 2013). And that also made it possible to look into the national past in terms of "mass protests" that recalled those of 1990 or 1996, and that in turn recalled another Plamen who had threatened to immolate himself (and who appeared in the exchange with which I began). This was Plamen Stanchev, who had allegedly threatened to do so if the communist star was not removed from the Communist Party headquarters. This edifice was the repository of the records of the secret service network in the period of authoritarian dictatorship, and it was alleged at the time that these records had vanished. Those spectral secret service ties of the past were now seen as morphing into the hydra of political and financial monsters with connections to organised crime. The fortuitous coincidence of the shared name suggested a mystic and affirmative link. Moreover, the name itself – Plamen – was found to have some symbolic significance, as it means "Flame" (see Childs and Terziev 2013). These circumstances were further accentuated by the fact that Goranov died on national Liberation Day (3 March), and, moreover, central government institutions announced a day of national mourning (6 March). National history and individual gesture seemed to converge on the axes of "memory", "heroism" and "love of freedom".

Various nudges were accordingly given to the story of Goranov's life as told after he died. Goranov's uncertain employment status was now presented as *his* refusal to be constrained by stable employment and bureaucracy, as his desire to remain free. Such free-spiritedness went hand in hand with Goranov's artistic temperament: that is, the freedom of the artist to express himself. So, much was made of Goranov's artistic sensibility as a photographer from early on. As further suicides and suicide texts accrued, Goranov's exceptional stature seemed further enhanced. Within the narrative of anti-corruption protests against oligarchic political elites, the idea that citizens could provide a moral compass in government became of paramount importance. In this regard too, Goranov was adopted as an icon: for example, in forming the grassroots initiative group "VazPLAMENyavane" (enFLAMEd). The initial aims of this were to counter "character assassination" attempts on Goranov while he was in hospital fighting for his life, to assist in finding volunteers for blood donations for his treatment, and to ensure that his political demands were realised. After Goranov's death and the success in achieving an immediate political goal (i.e. the resignation of the mayor), the activist efforts became increasingly geared towards preserving Goranov's legacy and the memory of his life and death. This proved significant as further suicides were reported and the discourse of protest shifted in the ways noted above.

In other words, narratives of Goranov's life, death and their significance went through certain institutional confirmations. By this I do not simply mean that the obvious rituals of memorialisation were performed. Indeed, plenty of those were undertaken, by protesters and by state and media functionaries. For instance, a gathering of citizens of Varna suspended protest actions for a more subdued memorialisation gesture by amassing a monumental heap of stones at the steps of the municipality amidst candles, flowers and images of Goranov. More importantly, while the "leaderless protests" of the winter had definitively rejected the idea of leadership, protesters at this stage attributed leadership qualities to Goranov that had not been discernible in life, and kept him at some distance from and above others who committed suicide-as-protest thereafter. This is well evidenced in the film *Burning Men of Bulgaria* (Vice Media 2013) shot in the summer/ autumn of 2013, which ponders the stories of two self-immolation survivors (Dimitar Dimitrov and Georgi Kostov), and in which the voiceover and spokespersons (friends, professionals, etc.) reaffirm the deeper significance of Goranov's self-immolation.

The institutional confirmations I have in mind came with the setting up of the Plamen Goranov Foundation in the spring of 2013 and the subsequent recognition of his status as an artist and representative of protesters as the "year of protest" unfolded. In the weeks immediately after his self-immolation, Goranov's photographs as creative expression and art had already become part of his identity as a protester. On 21 June, the foundation bearing his name, set up by a close circle of his friends, formally inaugurated itself by opening an exhibition with nine of his photographs at Varna art gallery. It announced its mission as one that aimed "to preserve Plamen Goranov's heritage and to encourage the

creative streak in all Bulgarians" (Kostova 2013), and the curator
of the event publicised the exhibits as follows:

> Plamen creates a utopian world in which reality – often uncomely
> and depressing – clashes with the optimism inherent in all
> people. In his works he succeeds in joining together the desired
> and the real world of his characters as if to breathe confidence in
> them that even on the canvas of misery dreams remain beautiful,
> free [of charge], and accessible. Plamen creates this world with
> found art, not with specifically designed artistic material [...]
> Plamen Goranov's tragic biography turned him into a symbol of
> an entire generation. His implacability in the face of social per-
> fidy culminated in an act the sacrificial power of which we are yet
> to fully comprehend. Focusing on symbolic value, however, may
> potentially lead to schematization. Turning towards the artistic
> world of Plamen is a way to preserve the substance of his
> presence. (Kostova 2013)

Three points seem noteworthy here. First, such an initiative was
aimed at "encouraging the creative streak in all Bulgarians", perhaps to counter collective destructive tendencies. Second, the art
was presented as transcending reality more than engaging with it:
as a bridge between the real and utopian, and seemingly enabling
optimism without seeking real change. Third, the art is decisively
imbued with Plamen's spirit, which seems disinvested of political
commitment – more mystically and symbolically meaningful than
rationally engaged. At a later stage, a film on Goranov appeared,
Plamen (2015), which also foregrounded his artistic sensibility
– and where being artistic was conceived to similarly depoliticising effect (see Gupta 2016).

A further turn of institutional confirmation was concerned with
the continuation of the citizens' agenda to act as a moral check on

compromised Bulgarian institutions. Calls for moral correctives to an oligarchic political class and corrupt institutions dominated the discourse of protest throughout the year. In that vein, the foundation followed "in the path" blazed by Goranov, applying public pressure for disclosure of the results of the investigation into the self-immolation by the prosecutors' office. Demands were made for video recordings of the act to be viewed by independent experts and a citizens' body. To achieve this aim, the Plamen Goranov Foundation circulated an open letter, which appeared in a number of media outlets:

> Plamen Goranov Foundation was set up by Plamen's closest friends who had known and loved him for years and for whom his death is a heavy and inconsolable loss. The foundation does not aim to valorise or politicise Plamen Goranov's personality, but to preserve the purity of his memory and his creative oeuvre and to contribute to popularising the ideas and values of this unique young man [...] Since we are Plamen Goranov's closest friends, we know his character and world view well and had been in close contact with him until the last days before the tragedy. It is our firm conviction that his catching fire in front of the building of Varna municipality is not an act of suicide but probably a fatal mistake in his daring plan to pose an ultimatum before the corrupt governing authorities of the seaside city. (*FrogNews* 2013)

Several reasons were cited in the letter to prove the point made above. To begin with, he had not shared his intention with any of his friends, including the ones he had been with the night before; on the contrary, he had plans to go with a group of friends to Antalya the following week. Further, "Plamen Goranov did not leave a suicide note [...] In the historically known cases of ritual self-immolations, such as Jan Palach and other Czech citizens in 1968 [sic], the protesters had inevitably left suicide notes." Apparently, the contents of the backpack he had with him when he set himself on fire suggested more protracted plans for agitating through the day and for setting an ultimatum later on. The interventions of guards and policemen on the spot were described, and their alleged actions and inaction were questioned. The testimony of one of the members of the medical team that took care of Plamen on the way to hospital was quoted: he testified that Goranov had said, "I don't want to die." After making these points, the open letter then went on to remind readers of the international coverage of the case (referring to the BBC, *The New York Times*, *The Wall Street Journal*, *Der Spiegel*, *Komsomolskaya Pravda*, *Asahi Shimbun*, etc.) and observed that, from an international perspective, not disclosing the contents of the final decision would be "risky for the already shaken reputation of the Bulgarian judicial system". Therefore, it insisted on the public release of the official report of the investigation and demanded that recordings of the incident should be viewed in the presence of individuals appointed by the foundation.

Despite seeming to suspect some sort of cover-up or conspiracy, the letter reiterated salient features of Goranov's heroic and patriotic convictions as these were now understood: continuous citizens' engagement with the practices of institutions at the regional or national level and recourse to citizens to ensure moral rectitude. More interestingly, this public intervention sought to delink *protest* and *suicide*, questioning whether Goranov's self-immolation was suicide while being categorical that it was protest. In the next section, I return to this studied delinking.

Such public pressure worked, and a month later the Regional Prosecution Office in Varna released its findings to public scrutiny. This effectively allowed the self-immolation archive of Goranov to include a confirmatory establishment closure, underlining the exceptional status of Goranov – no other similar investigative report has been published. The inquiry into the case was undertaken against persons unknown for a crime defined by article 127, paragraph 1 of the Penal Code and was terminated with the decision of the supervising prosecutor on 29 July 2013 for lack of grounds in accordance with this article. Given the public interest in the case, the decisions were reported in the media. The *Blitz* news article was entitled "The Prosecution: Plamen Did Not Want to Kill Himself" (2013). The lengthy legal document contained a detailed description of findings at the scene, witness testimonies, biographical details about the deceased, and a retrospective psychological evaluation based on accounts from family members and close associates. The final lines of this decision read as follows:

Dousing himself with petrol was his ultimate form of protest. There is no verbal or written evidence to support a thesis that he had another motive for such a protest (i.e. unsolved personal administrative problems), apart from his clearly formulated civil position. The conclusion about the unusual form of reaction against the state administration in the face of the mayor, the municipal council and other structures has been supported by the conclusions of the posthumous psychological-psychiatric expert evaluation that was conducted. The testimony of the witnesses and the conclusions of the psychological-psychiatric expert opinion give grounds to acknowledge that in Plamen Goranov there had not been shaped ideas of suicide, whether planned or impulsive. At the moment of self-immolation he was

aware of everything around him and was in a state of extreme
tension and excitement. The specific traits of his character
in terms of refusing the influence of other persons, especially
when defending an idea, as well as the fact that the police officer
approached him, taking from his left hand the 11-litre plastic
container, led to his taking an exceedingly high risk, overestimat-
ing the situation and producing a spark by pressing the lighter
which he held in his folded right hand. The actions of all persons
connected to extinguishing the flames and the ensuing medical
activities give grounds to accept that timely measures aimed at
preventing dire consequences were undertaken. Irrespective of
the medical measures taken in accordance with good medical
practice, there developed multiple organ failure resulting in his
death. Prosecutor Desislava Yotova, Speaker of the Regional
Prosecution – Varna. (*Blitz* 2013)

In short, Goranov had not harboured suicidal thoughts. He
was lucid, felt strongly about ideas that did not necessarily
entail a personal agenda, and was inclined to be overly firm in
his convictions. The establishment thus also recognised that he
had acted in protest insofar as dousing himself with petrol was
concerned. But self-immolation was unintended, it officially
concluded.

Professionals and institutions
Needless to say, speculation on individual mental states, with
occasional references to alleged diagnoses, and, subsequently,
a "wave of imitation" are part of the Bulgarian self-immolations
archive. States of mind were mentioned in initial media reports
in relation to Marechkov, and also in relation to Plamen while he
was still fighting for his life in hospital. A typical example goes as
follows:

"People's life of misery influences them not only because of the enormous stress, but also psychologically," observed psychiatrist Tsveteslava Galabova, MD, to explain the actions of the young man. She added that the ostentatious act is a sign of desperation in most cases of self-immolation, while a life full of problems is a reason for the weakening of the entire organism of a person. (*News.bg* 2013)

Yet these were quickly overtaken by protest narratives – that is, narratives that recognised self-immolations as a form of protest and the people who set themselves on fire as protesters who convey a poignant social or political message. Also, although these self-immolations were initially regarded as a form of "collective malaise", they were also considered as calling for reflection – with social lessons to be learned. "Self-immolation is simultaneously a manifestation of an impasse and protest" (BNT 2013), according to an interview republished in a number of articles. The following views of a social anthropologist in news comments represent the norm at the time:

People who feel they are isolated and have no prospect or hope in their lives, and are therefore deeply depressed, are trying to get their feeling of being alive back by this terrible form of self-destruction: the act of self-immolation. Therein lies the ominous paradox – their suicide is an attempt to erase the social non-existence they suffer. When a person feels totally disregarded, like an isolated outcast, and the only message they get from society is that they are unwanted and useless, then this person does not feel alive. They make a dramatic gesture to put an end to their life in a way that cannot go unnoticed. This is exactly what is happening in Bulgaria now. And the moral of all this is that we have created a society where many people do not see a reason to live and have no other means to take part in social life other than to commit suicide. (ITN 2013)

Among the various professional commentaries on the "collective phenomenon", most did not read it as arising from individual dysfunction but from a collective one. That tendency was neutralised to a considerable degree, after the first few cases, by labelling the rest a "wave of imitation" (Grozeva 2013).

At the other end of the spectrum of commentaries, the phrase "Werther's syndrome" (referring to Goethe's novel *The Sorrows of Young Werther*, 1774) became firmly established in the popular vocabulary in Bulgaria with regard to self-immolation waves by 2014. In fact, the activist newspaper *#Protest*, set up as an extension of the grassroots formation *#Protestna mreja* (Protest network) which emerged to overturn the appointment of Peevski, put "Werther's syndrome" as number one in its list of "10 Facts about Suicides and Self-immolations" (Gatev 2014). This article favoured the notion that only the first few self-immolations were for political reasons and the rest were imitations inspired by media exposure. A connection between self-immolation and the "economic recession" (i.e. the financial crisis) came a low eighth out of the ten things, only to suggest that this is "not only relevant to our context" but also to "Western contexts". The piece concluded by briefly registering tendencies in overall suicide rates in Bulgaria. As a whole, the article is useful for charting shifts that had taken place in the Bulgarian self-immolations archive between summer 2013 and late 2014. To put it succinctly, in the interim a wedge had been driven between self-immolation and protest – by pointing to "other contexts", by turning it into a somewhat indulgent "syndrome", by moving from "authenticity" to "imitation", by gradually emphasising the psychological over the social. These shifts had in fact already been set in motion by April 2013.

Initially it was left to the discretion of individual members of the Bulgarian clergy of different denominations to find a balance between the theological canon, which forbids suicide, and the practice of offering solace to relatives of the deceased in individual memorial services (as in the cases of Marechkov and Goranov). Then the new Orthodox Church leadership was called upon to consolidate a position and become more active. The church was one of the few functioning national institutions at the time (for a period only the presidential office appeared to be functional), and the newly elected Patriarch Neofit (who became head of the church on 24 February 2013) had appeared in various public forums to denounce suicide and urge people to turn to their faith. After meeting with the new caretaker premier Marin Raykov, the Patriarch was quoted as saying: "Do not take your life under any circumstances. There are other ways to solve problems than through monstrous death." He also urged people "not to fall prey to the lack of hope but seek strength in God" (AFP 2013). As the number of self-immolation fatalities grew and social unrest resurged after a brief respite of a week for the caretaker government to "settle into office", on 4 April President Rosen Plevneliev appealed to church leaders of different denominations to ask the people of Bulgaria not to succumb to desperation, and to jointly hold three days of prayers for "the peace, health and well-being of the Bulgarian people". The church leaders accepted the appeal, and as services were held over the following days (BBC 2013b), Plevneliev gave the following statement:

> [A] desperation [has] gripped Bulgarians and we have seen its consequences in the last weeks, not only with the increased number of self-immolations across the country but also with the wave of suicides we witness [...] In overcoming the hardships, we should

all, together, learn a lesson, to have more faith. Faith has preserved us as a people throughout centuries [...] In this difficult situation for Bulgaria it is very important that all of us – the state institutions, the citizens, the spiritual leaders – unite and seek the right decisions for the country and the people. To pray for the lonely ones and to show solidarity. In Bulgaria there exists a strong basis among all religious communities for understanding, tolerance, and mutual support. The voice and authority of the religious institutions in Bulgaria are very important. These should become ever more important and significant and I, in my capacity as president, will work towards that. Bulgarian society is supported by three fundamental pillars – religion, school and family – and I would like to continue working so that each of them remains a solid basis of the nation. (Presidential Statement 2013)

These appeals evidently resonated not only with the church leaders, who stepped in at that point as voices of authority, but also with public sentiment.

The political aspect of public self-immolations thereafter also acquired different dimensions. They had already been placed frequently within the frame of economic depression but now they were also increasingly related to lack of spiritual guidance or personal spiritual conviction, the failure of familial support networks, and so on. In April there was a break of several weeks in the pattern of self-immolations established by this time. Those that followed during the second half of the year were differently positioned, both in performance (chosen venue) and in reception after the fact. Several suicide attempts in public or institutional spaces were prevented in the summer, while fatalities and survivors of subsequent self-immolations were mostly in smaller towns and villages, often in residential areas or in people's houses. For the most part they failed to be recognised as *protest* suicides (I return to this later), while still being registered as resulting from prolonged conditions of unemployment, financial strain and family debt, among other reasons. The overall suicide rates in the country began to be foregrounded instead of individual cases, subsuming self-immolations as numbers within the category of suicide attempts in general.

Also, the perspective of social psychology began increasingly occupying public discourse, with much rumination on the history and effects of "Werther's syndrome". In fact, as early as January 2013 psychologists had warned about potential dangers along such lines, not in relation to self-immolations but in relation to two murder-suicides, in both of which retired military men were involved (Konstantinov 2013). With the registered "epidemic" at hand later in the year, the rationale of suicide prevention gradually took centre stage. On the basis of tendencies in overall suicide rates in the country since 2008, a national prevention programme had been drafted and submitted to the Ministry of Health for consideration in 2011. This was transformed into the "National Programme for Suicide Prevention and Suicide Prophylactics in the Republic of Bulgaria 2013–2018", which was proposed for official public discussion in April 2013 (see *Zdrave.net* 2013) under the caretaker government, and approved by the Council of Ministers in August 2013 under the BSP coalition government of Oreshar-ski. This was initially financed with annually approved budget allocations, and it envisaged an action plan as well as activities aimed at educating a cohort of general practitioners across the country who were identified as primary points of medical contact for citizens who were potentially at risk. This programme was financed by the Norwegian financial mechanism from December 2014 (Ministry of Health 2013).

Based on ongoing research (Nakov and Donchev 2015), various trends in suicide prevention can now be registered in relation to suicide rates in Bulgaria. Until 2013, Bulgaria had been experiencing a steady growth in overall suicide attempts; in 2013, in fact, a small drop was found in the overall tendency of increasing suicide rates in the years after the financial crisis of 2007–08. The same year was marked as one in which the usually higher summer and spring overall suicide attempts were equalised with those in the winter (in contrast to previous years). Further, while suicide rates do not usually show a straightforward connection between poverty and suicide, in 2013 suicide attempts in villages to the north-west, the poorest region in Bulgaria, were the highest in the country. A presentation by Vladimir Nakov (ibid.), summarising his findings for the period 2008–13, showed decreased suicide attempts where support from family and associates was available – in other words, this suggested that suicides are not necessarily related to unemployment or uncertain employment. To summarise, the spring of 2013 marked not only the moment when decisive institutional measures were undertaken with regard to suicide prevention, but also when the voices of medical professionals began to be called upon regularly. So, for instance, in the interview programme "Dr. Vladimir Nakov: People who Intend to Commit Suicide Send Warning Signals" on Bulgarian National Radio (BNR 2015), medical expertise was sought in view of three suicides occurring on the same night in Sofia.

In addition, medical and government institutions and professionals sought to involve journalists in a series of educational round tables that took place over the course of 2013, advocating responsible journalism and drawing attention to the ethics code for media professionals in Bulgaria. Among other commentary, the "Media" section of *Sega* newspaper (2013b) elaborated on guidelines of professional conduct and mentioned a series of initiatives that the Council for Electronic Media (CEM) was undertaking in cooperation with the Ministry of Health. So, it was in the spirit of "lessons learned" that the news media buzz around the self-immolation of thirty-eight-year-old Lidia Petrova, a photojournalist, in front of the presidency building in Sofia on 3 November 2014 quickly mobilised professional circles and institutions within the country. In the midst of negotiations to form yet another new government (GERB failed to achieve a clear majority in snap elections following the resignation of Oresharski's cabinet), this self-immolation was felt to have tarnished Bulgaria's image in the international media and seemed a regression to 2013. The AFP, RT and BBC, among other media outlets, reported it and made references to six or seven previous self-immolations and the overall poverty and deprivation in Bulgaria, "the poorest country in the EU". Tatyana Vaksberg's appeal in *Deutsche Welle* (Bulgarian edition) was, not uncharacteristically at the time, for professional rectitude among reporters:

> The ethics code of Bulgarian media contains a separate chapter entitled "Suicides". Its contents reveal how the media should cover them: "when reporting on suicides we will avoid disclosing details about the way they were committed, so as to limit the risk of imitation". The essential words in this text are "so as". They indicate that there is sufficient clarity in terms of what the risks entailed in detailed information are – you may create followers. Bluntly put, if you show a person who set himself or herself on fire, it might lead to the self-immolation of another person. (Vaksberg 2014)

Vaksberg also acknowledged some persistent analytical voices that were becoming sidelined and that should be taken more seriously, such as that of Alexey Pamporov, who kept insisting that socio-economic marginalisation was still pervasive in Bulgaria and that self-immolation had become a social trend reflecting it. Vaksberg observed ruefully that: "For a European country however, even if the poorest in the EU, the concentration of 17 self-immolations in less than two years is a fact that is almost impossible to comprehend." Note the rather remarkable difference in the numbers of self-immolations given in this domestic source compared with the international news. In this instance, around a year and a half after protests peaked in 2013, experts in social psychology were called upon to give advice on prevention of further cases and appropriate handling of information. Nikolay Mihailov, for example, appeared on "The Day Begins" morning show of BNT on 4 November 2014, as well as in other media, and spoke as follows:

> Let us avoid the illusion that we know the motives fully […
> When] this tragedy is transferred from the reality of the physical person to media coverage, then this stylisation of the motive happens, it is glamorised and valorised, and then we have a model for imitation constructed by the media and a repetition of the tragedy. This should be suppressed. This is what I want to say and this is where I put the emphasis. Let us be careful and economical in this […] Such a case must not be underestimated in terms of how radical a question it poses before the whole of society. This, after all, is a clear manifestation of our communal failure before the tragic fate of this woman. We can't help but think about our own responsibilities. But we must not look for them irresponsibly and aggressively in terms of our own political bias […] This is a very big risk and is a sign of low existential culture, I would say, it reveals a low level of civilization. (BNT 2014)

Meanwhile, new turns had appeared in narratives of self-immolation. Since the first self-immolator in the capital, the fifty-one-
year-old blacksmith Dimitar Dimitrov, had survived, it was possible to add his "authentic" voice to his own suicide text after the
act. Indeed, that was what some media outlets did immediately
afterwards, and Dimitrov featured in the documentary *Burning
Men of Bulgaria* (Vice Media 2013). In these appearances, he
revealed a distinctive political consciousness and held the political class responsible for the prevailing socio-economic woes in
Bulgaria. Almost a year after his suicide attempt, on 16 February 2014, he appeared on the bTV "Morning Show" and was
interviewed by Kristina Vladimirova. He was announced as the
man who set himself on fire two hours after the president gave the
mandate to form the interim government when Borisov's cabinet
stepped down. Dimitrov said:

> I had paid the fees for the first term of study for my daughter
> and didn't have the money for the second. I must have been
> very desperate, Krissi, must have had enough at that point ...
> In a certain moment you see the dead end you are at ... What
> can I tell you? You are 50 years old, nothing before you, after
> yourself you have left many, many, many things ... [...] so it
> was consciously thought through, since I had left home with
> the gasoline and everything ... [...] and I had decided on the
> presidency because the flame will be visible ... Here, in the
> field, who will see me?! ...

He went on to recount how he had planned his suicide but had
realised how much his close family circle would miss him. He
described the present as "wolf times" and said he had no fear of
fire – he had returned to his workshop several days before the
interview. Then the interview concluded thus:

Interviewer: This, however, will be one of the last days he will be spending in his workshop. He started building it about 20 years ago. The EU standards, however, forced him to close it down. He will soon give his entire equipment to scrap metal.

Dimitrov: I love what I do and I invest my soul in it. But what can I tell you ... When they don't allow you ... when you can face thousands of leva in fines ... What to do? ... Well, I stop ... I nail planks, layer slates or bricks for some [neighbour] ... make 10 leva ... I will go now to Popino near Silistra ... Vines, apricot trees, a field ... Will be helping them in the village ... Well, we will survive ... [...] The recap of the year? Well, just like any other year. Nothing will change. I won't become a millionaire, I don't play the lottery, I am healthy, I live for my children ... (bTV 2014)

It appeared, then, that with hindsight a survivor's sense of politically charged pressure and social disaffection had dissipated to a significant extent. Unlike his earlier interviews (Esslemont 2013), this one suggested that poverty can be overcome by family love and a will to endure. The discourses of suicidology and suicide prevention programmes seemed confirmed. At the same time, the interviewer's reference to EU regulations for small business owners seemingly pushed culpability for remaining causes of dissatisfaction somewhere outside the local or national sphere, to an extrinsic source – although, in fact, the mediators of EU policy in Bulgaria were not too far away. This interview at the very least suggests a sort of retraction, a pulling away from interpretative possibilities that the suicide attempt had opened up. This turn, however, was not confined to self-immolation survivors; such diffusions, retractions and retreats had already spread across the self-immolations archive in Bulgaria, for fatalities as well.

Over the course of the second half of the "year of protest", the continuous increase in self-immolation acts was increasingly delegated to the "private sphere". The social and political factors continued to be contemplated, but the framing of self-immolations had shifted from the dynamism of protests to temperate concern with functioning and socially oriented government institutions. Accentuating that shift, reports on the later self-immolators often alluded to domestic disputes and existing psychiatric conditions, previous suicide attempts, family tragedies and "loneliness" (i.e. lack of a support network, whether provided by social services or simply neighbours). Further, the "public" had also been removed from them, or, alternatively, they had removed themselves from "the public": the acts were largely committed now away from public buildings, institutions and squares filled with protesters, and undertaken in the seclusion of homes, yards and vehicles, in smaller towns and villages across the country. When, in December 2013, twenty-one-year-old Sabin Sabinov died by self-immolation in Varna, the case was reported and received in a quite different spirit from earlier cases (*Trud* 2013b; *Vesti.bg* 2013). Sabinov had been raised by his grandparents as his divorced parents had been working abroad (reportedly in Germany); it was felt that his must have been an isolated upbringing. Public opinion sided mostly with the view that the young man was part of a group with mental disorders, distant from any connection to public protest. This was a departure from the earlier consensus that it is not easy to establish a direct link between psychiatric illness and self-immolations in Bulgaria:

> According to a literature review of deliberate self-burning (DSB) over a 20-year period, conducted by Medecins Sans Frontiers [sic] in 2003, Bulgaria had an average of 7.4 cases per year

(between 1983–2002) and a total number of cases that was only
surpassed among European countries studied by the Nether-
lands. The report, which draws a distinction between psychiatric
illness and political motivation as a causal factor, notes that
Bulgaria had the lowest correlation to mental illness among
European countries studied, with only a third of immolations
stemming from clinical psychiatric disorders. (Hannun 2013)

Perhaps more striking than the weakness of the correlation
between psychiatric conditions and self-immolation in that report
is the observation that between 1983 and 2002 there had been 7.4
cases of self-immolations each year. Evidently, the context deter-
mines whether such cases are noticed or not, and how they are
signified and understood.

Nothing in common

Three years after Goranov's death, some media outlets published
short news items to mark the occasion. I draw on one of them
to signpost how the exceptional suicide archive of Goranov as
protester, and more generally of Bulgarian self-immolations-as-
protest, had fared. On 3 March 2016, *Dnevnik* newspaper published a feature entitled "Today It's Three Years Since the Death
of Plamen Goranov in Varna". After reminding readers of the
details and circumstances of the case, the article continued:

> In memory of Plamen and demanding the removal of Kiril Yor-
> danov, the citizens of Varna had amassed a heap of stones under
> the window of the mayor's office [in 2013]. It disappeared in the
> late hours of 12 February this year under the pretext that there
> are construction works on the sidewalk in front of the municipal-
> ity in Varna. This caused an acute public reaction, since the heap
> was erected during the most massive civic protests in the winter
> of 2013. (*Dnevnik* 2016)

Some of the comments following the article expressed scepticism about the "acuteness" of the public reaction. It was averred that some people had objected during a vigil held on the site, but the numbers of people present were not numerous enough to constitute a *public* reaction, let alone an acute one. Other comments included one that expressed a sort of surprise that it was "indeed on this date" and added "God rest his soul"; "God rest his soul! Stop elevating as heroism the suicide of a sick person, suicide is the gravest sin"; "The man had psychological problems, but evidently nobody wants to admit this"; "Sheep-like Bulgarians (especially petty bourgeoisie like Varna residents) do not deserve to have their Jan Palach. This is why his deed did not lead anywhere"; "There was no point in such a hopeless deed, may he rest in peace!!! There is no point also in amassing stones into some heap; Varna, after all, is a tourist city, this is in the centre of town, and makes the street ugly – what will that lead to?" A few were saddened or outraged by such dismissive sentiments, but the overwhelming majority were along the lines quoted.

It seems that, in the intervening period, Goranov's exceptional status had been largely withdrawn, and he had joined the ranks of the other self-immolators as "simply suicides", all with doubtful soundness of mind – all of whom could be quickly commended to heaven and forgotten.

References

AFP (2013) "Bulgarian Church Leader Decries Self-immolations". Agence France-Presse (AFP), 14 March.

Anderson, Biserka (2013) "Misinformation and Propaganda: British Media Coverage of the Bulgarian 'Problem'". *Spinwatch*, 6 March. http://www.spinwatch.org/index.php/blog/item/5473-misinformation-and-propaganda-british-media-coverage-of-the-bulgarian-problem.

BBC (2013a) "Bulgaria Protests: New Self-immolation in Sofia". BBC News, 13 March. http://www.bbc.com/news/world-europe-21771229.

BBC (2013b) "Bulgaria Holds Prayers to End Suicides and Despair". BBC News, 5 April. http://www.bbc.com/news/world-europe-22039182.

Bechev, Dimitar (2013) "Bulgaria's Anger, the Real Source". Open-Democracy, 14 March. https://www.opendemocracy.net/dimitar-bechev/bulgaria%E2%80%99s-anger-real-source.

Bigg, Claire (2013) "Bulgarian Students Intensify Effort to Topple Government". RadioFreeEurope Documents and Publications, 14 November. http://www.rferl.org/content/bulgaria-unrest-protests-students/25167938.html.

Blitz (2013) "The Prosecution: Plamen Did Not Want to Kill Himself". Blitz, 21 October. http://www.blitz.bg/news/article/229064.

BNR (2015) "Dr. Valdimir Nakov: People Who Intend to Commit Suicide Send Warning Signals". Interview, translated by Kostadin Atanasov. Bulgarian National Radio, 26 May. http://bnr.bg/en/post/100561338/dr-vladimir-nakov-people-who-intend-to-commit-suicide-send-warning-signals.

BNT (2013) "Haralan Alexandrov: Self-immolation Is Protest and an Accusation to All of Us". BNT, 21 March. http://news.bnt.bg/bg/a/97485-haralan_aleksandrov_samozapalvaneto_e_protest_i_obvinenie_kym_vsichki_nas.

BNT (2014) "How Should the Media Report Grave Suicide Acts, Such as Self-immolation". "The Daily Show", BNT, 4 November. http://bnt.bg/part-of-show/kak-tryabva-mediite-da-otrazyavat-tezhki-samoubijstveni-aktove-kato-samozapalvane.

Borba (2013) "A 26-year-old Person from Turnovo Set Himself on Fire Because of Poverty". Borba 35, 20 February. http://www.borbabg.com/2013/02/20/26-%D0%B3%D0%BE%D0%B4%D0%B8%D1%88%D0%B5%D0%BD-%D1%82%D1%8A%D1%80%D0%BD%D0%BE%D0%B2%D0%B5%D1%86-%D1%81%D0%B5-%D1%81%D0%B0%D0%BC%D0%BE%D0%B7%D0%B0%D0%BF%D0%B0%D0%BB%D0%B8/.

bTV (2013) "Self-immolations Show the Need for a Change for the Better". bTV, 17 March. http://m.btvnovinite.bg/article/bulgaria/samozapalvaniyata-posochvat-nuzhdata-ot-promyana-kam-dobro.html.

bTV (2014) "Second Life for the Blacksmith who Set Himself on Fire in Front of the Presidency". "Morning Show", bTV, 16 February. http://btvnovinite.bg/video/bulgaria/obshtestvo/vtori-zhivot-za-kovacha-koito-se-samozapali-pred-prezidentstvoto.html.

Childs, Margaret and Kostadin Terziev (2013) "Plamen Goranov – Martyr of the 'Bulgarian Spring'". The Vienna Review, 8 April. http://www.

viennareview.net/news/central-europe/plamen-goranov-martyr-of-the-bulgarian-spring.

CNN (2013) "Six in Bulgaria Die by Self-immolation". CNN, 22 March. http://edition.cnn.com/videos/world/2013/03/22/intv-bulgaria-self-immolation-radeva.cnn.

Dnevnik (2016) "Today It's Three Years Since the Death of Plamen Goranov in Varna". Dnevnik, 3 March. http://www.dnevnik.bg/bulga ria/2016/03/03/2716580_dnes_se_navurshvat_tri_godini_ot_smurtta_ na_plamen/.

Dress Code (2013) Plamen. [Flame.] Available at https://vimeo.com/ 129381629.

Esslemont, Tom (2013) "Poverty in Bulgaria Drives More to Make Ultimate Sacrifice". BBC News, 8 May. http://www.bbc.com/news/ world-europe-22439961.

FrogNews (2013) "We Want the Truth about the Death of Plamen Goranov". FrogNews, 24 September. http://frognews.bg/news_59124/ Iskame-istinata-za-smartta-na-Plamen-Goranov/.

Ganev, Venelin I. (2014) "The Legacies of 1989: Bulgaria's Year of Civic Anger". Journal of Democracy 25 (1): 33–45.

Gatev, Hristo (2014) "10 Facts about Suicides and Self-immolations". #Protest: the newspaper of the active person, 29 November. http:// vestnikprotest.com/analizi/deset-fakta-za-samoubiistvoto-i-samozapalvaneto/.

Grozeva, Yana (2013) "Death Because of Imitation is a Sickness! (This is Werther's Syndrome Dating Back to the 18th century)". Blitz.bg, 19 April. http://www.blitz.bg/article/34018.

Gupta, Suman (2014) "'Financial' or 'Economic' Crisis? Note on Protests in Bulgaria". Framing Financial Crisis and Protest: Comment and Debate, November. http://www.open.ac.uk/arts/research/finance-crisis-protest/ observations/bulgarian-protests.

Gupta, Suman (2016) "Protest Suicide and the Function of Art". Framing Financial Crisis and Protest: Comment and Debate, March. http://www. open.ac.uk/arts/research/finance-crisis-protest/comment-and-debate/ protest-suicide-and-function-art.

Hannun, Marya (2013) "Self-immolation in Bulgaria Isn't as New as You Might Think". Foreign Policy, 14 March. http://foreignpolicy.com/2013/03/14/ self-immolation-in-bulgaria-isnt-as-new-as-you-might-think/.

Hristov, Ivo (2013) "The Roots of Rebellion: Restarting Democracy". Occupy.com, 26 February. http://www.occupy.com/article/roots-rebellion-restarting-democracy-bulgaria.

ITN (2013) "Bulgaria: Bulgaria Suffers Spate of Self-immolations over

Corruption". ITN Newswire, 22 March. http://www.itnsource.com/en/shotlist/RTV/2013/03/22/RTV010193909/?s=Bulgaria suicide.

Ivancheva, Maria (2013a) "The Bulgarian Winter of Protests". *OpenDemocracy*, 15 March. https://www.opendemocracy.net/mariya-ivancheva/bulgarian-winter-of-protests.

Ivancheva, Maria (2013b) "The Bulgarian Wave of Protests 2012–2013". *CritCom*, 7 October. http://councilforeuropeanstudies.org/critcom/the-bulgarian-wave-of-protests-2012-2013/.

Katsarska, Milena (2015) "Framing the Bulgarian Year of Protest". *Framing Financial Crisis and Protest: Comment and Debate*, March. http://www.open.ac.uk/arts/research/finance-crisis-protest/framing-bulgarian-year-protest.

Katsarska, Milena (2016) "*#The Protest*: Anthologizing, Branding and Institutionalizing Protest". *Bulgarian Ethnology*, "Cultures of Protest" thematic issue, edited by Mila Maeva and Daniela Koleva, pp. 104–21.

Konstantinov, Mihail (2013) "Werther's Syndrome". *Politika*, 25 January. http://www.politika.bg/article?id=30556.

Kostova, Stela (2013) "Opening of Plamen Goranov Foundation". *Facebook*, 21 June. https://www.facebook.com/events/185869884911242/.

Krastev, Ivan (2013) "Why Bulgaria's Protests Stand Out in Europe". *The Guardian*, 30 July. http://www.theguardian.com/commentisfree/2013/jul/30/bulgaria-protests-europe.

Kristeva, Julia (2002) *Intimate Revolt: The Powers and Limits of Psychoanalysis*. Translated by Jeanine Herman. New York NY: Columbia University Press.

Lessenski, Marin (2013) "Bulgaria's Leaderless Protests in the Winter of 2013: The Causes and Consequences Are Here to Stay". Policy Brief 38. Sofia: Open Society Institute, European Policies Initiative. http://eupi.osi.bg/fce/001/0070/files/LeaderlessProtests_EuPIPolicyBrief38March2013.pdf.

Ministry of Health (2013) "Project Has Been Launched to Improve Mental Health Services in Bulgaria". Sofia: Ministry of Health, National Centre of Public Health and Analyses. http://www.ncpha.government.bg/en/news-2/1121-projecthas-been-launched-toimprove-mental-health-services-in-bulgaria.html.

Moftah, Lora (2013) "Bulgarian Mayor Resigns after Self-immolation Protest". *Blouin Beat: Politics*, 6 March. http://blogs.blouinnews.com/blouinbeatpolitics/2013/03/06/bulgarian-mayor-resigns-after-self-immolation-protest/.

Morris, Harvey (2013) "Poverty Blamed for Bulgaria's Suicide Wave". *The New York Times* blogs, 23 March.

Nakov, Vladimir and Tony Donchev (2015) *Suicides in Bulgaria 2009–2013*. Sofia: Military Medical Academy.

Nedeva, Irina (2015) "The Special Issue of *Piron* Is Dedicated to the New Forms of Revolt". Interview with Kamelia Spasova and Darin Tenev, Bulgarian National Radio, 11 June. http://bnr.bg/horizont/post/100567845/izvanredniat-broi-na-spisanie-piron-e-posveten-nanovite-formi-na-bunt.

News.bg (2013) "Plamen from Varna who Set Himself on Fire Already Breathes on his Own". *News.bg*, 2 March. https://news.bg/regions/samozapaliliyat-se-plamen-ot-varna-veche-disha-sam.html

O'Brennan, John (2013) "Bulgarians Confront the Oligarchs". *OpenDemocracy*, 26 June. https://www.opendemocracy.net/johnobrennan/bulgarians-confront-oligarchs.

Petkova, Mariya (2013) "Protests in Bulgaria and the New Practice of Democracy". *Al Jazeera*, 21 February. http://www.aljazeera.com/indepth/opinion/2013/02/201322163943882279.html.

Presidential Statement (2013) "Presidential Statement of Rosen Plevneliev after Meeting Representatives of Religious Communities". Catholic parish St Joseph, Sofia, 4 April. http://sofia.capucini.bg/index.php?option=com_content&view=article&id=264%3A2013-04-07-07-29-23&catid=43%3Az-glosu&Itemid=105&lang=bg.

Sega (2013a) "The Self-immolated Ventsislav Vasilev from Radnevo Died". *Sega*, 10 March. http://www.segabg.com/article.php?id=640060.

Sega (2013b) "Werther's Syndrome, or How Contagious Suicides Are". *Sega* 4655 (78), 2 April. http://www.segabg.com/article.php?id=643246.

Siderov, Yavor (2013) "What a Terrible Time for Europe to Show Bulgaria the Cold Shoulder". *The Guardian*, 6 March. http://www.theguardian.com/commentisfree/2013/mar/06/bulgaria-europe-plamen-goranov.

Spasova, Kamelia and Darin Tenev (2015) "Editorial". *Julia Kristeva. Form and Meaning of Revolt* 10. http://piron.culturecenter-su.org/category/broi-10-julia-kristeva-forma-i-smisul-na-bunta/.

The Economist (2013) "Bulgaria's Crisis: Poverty Protests. Desperate Demonstrations against an Ephemeral Government". *The Economist*, 23 March. http://www.economist.com/news/europe/21574034-desperate-demonstrations-against-ephemeral-government-poverty-protests.

Toshkov, Veselin (2013a) "Bulgaria Experiencing Spate of Self-immolations". Associated Press, International News, 14 March.

Toshkov, Veselin (2013b) "Desperate Bulgarian Man Sets Himself Ablaze". Associated Press, Business News, 20 March.

Trud (2013a) "Plastic Shaped like a Dove Remained from the Jacket of Self-burnt Trayan". *Trud*, 17 March. https://www.24chasa.bg/Article/1847633.

Trud (2013b) "Sabin Who Set Himself on Fire Asked his Grandmother for Money and Bought Petrol". *Trud*, 9 December. http://bg.time. mk/c/9ca2638aac/zapalilijat-se-sabin-poiskal-pari-ot-baba-si-kupil-si-benzin.html.

Tsolova, Tsvetelina (2013) "Bulgarians Protesters Demand Stop of State Railway Sale". Reuters, 10 March. http://www.reuters.com/ article/bulgaria-government-protests-idUSL6N0C230D20130310.

Vaksberg, Tatyana (2014) "Don't Show Lidia!" *Deutsche Welle Bulgaria*, 5 November. http://www.dw.com/bg/%D0%BD%D0%B5-%D0%BF% D0%BE%D0%BA%D0%B0%D0%B7%D0%B2%D0%B0%D0%B9% D1%82%D0%B5-%D0%BB%D0%B8%D0%B4%D0%B8%D1%8F/a-18040002.

Vesti.bg (2013) "The 21-year-old Sabin Who Set Himself on Fire in Varna Died". *Vesti.bg*, 13 December. http://www.vesti.bg/bulgaria/incidenti/ pochina-21-godishniiat-sybin-samozapalil-se-vyv-varna-6000711?page= 0#commentsContainer.

Vice Media (2013) *Burning Men of Bulgaria*. Produced by Wesby Enzinna. Available with English subtitles on YouTube. https://www.youtube. com/watch?v=WqxyogULa3U.

Zdrave.net (2013) "National Programme for Suicide Prevention: How Far Are We from Realizing It?" *Zdrave.net: The Bulgarian Health Portal*, 10 April. http://www.zdrave.net/news/aktualna-tema-211/natsionalna-programa-preventsia-samoubiystvata-57062.

TABLE 4.1 Self-immolations, attempted self-immolations and prevented attempts in Bulgaria, 2013–15

Date	Name	Age	Town/village	Location	Status
18 Feb. 2013	Trayan Marechkov	26	Veliko Turnovo	In the street	Fatality
20 Feb. 2013	Plamen Goranov	36	Varna	In front of the municipal building	Fatality
26 Feb. 2013	Ventsislav Vasilev	53	Radnevo municipality	In the municipal building	Fatality
13 Mar. 2013	Dimitar Dimitrov	51	Sofia	In front of the presidency building	Survived
15 Mar. 2013	Daniela Nakova	45	Plovdiv	On Youth Hill	Fatality
20 Mar. 2013	Todor Yovchev	40	Village of Sitovo	In the stadium	Fatality
24 Mar. 2013	Unnamed male	73	Sofia	In front of the presidency building	Prevented
27 Mar. 2013	Nikolay Gatsev	48	Botevgrad	In front of the flat of a person under eviction notice	Prevented
1 May 2013	Ventsislav Kozarev	47	Smolyan	In front of a supermarket	Fatality
5 June 2013	Georgi Kostov	31	Dimitrovgrad	At home	Survived
11 June 2013	Todor Dimitrov	59	Harmanli	In the yard of his home	Fatality
11 July 2013	Chavdar Yanev	55	Sofia	In front of the Supreme Judicial Council building	Prevented
18 July 2013	Unnamed male	Not stated	Sofia	Eagle Bridge, in rally crowd	Prevented
23 July 2013	Unnamed male	48	Dupnitsa	At home	Survived

TABLE 4.1 *Continued*

Date	Name	Age	Location	Place	Outcome
7 Aug. 2013	Unnamed male	41	Sofia	In the underpass of the National Palace of Culture	Prevented
12 Aug. 2013	Unnamed female	37	Sofia	In the Slatina residential area, in the street	Survived
15 Aug. 2013	Nadezhda Sultova	74	Village of Ploski	At home	Fatality
16 Aug. 2013	Unnamed female	Not stated	Kazanluk	In a mobile operator service centre	Prevented
15 Sep. 2013	Nikolay Kumanov	42	Village of Stezherovo	In his car	Fatality
16 Sep. 2013	Milko M. and Zhivka M.	52 and 49	Village of Nikola Kozlevo	At home	Survived
27 Oct. 2013	Atanas Atanasov	38	Dupnitsa	At home	Survived
9 Dec. 2013	Sabin Sabinov	21	Varna	On the green near the TB clinic	Fatality
13 Jan. 2014	Todor Atanasov	61	Pazardjik	In the office of the Territorial Expert Medical Commission	Survived
15 Jan. 2014	Georgi Ivanov	37	Glavinitsa, Silistra region	At home	Fatality
5 Feb. 2014	Gospodin Dimitrov-Zaksa	Not stated	Burgas	In prison	Prevented

Date	Name	Age	Location	Place	Outcome
1 June 2014	Unnamed male	58	Village of Krushare, near Sliven	In the street	Survived
27 July 2014	Unnamed male	25	Sofia	In the Lyulin residential area, in front of the block of flats where he lived	Fatality
12 Sep. 2014	Dimitar Zhelev	42	Near village of Mirolyubovo	On the road near the village	Fatality
3 Nov. 2014	Lidia Petrova	38	Sofia	In front of the presidency building	Fatality
11 Nov. 2014	Todor Barzashki	30	Koinare	At home	Survived
19 Nov. 2014	Desislava Koleva	28	Pernik	In a garage	Fatality
8 Dec. 2014	Unnamed female	32	Stara Zagora	In the street	Fatality
26 Dec. 2014	Stanka Yankova	82	Village of Varbovka	At home	Fatality
3 Feb. 2015	Unnamed male (B. P.)	45	Village of Poibrene	In his car	Fatality
11 Apr. 2015	Unnamed male	Not stated	Sofia	On the green between blocks of flats	Fatality
4 May 2015	Unnamed male	Not stated	Kazanlak	At home	Fatality

FIVE | Self-effacing suicides and troubled talk

Suman Gupta

The individual life

The suicide archives discussed in the previous chapters gathered and grew around a particular idea: that those committing suicide were apparently doing so as individual acts of political protest. This notion was variously accentuated, honed, contested and dispersed through the suicide texts that accumulated after Mohamed Bouazizi's self-immolation in Tunisia, Dimitris Christoulas's suicide by publicly shooting himself in Greece, and amidst a series of self-immolations in Bulgaria. Discussions of these cases developed, at least initially, by conferring a resistant and anti-establishment political agency on the persons committing suicide. Understood as politically active gestures, these suicides could be called upon to activate anti-establishment mobilisations and protests, or their effects had to be managed by establishment authorities, according to contextually specific pressures.

At a broader level, the political resonances of these acts of suicide as traced in their archives, although ultimately manageable and unfailingly pacified in various ways, have a similar ideological significance. They transiently but powerfully disturbed the dominant political order of the present, not only in local settings but also in terms of the ideological principles that underpin that order, so with global ripples. That is to say, the political

resonances of these suicides served to render establishment ideological principles opaque both locally and globally, sharpened
awareness of their import, and clarified their contradictions and
their consistent complicity with coercive power – a complicity that is usually either emphatically denied or presented as an
exceptional and pragmatic necessity. State policy directives,
party-political rhetoric, media framings, commercial interests,
religious sanctions, specialist (especially juridical and public
health) processing, and certain kinds of academic interpretations
are intricately woven into each of the suicide archives discussed
in previous chapters. Their interpenetrations articulate the local
contexts of the suicide archives in question, and they coalesce
along the lines of the prevailing global ideology and dominant
political order of our time; these have been prolifically discussed
already as a neoliberal ideology and order. Through the refrac-
tions of different contexts, these suicide archives converge and
are grounded in a pervasive neoliberal condition, within which
the economic squeezing of (and systematic increase in insecurity
among) ordinary people interlocks with a close control of ordinary
lives, at the behest of locally ensconced elites and for the benefit
of a global alignment of elites. The pervasiveness of this condition thus appears to be a natural or inevitable political and economic order. The suicide archives also show that this neoliberal
order is constantly naturalised through moral claims and coun-
ter-claims, with all sides championing "freedom", "democracy",
"rights", "dignity", "peace" and so on in contradictory ways. It
seems that moral claims and desires themselves then become a
means of both upholding and challenging the establishment, in
ways that ultimately reaffirm the dominant neoliberal ideology
from all directions, or at least empty resistance of its ideological

content. No regime change could then be very much more than a replacement of what preceded it, perpetuating the essential neo-liberal economic and political order and its ideological discourse. The suicide archives examined in this book also reveal that the contemplation of suicide-as-protest – the association of suicides with resistance – does, however, *disturb* the prevailing establish-ments and their global partners. It does call for an uneasy pause – though not for long, only for as long as it takes for establishment systems to manage the moments of disturbance. Nevertheless, these suicide archives offer unsettling fissures in the smooth sur-face gloss of the pervasive neoliberal condition.

Arguably, these fissures surface irresistibly, even if transiently, because of the manner in which individual life is inscribed in the neoliberal condition and its establishment discourses and moral claims – the manner in which individuals are recognised and talked about. By way of a conclusion, a few notes follow on how talking about the individual apropos of suicide and politics structures the suicide archives in our time. This is facilitated by considering a different perspective on the political resonances of suicide; another kind of individualised suicide archive with polit-ical resonance is therefore discussed below, distinct from those where suicide is received as an act of protest. These are individual suicides that seem politically noteworthy, and that may be aligned with discourses of protest, but which are not considered acts of protest in themselves. The reception of this kind of suicide offers scope for examining the limits of acceptable ways of talking about individual suicides and politics within neoliberal discourse, and the tensions and discomfort that are found even within those lim-its, and the potentials that arise for exploding those limits. I think of these as *self-effacing suicides* with political resonances, such as the so-called "economic suicides" in Italy and "eviction suicides" in Spain. A section is devoted to each of the latter in this chapter, and then some general observations on ethical concerns and anxieties involved in reporting and discussing suicide are offered.

"Economic suicides" in Italy

One of the points made in each of the preceding case-specific chapters is that the focalised suicide-as-protest always appeared as a singularity among other less-noted or publicly neglected suicides. That is, it appeared as one among other suicides that could similarly have been construed as acts of protest, thus calling into question why this one was highlighted in particular. More importantly, the highlighted suicide-as-protest seemed rather unfairly to divert attention away from a great many other suicides that were not acts of protest but which were perhaps equally indicative of social malaise and disaffection – suicides that could be considered passive symptoms of a political condition rather than gestures of protest against that condition. So, it was observed that before Bouazizi's or Christoulas's defiant self-killings there were numerous other inarticulate and self-effacing suicides with passive political resonance. In Bulgaria, the form of self-immolation assumed proportions that seemed to drown out the political resonance of self-effacement in suicide, which meant that eventually self-immolation itself – despite its spectacular and affective character – appeared to become dumbed down to passive political significance. The individual case of suicide as concerning a passive victim of prevailing political and economic conditions, not voluntarily acting but tragically surrendering, fits into the most neutral way of tracking the incidence of suicide in relation to socio-economic factors: in terms of suicide rates and statistical trends. Such individual suicides could be thought of as anonymous points on the line in the graph that tracks suicide rates. And tracking suicide rates could be regarded as evidence of the conscientiousness of the prevailing ideological establishment (if not the specific regime in power), a sign of its determination to detect social anomalies and act upon them through its own beneficent volition. So, when even such passive self-effacing suicides occasionally become individualised and accrue political resonance through suicide texts, a discomfort in talking about suicide becomes manifest – and that discomfort appears in painfully contriving acceptable limits on such talk.

One of the breaking news articles on Christoulas's suicide discussed in Chapter 3 (in *The Telegraph* on 4 April 2012) ended by moving from Greece to Italy:

> The high-profile suicide [Christoulas's suicide] came a day after a 78-year-old Italian woman threw herself from the balcony of her third-floor apartment in protest against a cut in her monthly pension from 800 euros to 600 euros. The pensioner, from the town of Gela in Sicily, was reportedly worried about how to make ends meet [...]
>
> Her death came a week after a 58-year-old businessman tried to commit suicide by setting himself alight while sitting in his car outside a tax office in Bologna in northern Italy. He was apparently protesting against the rejection of his appeal against a claim for unpaid tax [...]
>
> A day later a 27-year-old Moroccan immigrant set himself on fire in protest at not being paid for four months. The construction worker doused himself in petrol outside the town hall of Verona, also in northern Italy. He too was treated in hospital for horrific burns. (Anast and Squires 2012)

In fact, such individual "economic suicides", as they came to be called, in Italy started being reported regularly from 2012, not just in Italian news media but in the international press too. These included the suicide of an elderly couple "after losing their home, jobs and dignity due to the crippling economic crisis", reported in *The Daily Express* (Moran 2012). The case of a forty-one-year-old publicity agent who killed his two children before committing suicide, along with two cases of public suicides, one by shooting himself in the head and another by self-immolation, were outlined to exemplify "more than 80 Italians whose suicides and deaths can be linked to austerity measures since the beginning of the year" in a *Newsweek* report (Nadeau 2012). Twelve austerity-related cases were individually detailed on the World Socialist Web Site (2013), by way of giving a sense of 30 similar cases that had occurred since January 2013:

> Those who committed suicide included chronically unemployed workers, some who recently lost their jobs or had been otherwise unable to make ends meet, as well as indebted small businessmen. They included individuals as well as couples and families, younger and older workers, immigrants and Italian nationals. Some of these incidents took place in public in shocking fashion, while more frequently people took their lives while hidden from view, leaving friends and neighbors to find their bodies. (WSWS 2013).

Three suicides were similarly outlined in an *Al Jazeera* report shortly afterwards (Scammell 2013). And so it continued ... "A pensioner in Civitavecchia, near Rome, hanged himself after his €100,000 investment in Banca Etruria was wiped out" (BBC 2015); "A 54-year-old man from Palermo committed a horrific suicide on Wednesday by setting himself on fire in his car at a busy fruit and vegetable market. Ferdinando Bosco spiralled into suicidal depression after losing his job" (*The Local* 2016).

Reports on such cases individualised the suicides sufficiently, albeit fleetingly: in each instance the age and occupation and sometimes the name were given, the circumstances of the suicide were outlined (occasionally with a statement from a family member or official), and the economic crisis-related cause was stated. But for none of these specific "economic suicides" – even where the suicide was publicly and spectacularly enacted – was there a serious suggestion that these were acts of political protest, against the prevailing establishment. Rather, they were cited and outlined to accentuate patterns larger than their individual instances, to characterise the effect of the economic crisis and austerity broadly, to gesture towards general conditions of impotency and helplessness (arising from unemployment, destitution, etc.), to put them amongst other such cases and, invariably, amongst such statistical indicators as seemed relevant. So the individual act repeatedly became part of a collective phenomenon. Nevertheless, they were individualised to a sufficient extent, and as individuals very few were anonymised – rather, each case appeared to float up vividly, but then to almost immediately drown within the larger phenomenon and pattern. It appeared that the individual instances needed to be kept in view not merely to accentuate but also to *confirm the larger pattern.* Perhaps more precisely, the individual instance appeared in these suicide texts to *reconfirm* patterns that readers would already have anticipated, or have accepted in advance. Any shock of a Great Refusal in such a suicide, which could release the energies of a political protest, was already neutered by a general discomfort; the individualisation of passive self-effacing suicides had the effect of articulating a simmering discomfort without quite allowing implosions.

To some extent, the affective appeal of "personal stories" that news reports exploit comes to mind as a ready explanation for such repeated individualisation of suicides. To that extent, it is routinised consumer behaviour and profiling – the appeal of the sensational – that is exploited in these suicide texts. While that was undoubtedly exploited, it was done with circumspection, briefly though repeatedly: the discomfort of noting the individual suicide as news carried more intent. Political expediency often played more of a part in the appearance of such news. The reporting of such suicides seemed to intensify at various junctures when austerity measures were being hotly debated and protests were being organised against them. Towards the end of Prime Minister Silvio Berlusconi's colourful career, in the face of a debt crisis, the Italian Senate approved a much contested austerity package in September 2011 – effectively reducing labour protections and public spending and increasing taxes. The effects were exemplified most frequently in terms of cases of suicides in the years 2012 and 2013. In October 2014, Prime Minister Matteo Renzi's Jobs Act was passed by the Senate, removing remaining protections for workers and increasing the powers of corporate employers. Such suicides were reported and cited before and after the event, and were picked up in various protests. A rally in October called by the Confederazione Generale Italiana del Lavoro (Italian General Confederation of Labour) was ironically dubbed "Italy's Economic Suicide Movement" in the *Wall Street Journal* (2014), ever the champion of neoliberal policies. However, the double-speak in that phrase was, in a way, apt: the reproach contained in evoking the self-effacing "economic suicide" could be played upon by both sides. For anti-austerity protesters, such evocations decried the effects of government policies; but, at the same time, these suicides could also be cited to underline the seriousness of the debt crisis that those measures were ostensibly meant to deal with. Either way, noting and citing such self-effacing "economic suicides" were not so much to voice anti-establishment positions as to articulate reproach, calling attention to the establishment's – the liberal state's – obligations. Suicide could be construed only as the "collateral damage" of either the debt crisis or austerity measures, not as a gesture calling the very validity of the establishment into question. Suicides could not be thought of as *protests* in themselves, but as material that could be cited for lobbying within the structures of the establishment: that is, the state, corporations and unions, all exhibiting concern about the lot of ordinary people.

There is, however, a further tacit emphasis in the individualisation of "economic suicides" in news suicide texts from, particularly, 2012 in Italy. After 2010, the official body for producing national statistics, the Istituto Nazionale di Statistica (Istat), stopped collating data on suicides, which, until then, had been provided together with an attribution of causes (including economic causes), on the grounds that such attribution is always uncertain. The move appeared to be an attempt by the government to de-recognize the economic causes of suicides, to try to muddy the waters insofar as relating statistical trends to the economic crisis and austerity was concerned. It then appeared that keeping track of this trend became a kind of activist-citizen's duty, and began to be undertaken by non-state bodies. Notably, sociologist Nicola Ferrigni, Director of the Laboratorio di Ricerca Socio Economica (Laboratory of Socio-Economic Research) of the Link Campus

University in Rome set up an Osservatorio sui Suicidi per Crisi Economica (Observatory of Suicides due to the Economic Crisis) in 2012 to record such suicides and produce periodic reports (see Link Lab 2015, covering data for 2012, 2013 and 2014; for an analysis of Istat data on suicides in relation to crisis until 2010, see Pompili et al. 2014). Various controversies and doubts have surrounded this project (detailed in Mackinson 2015), but its activities underlined the withdrawal of official provision and kept the issue alive – and, of course, fed news reportage. Although data such as that provided by Link Lab does not describe individual instances, its unsanctioned effort seems aligned with the gaze of the public – seeking and providing confirmation of what can be exemplified by ordinary experience. Noting the individual cases and totting them up as a matter of conscience appears – regretfully – to have become the duty of citizen-activists as a reproach to the state, to emphasise the discomfort of seeing what the state apparently does not want to see. To some degree, unease about contemplating suicides underpins the duty to enumerate them here, both by keeping numerical track of them and by facing up to the discomfort of their individual and specific circumstances.

"Eviction suicides" in Spain

This discomfort in talking about similar self-effacing suicides appeared with a somewhat distinctive character in Spain, amidst the throes of the financial crisis after 2008. Reports of individual self-effacing suicides due to financial pressures, and especially threats of eviction, have simmered persistently despite – and perhaps due to – a widespread reluctance to talk about them while in fact talking about them. Initially, rising suicide rates were intermittently reported as the financial crisis worsened after 2008, and especially as stringent austerity measures were imposed and a powerful anti-austerity movement appeared. The large-scale anti-austerity demonstrations of 15 May 2011 (the Indignados or 15M Movement), with orthodox estimates of participation across the country exceeding 6 million, were attended and followed by some notice of rising suicide rates and the difficulty of obtaining reliable information on the causes and figures. The information website arising from this movement, 15Mpedia, offers a listing of "suicides related to the crisis" from 2008, referring in most instances to news reports in which itemised cases were mentioned (15Mpedia 2016). These, then, are reported cases, although it is widely accepted that many more were not reported; at the time of writing, fifty-nine are listed on the website as being related to the financial crisis and occurring between 2008 and 2016, of which thirty-nine are due to eviction orders. Particular interest was evinced throughout in the "eviction suicides", and sometimes there was a particular focus on individual cases of eviction suicide. Political expediency played its part here, somewhat going against the natural inclination of both the government and the principal social movement mobilising against evictions – the Plataforma de Afectados por la Hipoteca (PAH or Platform for People Affected by Mortgages). The PAH had been formed in February 2009, building upon an earlier (from 2006) movement campaigning for the right to housing, V de Vivienda (H for Housing). The PAH had participated energetically in the 15 May 2011 demonstrations (for accounts of the social movement's goals and trajectory, see Colau and Alemany 2014 [2012]; Fominaya and Jimenéz 2014; de Andrés et al. 2015). One of the PAH's founders and principal spokespersons, Ada Colau, was elected Mayor of Barcelona in June 2015, representing the citizens' platform Barcelona en Comú.

The issue of evictions, and the cases of suicide related to evictions, had a particular purchase in the context of the anti-austerity protests in Spain. Unusually, according to Spanish law, mortgage holders who are unable to keep up payments may not merely have their homes repossessed by lenders (banks), but might continue to be liable for the loan to the lender if such a condition appears in the mortgage agreement. This means that even after eviction, dispossessed homeowners can be expected by law to repay the loan, effectively entering a condition whereby they are unable to ever own anything again – unless they suddenly become affluent enough to pay off the loan. This legal position underlined the iniquities at the heart of the financial crisis of 2008, which to a significant extent related to sub-prime mortgage lending by banks exacerbated by growing poverty and unemployment due to austerity policies. Moreover, the law revealed the character of neoliberal governance, whereby the state protects the interests of private sector financial organisations such as banks at the expense of the interests of ordinary citizens. It seemed fundamentally irrational that the debt was not necessarily cancelled if the security (the home) against which the loan (mortgage) was given was handed over to the lender (the bank). Elsewhere, for example in the USA, where sub-prime lending and the financial crisis were directly linked, mortgage foreclosure automatically frees the dispossessed homeowner of the debt. One of the basic demands of the PAH was to change the law in Spain so that evicted homeowners could not continue to be in debt to banks, to effect a *dación en pago* or having foreclosure equated to repayment (Colau and Alemany 2014 [2012]: 103–4). The issue of evictions, then, assumed especial significance as symptomatising all that was wrong with neoliberal regimes and austerity measures. As vigorous protests against evictions led by the PAH grew through 2012, calls for reform of the law were heard from various sides, and the matter was raised in parliament in February 2013. However, the ruling party of the time, the Partido Popular (PP or People's Party), opted to keep the law in force on the grounds that revoking it could lead to the financial crisis spiralling out of control, as had happened in the USA. In March 2013, the European Court of Justice ruled that this legal position gave "incomplete and insufficient" protection for mortgage holders, and held that Spanish courts should be able to halt eviction processes when mortgage contracts were challenged in court (Buck 2013). However, the law was not reformed.

Amidst such concerns and protests, the growing incidence of eviction suicides and the accrual of individual tragedies they evidenced naturally drew attention. However, throughout, such attention was accompanied by a reluctance to address the issue, by a sort of principled caution – which, interestingly, both served to keep the issue afloat and became a concern in itself. That the government would be reticent was, of course, only to be expected; so there is no official accounting of statistics relating to possible causes. It was widely suspected initially, in 2011 and 2012, that the media was being overly restrained about crisis suicides (this turned into a news story itself in the right-wing, but critical of PP, *Alerta Digital* (2012)). However, this evidently did not deter a very significant number of reports from appearing, as the 15Mpedia list mentioned above shows, and as is apparent below. And almost all such reports capitalised on the tragic appeal of individual cases of eviction suicide, usually fleetingly outlined as self-effacing victims of larger circumstances. If there was any caution in journalistic circles about the issue, it may have had a great deal to do with cultural qualms (religious qualms, really) about valorising suicide, and, possibly, fear of getting on the wrong side of their establishment sources. Eventually, the government's attitude hardened towards the inconvenient use of media technologies for arousing dissent, and a clampdown followed with the introduction of the Public Security Law in 2014 and its adoption in 2015 (dubbed the *Ley Mordaza* or Gag Law). This introduced punishments for disseminating photographs of police officers that endanger them or are considered obstructive, individuals participating in unauthorised demonstrations outside parliament buildings and in other significant areas, using social media to organise protests and obstructing evictions, among other acts. In a professional vein, reticence about eviction suicides in the media may also be connected to ethics codes on reporting suicides (an issue that arose in the Bulgarian context as discussed in Chapter 4, and of which I have more to say in the next section). Such ethics codes are largely informed by fears about possible copycat suicides, and are strongly endorsed by suicide prevention bodies and mental health experts (as discussed in Chapter 1). Paradoxically, though, one of the responses to the painful public awareness of eviction suicides from suicidologists in Spain was to encourage *more* talk of suicide, exhorting those contemplating suicide due to financial or other pressures to break the "taboo" and speak out. That, too, became part of media narratives at times, occasionally enabling individual cases of crisis and eviction suicides to be singled out for brief attention. At any rate, several television documentaries and reports featuring mental health experts calling attention to suicides appeared (*Informe Semanal* 2012; Documentos TV 2013; Hermida 2016).

Similar caution was also exercised by the main body heading anti-eviction protests, the PAH. So, there was no mention of eviction suicides in the book *Mortgaged Lives* (2014 [2012]), which Ada Colau co-authored with Adrià Alemany, and which lay out the background of mortgage laws in Spain and the PAH's agenda. In the generally upbeat and empowering tone that social movement manifestos prefer, the few individual cases presented were success stories of the movement, and were underpinned by a desire to differentiate them from the sensationalistic tragic personal stories that appeared in the news media:

> The specific cases of people affected, which are referenced throughout the book, are all real. However, apart from the names we avoided including personal data because we consider it unnecessary. While we want to explain the importance of the lives that are at play within the mortgage crisis, we do not want to abuse their personal stories. This is what the media usually looks for, what they call *human interest stories*, and almost never give space for the investigation of the structural causes, nor of the collective struggle over the last three years that has made it possible to begin to listen to much of these individual complaints. (Colau and Alemany 2014 [2012]: 25, emphasis in the original)

The actual incidence of suicide was elided in this, and the discussion only briefly touched on it as a risk among other health problems that eviction threats cause: "The anxiety felt before an impending eviction and the financial death of families causes severe psychological disorders, which on occasion result in, among others, violent episodes, alcoholism, child neglect, family tensions, increase in domestic violence and suicide attempts" (ibid.: 35).

Despite such all-around anxiety and caution in talking about individual cases of eviction suicides, filtered through disquiet about such reserve itself, a few such cases did surface prominently in news media – as suicides that, though not protests in themselves, carried political resonances that could be aligned with ongoing protests, especially at the appropriate political juncture. The suicide of fifty-three-year-old Amaya Egaña, who threw herself out of her fourth-storey apartment in Barakaldo in the Basque region on 9 November 2012 when bailiffs arrived with eviction orders, was widely covered. It was detailed and discussed extensively in Spanish newspapers: in the largest daily, *El País* (Rivas 2012), in the second largest, *El Mundo* (Iglesias et al. 2012), in the left-wing *Público* (2012), and in the Basque-country paper *Naiz* (2012), among others. It was also mentioned cursorily but widely in international English-language news: for example, on 12 November in the *Financial Post* (Davies 2012), *The Guardian* (Roberts 2012) and *The Telegraph* (2012), and in *Bloomberg* (Smyth 2012) on 16 November. Without going into the particular circumstances of Egaña's suicide and the nuances of specific reports, it is possible to speculate on explanations as to why this case was highlighted. Egaña's suicide occurred at a moment when calls for reforming the law for mortgage foreclosure were multiplying from various sides outside activist circles and opposition political parties, even from within the judiciary in Spain and from a range of external observers in the financial sector. The international coverage pinned the significance of this suicide on those broader debates. Between the lines of the Spanish reportage, there was another political nuance – an ideological aspect – to this case that played a part. Egaña had been a councillor for the Partido Socialista de Euskadi (PSE or Socialist Party of the Basque Country) in Eibar, in the province of Gipuzkoa, in the 1980s. Her father was Ramon Egaña, mayor and for many years president of the Socialist Group Eibar. Her husband, José Manuel Asensio, had also been a PSE councilman in Barakaldo between 1995 and 2003.

So Amaya Egaña had not merely shown a personal commitment to socialist principles, but also represented a lineage of socialist political engagement. Her suicide resonated symbolically as the death throes of an equalitarian political ideology in Spain (or at least in the Basque country) under a conservative and neoliberal state. An opinion piece by Rafael Martínez-Simancas (2012) observed that, before Egaña's suicide, the issue had not been significantly on the government's or other political parties' agenda. But her suicide had changed all that, and revealed "that something has gone awry in the environment, has broken the citizens' respect for the big banks and clarified how the cutbacks and efforts to strengthen the financial system and banks are proceeding without sensitivity for them and their families".

Other individual cases of eviction suicides also surfaced in less prominent but nevertheless telling ways because of their particular political resonances – and became peculiarly aligned with anti-eviction protests. Two examples suffice to make this point. On 8 February 2013, thirty-eight-year-old Francisco J. Lema Breton, an unemployed PAH activist, committed suicide by cutting his throat in Córdoba after receiving an eviction notice (Camacho 2013). His involvement with the PAH naturally troubled the upbeat tone of the social movement found in Colau and Alemany's book (2014 [2012]) and seemed to dim its optimism. An article in the anti-capitalist newspaper *Diagonal* (Paratcha 2013) reported several cases of eviction suicide along with this one, and quoted a statement on Breton's case from the Stop Evictions Group of the Assembly of Granada 15M, denouncing it as an instance of "financial genocide":

> The death by suicide in Córdoba of Francisco J. Lema Breton is actually a murder for which all organisations and institutions are

responsible. It is caused by the "state terrorism" being carried out by judicial authorities, by bankers, by politicians and the government of the Spanish state. (Quoted in Paratcha 2013)

The tone of PAH activists darkened with the growing incidence of eviction suicides through 2012 and 2013, and the slogan that these suicides were murder, reminiscent of slogans raised after Dimitris Christoulas's suicide in Athens in April 2012 (see Chapter 3), was not uncommon. As Fomaniya and Jimenéz put it: "Activists in Spain, including the PAH, have reacted to eviction-related suicides by arguing that 'It's not suicide, it's homicide' or, in another version, 'austericide'" (2014: 34). Four days later, on 12 February 2013, an unnamed retired couple – a sixty-eight-year-old man and a sixty-seven-year-old woman – committed suicide together in Calvià on the island of Mallorca (*La Sexta* 2013; Díez 2013; *Daily Express* 2013). They left a suicide note explaining that they were killing themselves because their home was to be repossessed. This double suicide occurred at a particularly heated juncture of political debates about reforming the mortgage law. On 12 February, the legal reform was debated in parliament amidst PAH protests inside the chamber. The ruling PP government had indicated in advance that its members would vote against any reform; reportedly, during the debate their resolve was momentarily shaken when the Basque MP Uxue Barkos informed the house of the double suicide. But PP MPs hardened their resolve very soon afterwards.

Codes for reporters

The discomfort about talking of individual cases of suicide tracked so far in this chapter – and indeed throughout this book –

derives to some degree from the institutionalised dominance of the suicidological approach outlined in Chapter 1, and the programme of preventing suicide. That entails regarding suicide as principally a mental health matter, essentially grounded in the individual psyche, with suicide rates and trends being indicative of causes that affect individual well-being but that need to be addressed at a social (policy) level. From this authority-bearing medical position, the individual condition that results in suicide is always one without volition, akin to a disease which the patient cannot understand and for which they cannot be considered responsible for the consequences. Any evidence of suicidal inclination should therefore be regarded as a symptom; and a patient exhibiting this symptom should be surrendered to (or surrender herself to) the expertise of a doctor (a mental health expert, a psychiatrist), and be helped through treatment and convalescence by friends, family and others (given social support). A normality of not wanting to die could thereby be re-established, a return to health.

In Chapter 1, I cited arguments that suggest that political resonances are released by conferring some degree of rationality and voluntariness to a decision to commit suicide, and that withholding those from cases of suicide is an active mode of depoliticising suicide. This study has not speculated on the causes or intentions that could be attributed to any case of suicide; the endeavour here has been to examine cases where political resonances have been found *after the fact*, which are tractable in the suicide archives that accrue after such acts. So, this study has no part in investigating suicidological assumptions in detail; its interest is in the politics of reception rather than in the political motives underpinning suicides. Nevertheless, suicidological assumptions are imbued in various ways in that reception and need to be addressed here insofar as this is the case. Crucially, they are imbued in some of the basic source material that stands at the interface of politically resonant acts of suicide and the gathering of suicide archives – in news reportage as a first line of suicide texts.

The suicidology and prevention-of-suicide establishment has gradually instituted codes of ethical practice in the public reporting of suicide; this has occurred mainly post-2000 and is particularly targeted towards news media. The argument has been that news reports of suicide could themselves become causes of suicides, may encourage copycat suicides, and need to be regulated accordingly to prevent suicide. Any person or act that is regarded as a "copycat" suggests a suspension of self, so a kind of endemic lack of voluntariness and reason is attributed (not far from being "brain-washed" or indoctrinated). A secondary consideration in these codes is that the well-being of the bereaved should be kept in view. Such ethical codes tend to be examined in terms of application rather than critically, so as to make them work, to train journalists, and so on. (A report by Norris, Jempson and Bygrave (2001, updated 2006) gives a comparative sense of application in various countries in 2001; and a paper by Machlin et al. (2012) discusses how well such codes work.) More importantly, such ethical codes are converted by authority-bearing bodies into lists of instructions for routinised usage, with which, presumably, reporters comply (or may be obliged to comply by their employers) when they produce their first line of suicide texts as news. It is possible that many news reports on suicide are influenced or moderated by these codes of ethics, so that such moderation is tacitly imbued in this first line of suicide texts and therefore into the suicide archive at large. The character of this invisible but probably pervasive influence of suicidological presumptions in the suicide archives is naturally a matter of analytical interest for this study. The very intractability and invisibility of this influence makes it difficult to factor in when analysing any suicide archive, and it has only been acknowledged tangentially at times rather than analysed in the preceding chapters. A bit more analytical weight can be brought to those acknowledgements by briefly but directly contemplating such ethical codes for routinised practice.

The World Health Organization and International Society of Suicide Prevention's *Preventing Suicide: A Resource for Media Professionals* (WHO 2008 [2001]), a set of guidelines for reporters, is possibly the most cited of such codes, and the following observations refer to it. Professional and government bodies in many countries offer more context-specific and detailed guidance, as codes of good practice or with stronger policy endorsement and legal force. Others that circulate widely are *Recommendations for Reporting Suicide* (AFSP 2015), produced by the American Foundation for Suicide Prevention with twenty partners (professional, academic and community bodies), and the Samaritans' *Media Guidelines for the Reporting of Suicide* (2013) – these are very like the earlier WHO *Resource*.

The WHO *Resource*, like its later equivalents, offers a series of instructions for reporters that are of interest to this study, along with a section on evidence of "imitative suicides" which I won't examine here. The document doesn't invite critical engagement: evidence is not presented to be critically examined but to be accepted, and instructions are categorically phrased to be uncritically followed. It is not an academic text, but it appears to exert academic authority by way of asserting bureaucratic authority

– the instructions are the point of this document. Some of its noteworthy directives are listed below.

Avoid language which sensationalizes or normalizes suicide, or presents it as a solution to problems: [...] Terms like 'increasing rates' should be used in preference to hyperbolic phrases like 'suicide epidemic', and caution should be exercised in using the word 'suicide' in headlines. [...] Out-of-context use of the word 'suicide' – e.g., 'political suicide' – may serve to desensitize the community to its gravity. Terms like 'unsuccessful suicide' imply that death is a desirable outcome and should not be used; alternative phrases such as 'non-fatal suicide attempt' are more accurate and less open to misinterpretation. The phrase 'committed suicide' should not be used because it implies criminality, thereby contributing to the stigma experienced by those who have lost a loved one to suicide and discouraging suicidal individuals from seeking help. Rather, one should refer to 'completed suicide'. [...] (WHO 2008 [2001]: 7–8)

Avoid prominent placement and undue repetition of stories about suicide: [...] Newspaper stories about suicide should ideally be located on the inside pages, towards the bottom of the page, rather than on the front page or at the top of an inside page. Similarly, broadcast stories about suicide should be presented in the second or third break of television news, and further down the order of radio reports, rather than as the lead item. [...] (WHO 2008 [2001]: 8)

Word headlines carefully: [...] Use of the word 'suicide' in the headline should be avoided, as should be explicit reference to the method or site of the suicide. (WHO 2008 [2001]: 9)

Exercise caution in using photographs or video footage: [...] pictures of an individual who has died by suicide should not be used. If visual images are used, explicit permission must be given by family members. These images should not be prominently placed and should not glamorize the individual. Also, suicide notes should not be published. (WHO 2008 [2001]: 9)

In the context of this study, these instructions are of greater interest than the underpinning assumptions of suicidology outlined in Chapter 1 and briefly summarised again above. These instructions are undergirded by preconceptions that have a direct bearing on the shape of any suicide archive, as understood and examined here. To begin with, the instructions carry a tacit conception of how language works: that is, how words and phrases are used and how they are strung together and presented (placed) in textual or audio-visual form. On the one hand, it is suggested that language has a dangerously autonomous drive – outside the control of a speaker or author. Language may do more than the speaker or author intended; indeed, it may work to quite the contrary effect of those intentions. On the other hand, it is suggested that listeners and readers are passive recipients of language, responding predictably and automatically to the stimuli of language – so they have no control on the work that language does either, and they are subject to its potentially dangerous misdirections. Given that sense of language, it is best to think of the message that is to be couched in language as somehow already there, prior to language, a pure and one-dimensional rational idea that has to be understood properly before it can be enunciated, and that can be enunciated thereafter in one appropriate way. Further, there is in the above instructions a conception of how information and knowledge should be disseminated. These consist in messages. There are those who understand the messages that need to be couched in language in advance (the authority issuing these instructions here), and those who may be trusted to do the couching if properly instructed (in this case, media reporters), and those who will receive the messages compliantly if those messages are appropriately couched (media consumers). There is a clear pedagogic hierarchy and top-down direction of the travel of knowledge, at least insofar as suicide goes: from, let's say, bureaucrat-specialist to reporter to news reader and audience. According to these instructions, then, the whole sphere of knowledge about suicide is disposed in a rigid hierarchy. Moreover, in those quoted instructions there is also a corresponding conception of the general public – the masses of media consumers, the people at the receiving end of the knowledge hierarchy, the readers and audiences in general. Let's call them the subjects and objects of this knowledge order: they are the base from which the message is extrapolated, about whom the message informs, and to whom the message has to be passed down in appropriately un-interfering language. This general public is constituted of individuals who have only an affective relationship to each other, not a rational one and therefore not a politically aware one. So, there are suffering, mentally disturbed, would-be suicides; there are bereaved people; there are caring people; there are traumatised people and helplessly imitative people and desensitized people; and there are people who may be affected by bad verbal hygiene (by simply beholding the words "suicide" or "political" in the wrong place). In brief, the general public is infantile and needs to be protected from themselves by those who have the message and their trusted functionaries. And, finally, there is a kind of performative conception that comes through these notions of language, knowledge and the general public: that social order is precarious and under constant threat. Vigilance needs to be maintained on everyone's behalf by elites who own the right message and by their trusted functionaries.

Insofar as these instructions represent the thrust of suicidological thinking with the agenda of preventing suicide, it would be fair to say that depoliticisation works here not merely with an effect on those who commit suicide; depoliticisation is tendentiously rendered pervasive. Language, knowledge and the general public are themselves pushed towards becoming disinvested of politics when it comes to talking of suicides. And, in fact, the WHO's production of documents with similar instructions for preventing suicide is not confined to media professionals, but also extends to teachers, physicians, firefighters and the police, prison officers, and indeed managers and workers in general (all post-2000; see http://www.who.int/mental_health/resources/preventingsuicide/en/).

The suicide archives and suicide texts examined in this book suggest that the underpinning preconceptions on which these codes are based are, simply, untenable. There is no way of controlling language or messages or readers and audiences so that political resonances vanish from the contemplation of suicides, even of individual self-effacing suicides. Such an expectation is a fantasy, but the fantastic expectation itself is worth considering further.

A descriptive project
The individualisation of self-effacing suicides with political resonance – the "economic suicides" in Italy, the "eviction suicides" in Spain – was momentary in news reports, and troubled by circumspection and caution about discussing suicide. This circumspection, however, did not stem the political resonances of such suicides – quite the contrary at times – but circumspection could perhaps be regarded as a nod towards the kind of authority-bearing codes of ethics exemplified above by the WHO *Resource*.

As the previous chapters show, when it came to individual suicides that were regarded as acts of protest, very little concession was made to such codes. There were bursts of garrulity in the news media with regard to Bouazizi's self-immolation, Christoulas's shooting himself, and Plamen's and a few others' self-immolations, wherein every point of the WHO *Resource* was directly contravened. The perception of individual suicides as political protest, it might be said, generates a sort of anxiety and fascination that both exacerbates and overcomes the discomfort of talking about suicide. While that discomfort lends at least some circumspection in reporting self-effacing suicides with political resonance, it intensifies when faced with suicides regarded as political protest and becomes a kind of compulsive logorrhoea. Talking about such suicides in a flow of suicide texts, in a rapidly accumulating suicide archive, becomes the path to pacifying this intensified anxiety. It would perhaps be mistaken to pin such production of talk on news media. More precisely, if news media usually overcome their ethical codes and injunctions when faced with suicides perceived as political protest, it is most likely because these suicides have already become reference points in intensive talk – they have already turned into spurs for political action and talk is buzzing in the streets and inside homes and online. The news media then blithely overcome their ethical constraints to join the buzz – otherwise they would lose their standing as conduits for news. In brief, the reading of suicide as political protest could become overwhelmingly and unmanageably news before the ethically conscientious news media could make, or refuse to make, the suicide into news. Also, of course, commercial pragmatism almost always manages to overtake ethical qualms in the daily life of media industries.

And yet, somewhat contrary to that speculation, there are distinctions to be made. Talking about Bouazizi's self-immolation caused fewer qualms than talking about Christoulas's and Plamen's and other suicides that appeared as political protest. The many "copycat suicides" reported after Bouazizi's simply provided fodder for talking some more about his suicide, for celebrating and honouring his self-immolation as protest for a year, and subsequently for gleefully turning it into farce and making him culpable for political disasters. No ethical circumspection kicked in there as far as the news media was concerned. However, after a spurt of anxious talk, reporting about Christoulas's or Plamen's or other putative suicides-as-protests did recall ethical concerns – very studiedly in Bulgaria, as observed in Chapter 4 – and soon the news media became, in a general way, respectfully reserved and dedicated to suicide prevention. Quite possibly, this impressionistically made point is centred on geopolitics. Suicide-as-protest that is apparently directed at the self-professedly liberal establishment in Europe calls for ethical rectitude; whereas suicide-as-protest apparently directed at the establishment in Africa or the Middle East, which is considered authoritarian or illiberal, cancels out ethical concerns. Ethical concerns about suicides such as those enjoined by the WHO *Resource* instructions are possibly lighter or heavier according to the ideological contexts of talk and suicides.

The anxious garrulity and uncomfortable persistence of talk with regard to suicides with differing political resonances that are tracked in this study, in geopolitical contexts that are ideologically differentiated to greater or lesser degrees, present a picture of the political economy of the suicide archive. This is a political economy of talk, organised within media, professional, judicial and academic discourses and institutional forms. The dynamics of this political economy are described by exploring the specific suicide archives to which the preceding chapters are devoted. In a general way, the principles of this political economy of talk are articulated here as being grounded in a pervasive neoliberal condition. They cohere with the operations of neoliberal economy and government, as summarised at the end of Chapter 1 and at the start of this final chapter. The character of neoliberalism is elaborated here – rather than theorised – by detailing how political and economic crises are refracted through the political resonances of suicide traced in these suicide archives. Details in the suicide archives described above dovetail into various theoretically nuanced examinations of neoliberalism as grounded in habit, in close-to-the-bone management of human subjectivity, in the conversion of persons into entrepreneurial beings, in the transformation of everyday life into a continuum of accountable production, in rendering all aspects of human life entrepreneurial, in state apparatuses designed to liberate economic activity from public interest, and in the atomisation of the very notion of public interest into individual culpability and responsibility. To the scholarly cognoscenti, each of those phrases will conjure a host of academic references following, especially, Michel Foucault's (2008 [2004]) characterisation of "neoliberalism" as a descriptive term for a political-economic order of the present in his 1978 lectures (I won't regurgitate numerous references here). To such cognoscenti, the preconceptions implicit in the WHO *Resource* delineated above may seem a fitting illustration of neoliberal vision. This book was conceived by the authors as predominantly a descriptive project. The larger conceptual implications of these descriptions will perhaps only become clear when they are slotted into careful historicist reckonings with the emergence of neoliberalism as organised practice and conceptual structure (such as, for the period covered in this book, Dardot and Laval 2013 [2009]; Mirowski 2013). Meanwhile, this book may be regarded as a prolegomenon for further conceptual effort in that direction. And, simply by having undertaken this description, it might disturb widely held notions about how the political significance of suicides should be talked about.

References

15Mpedia (2016) "Lista de suicidios relacionados con la crisis". Updated page of 20 June. https://15mpedia.org/wiki/Suicidio_crisis.

AFSP (2015) *Recommendations for Reporting Suicide*. New York NY: American Foundation for Suicide Prevention and 20 partners. http://reportingonsuicide.org/recommendations/.

Alerta Digital (2012) "Alarmante incremento del número de suicidios en España motivados por la crisis y silenciados por los medios". *Alerta Digital*, 29 July. http://www.alertadigital.com/2012/07/29/alarmante-incremento-del-numero-de-suicidios-en-espana-motivados-por-la-crisis-y-silenciados-por-los-medios/.

Anast, Paul and Nick Squires (2012) "Austerity Suicide: Greek Pensioner Shoots Himself in Athens". *The Telegraph*, 4 April. http://www.telegraph.co.uk/news/worldnews/europe/greece/9186568/Austerity-suicide-Greek-pensioner-shoots-himself-in-Athens.html.

BBC (2015) "Italy Bank Rescue Marred by Suicide and Lost Savings". BBC News, 10 December. http://www.bbc.co.uk/news/world-europe-35062239.

Buck, Tobias (2013) "EU Court Strikes Down Spain's Eviction Law". *Financial Times*, 15 March. http://www.ft.com/cms/s/0/16e37aca-8ca5-11e2-8ee0-00144feabdc0.html#axzz4GvX1zS5h.

Camacho, Julia (2013) "Un hombre se suicida en Córdoba tras reclamarle un pago por su casa". *Diario Córdoba*, 8 February. http://www.diariocordoba.com/noticias/cordobalocal/se-suicida-en-calle-cartago-un-activista-de-stop-desahucios_781290.html.

Colau, Ada and Adrià Alemany (2014 [Spanish ed. 2012]). *Mortgaged Lives*. Translated by Michelle Teran. *Journal of Aesthetics and Protests* (Los Angeles). http://joaap.org/press/mortgagedlives.html.

Daily Express (2013) "Spanish Couple in Eviction Suicide". *Daily Express*, 12 February. http://www.express.co.uk/news/world/377330/ Spanish-couple-in-eviction-suicide.

Dardot, Pierre and Christian Laval (2013 [French ed. 2009]) *The New Way of the World: On Neoliberal Society*. Translated by Gregory Elliott. London: Verso.

Davies, Nigel (2012) "Spain Pledges to Spare Needy from Eviction after Homeowner Jumps to her Death as Bailiffs Arrive". *Financial Post*, 12 November. http://business.financialpost.com/news/economy/spain-looks-at-eviction-reform-after-homeowner-woman-jumps-to-her-death-as-bailiffs-arrive.

de Andrés, Eva Alvarez, María José Zapata Campos and Patrik Zapata (2015) "Stop the Evictions! The Diffusion of Networked Social Movements and the Emergence of a Hybrid Space: The Case of the Spanish Mortgage Victims Group". *Habitat International* 46: 252–9.

Díez, Anabel (2013) "PP Does U-turn on Eviction Initiative in Congress". *El País*, 12 February. http://elpais.com/elpais/2013/02/12/ inenglish/1360691620_479968.html.

Documentos TV (2013) "La muerte silenciada: Suicidio, el último tabú". TVE, 8 September. http://www.rtve.es/alacarta/videos/documentos-tv/ documentos-tv-muerte-silenciada-suicidio-ultimo-tabu/1692885/.

Fominaya, Cristina Flesher and Antonio Montañés Jimenéz (2014) "Transnational Diffusion Across Time: The Adoption of the Argentinian Dirty War '*Esrache*' in the Context of Spain's Housing Crisis" in Donatella della Porta and Alice Mattoni (eds) *Spreading Protest: Social Movements in Times of Crisis*. Colchester: European Consortium for Political Research.

Foucault, Michel (2008 [2004]) *The Birth of Biopolitics: Lectures at the Collège de France 1978–1979*. Translated by Graham Burchell. Basingstoke: Palgrave Macmillan.

Hermida, Xosé (2016) "Suicidio, el gran tabú". *El País Semanal*, 10 July. http://elpaissemanal.elpais.com/documentos/suicidio-el-gran-tabu/.

Iglesias, Leyre, Marta G. Coloma and Rafael Dawid (2012) "Una ex concejal socialista de 53 años se suicida en Barakaldo cuando iban a desahuciarla". *El Mundo*, 9 November. http://www.elmundo.es/elmundo/2012/11/09/ paisvasco/1352452216.html.

Informe Semanal (2012) "Suicidios, la ley del silencio". TVE, 14 April. http://www.rtve.es/alacarta/videos/informe-semanal/informe-semanal-suicidios-ley-del-silencio/1376327/.

La Sexta (2013) "Un matrimonio de jubilados se suicida cuando iban a desahuciarles en Mallorca". *La Sexta*, 12 February. http://www.lasexta.

com/noticias/sociedad/matrimonio-jubilados-suicida-cuando-iban-desahuciarles-mallorca_2013021257280e3c4beb28d446037eb1.html.

Link Lab (2015) *Osservatorio suicidi per crisi economica*. Rome: Laboratorio di Ricerca Socio Economica. http://st.ilfattoquotidiano.it/wp-content/uploads/2015/07/Suicidi-crisi-economica-2012-2013-2014-2015-DEF.pdf.

Machlin, Anna, Jaelea Skehan, Melissa Sweet, Alexandra Wake, Justine Fletcher, Matthew Spittal and Jane Pirkis (2012) "Reporting Suicide: Interpreting Media Guidelines". *American Journalism Review* 34 (2): 45–56.

Mackinson, Thomas (2015) "Crisi, è il 'semestre nero dei suicidi economici': Ma l'Istat non li conta più". *Il Fatto Quotidiano*, 24 July. http://www.ilfattoquotidiano.it/2015/07/24/crisi-e-il-semestre-nero-dei-suicidi-economici-ma-listat-non-li-conta-piu/1902144/.

Martínez-Simancas, Rafael (2012) "Amaya Egaña". *La Gaceta de Salamanca*, 11 November. http://www.lagacetadesalamanca.es/opinion/2012/11/11/amaya-egana/77436.html.

Mirowski, Philip (2013) *Never Let a Serious Crisis Go to Waste*. London: Verso.

Moran, Lee (2012) "'We Dedicate Our Deaths to Silvio Berlusconi': Italian Couple Ruined by Economic Crisis Commit Suicide in Hotel Room after Writing to Former PM". *The Daily Mail*, 13 January. http://www.dailymail.co.uk/news/article-2086085/Italian-couple-ruined-economic-crisis-commit-suicide-hotel-room.html.

Nadeau, Barbie Latza (2012) "Debt Most Deadly: Recession and Austerity Fuel Suicide in Italy". *Newsweek*, 18 June. http://europe.newsweek.com/debt-most-deadly-recession-and-austerity-fuel-suicide-italy-65241.

Naiz (2012) "Amaia Egaña se quita la vida en Barakaldo cuando iban a proceder al desahucio de su vivienda". *Naiz*, 9 November. http://www.naiz.eus/en/actualidad/noticia/20121109/una-mujer-se-suicida-en-barakaldo-cuando-iban-a-proceder-al-desahucio-de-su-vivienda.

Norris, Bill and Mike Jempson, with Lesley Bygrave (2001, updated by Einer Thorsen 2006) *Reporting Suicide Worldwide: Media Responsibilities*. Bournemouth: Bournemouth University. http://eprints.bournemouth.ac.uk/13503/.

Paratcha, Diego Sanz (2013) "El relato torcido de los suicidios". *Diagonal*, 19 February. https://www.diagonalperiodico.net/panorama/relato-torcido-suicidios.html.

Pompili, Maurizio, Monica Vichi, Marco Innamorati, David Lester, Bijou Yang, Diego De Leo and Paolo Girardi (2014) "Suicide in Italy During a Time of Economic Recession: Some Recent Data Related to Age and

Gender Based on a Nationwide Register Study". *Health and Social Care in the Community* 22 (4): 361–7.

Público (2012) "Es la segunda muerte vinculada a un desahucio que se produce en las últimas semanas". *Público*, 9 November. http://www. publico.es/espana/mujer-suicida-barakaldo-iba-desahuciada.html.

Rivas, Javier (2012) "Una exedil socialista se suicida cuando iba a ser desahuciada de su vivienda". *El País*, 9 November. http://politica. elpais.com/politica/2012/11/09/actualidad/1352452631_706772.html.

Roberts, Martin (2012) "Spanish Banks to Restrict Evictions after Suicides". *The Guardian*, 12 November. https://www.theguardian. com/world/2012/nov/12/spanish-banks-evictions-suicides.

Samaritans (2013) *Media Guidelines for the Reporting of Suicide.* London: Guardian News and Media Limited. http://www.samaritans. org/media-centre/media-guidelines-reporting-suicide.

Scammell, Rosie (2013) "Suicides Rise as Italy's Economy Slumps". *Al Jazeera*, 3 August. http://www.aljazeera.com/indepth/features/2013/07 /2013731174919956289.html.

Smyth, Sharon (2012) "Spain Suicides Spark Law Risking Bank Losses: Mortgages". *Bloomberg*, 16 November. http://www.bloomberg.com/ news/articles/2012-11-15/spain-suicides-spark-law-risking-bank-losses-mortgages.

The Local (2016) "Jobless Man Burns Himself to Death in Car at Italian Market". *The Local*, 11 February. http://www.thelocal. it/20160211/unemployed-italian-burns-himself-to-death-at-sicily-market.

The Telegraph (2012) "Spain Set to Agree Measures to Stop Evictions after Suicide". *The Telegraph*, 12 November. http://www.telegraph.co.uk/ news/worldnews/europe/spain/9671777/Spain-set-to-agree-measures-to-stop-evictions-after-suicide.html.

Wall Street Journal (2014) "Italy's Economic Suicide Movement". *Wall Street Journal*, 26 October. http://www.wsj.com/articles/italys-economic-suicide-movement-1414348445.

WHO (2008 [2001]) *Preventing Suicide: A Resource for Media Professionals.* Geneva: World Health Organization (WHO) and International Society of Suicide Prevention. http://www.who.int/mental_health/prevention/ suicide/resource_media.pdf.

WSWS (2013) "Wave of Suicides in Italy as Social Conditions Deteriorate". World Socialist Web Site (WSWS), 21 June. https://www.wsws.org/en/ articles/2013/06/21/suic-j21.html.

Index